SMALL PLOT
BIG HARVEST

SMALL PLOT
BIG HARVEST

Lucy Halsall

DK

LONDON, NEW YORK, MUNICH, MELBOURNE, DELHI

Senior Editor Chauney Dunford
Editor Becky Shackleton
Senior Art Editor Alison Shackleton
Jacket Designer Nicola Powling
Production Editor Raymond Williams

Managing Editor Penny Warren
Managing Art Editor Alison Donovan
Publisher Mary Ling
Art Director Peter Luff
Publishing Director Mary-Clare Jerram

Picture Research Susie Peachey
Photography Mark Winwood

US Editors Rebecca Warren, Kate Johnsen
US Consultant Lori Spencer

First American Edition, 2012

Published in the United States by DK Publishing, 375 Hudson Street,
New York, New York 10014

12 13 14   10 9 8 7 6 5 4

008–183129–March/12

Published in Great Britain by Dorling Kindersley Limited.

A catalog record for this book is available from the Library of Congress.

ISBN 978-0-7566-9055-7

DK books are available at special discounts when purchased in bulk for sales promotions,
premiums, fund-raising, or educational use. For details, contact: DK Publishing Special Markets,
375 Hudson Street, New York, New York, 10014 or SpecialSales@dk.com.

Printed and bound by South China Printing Co. Ltd., China

Discover more at **www.dk.com**

Contents

Your growing space

Planning your plot

Lucy Halsall is editor of *Grow Your Own* magazine, a dream job for her. She describes it as *The Good Life* TV series in magazine format. Before this she worked at the RHS Garden Wisley and as the gardening editor at *Amateur Gardening* magazine. Lucy was raised on her family's small farm and has been cultivating salads and vegetables since her teenage years. Lucy describes her own garden as "small, yet very productive!"

Grow your own vegetables

Grow your own fruit

Problem solver

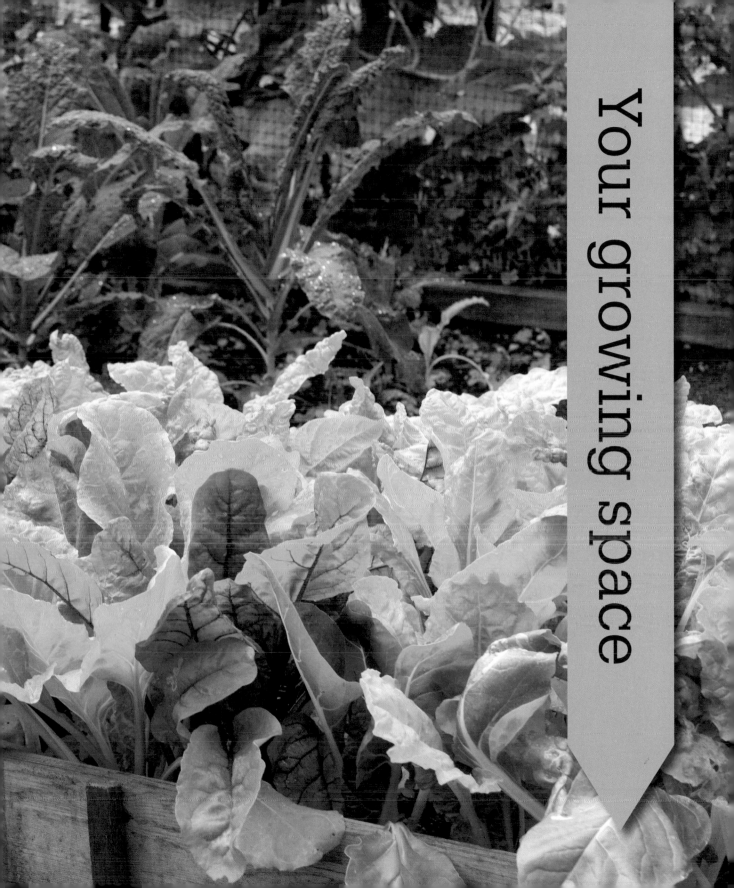

Your growing space

Why grow your own food?

Anyone who has ever picked fresh strawberries will know how unlikely it is that the first harvest will reach the kitchen. The urge to eat them then and there usually wins out over all but the strongest wills, reflecting one of the main reasons to grow your own—taste. Freshness equates to flavor, and growing your own crops allows you to pick them at their best. Compare store-bought green beans to your own, and you'll never buy them again. However, there are also many other reasons to grow your own crops, whether it's for your health and that of your family, for environmental concerns, or for the pleasure of it.

Fresh and healthy

The positive health effects of eating fruits and vegetables has long been known, but there are also direct benefits of actually growing them yourself. Vitamin and antioxidant levels are at their highest when crops are first picked, with the levels falling by half after 7–14 days from harvest. Although supermarkets sell fresh produce, you can rarely tell how long ago it was picked or how well it has been stored, especially if it has been imported or kept in refrigeration. Growing your own food means you can pick fruits and vegetables no sooner than is really necessary, ensuring they are as fresh, tasty, and nutrient-packed as possible.

Growing fitter

In addition to eating more healthily, the tasks involved in growing your own crops also provide good exercise, improving fitness, stamina, and flexibility. Just one hour's digging can burn off over 300 calories, while even light puttering means being active.

Good for the environment

Local and global concerns have driven many people to assess the impact of food production on the environment, and terms such as "food miles" and "carbon footprint" have become synonymous with a responsible, ecologically-minded attitude. Producing your own food at home embraces both these concepts—food miles are zero, and the carbon footprint is negligible.

Growing your own fruit and vegetables isn't just about jumping on the latest bandwagon however, it's pretty fundamental—people need food. By growing it in your own back yard or garden plot, you are reducing the strain on global supplies. You will also know exactly how "green" it is or how ethically it has been produced—organically perhaps. You can also share your surplus, helping to reduce the global impact of others.

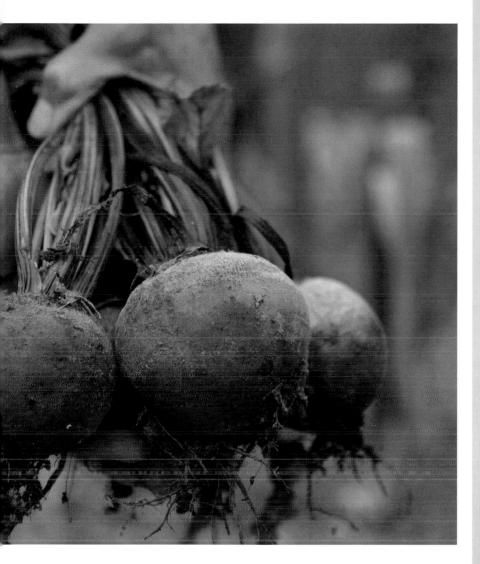

Space to grow

Growing fruits and vegetables does require a reasonable amount space, but that doesn't mean having a large garden of your own—or even a garden at all. Community gardens have surged in popularity over the last decade, with friends now commonly sharing areas to beat the waiting lists. The community spirit found at most shared garden sites makes them ideal for beginner growers, with neighbors freely sharing their knowledge, experience, tools, and surplus produce.

If you have a garden, or access to one, use every inch of space. Walls, balconies, and fences are all suitable for growing crops, as are containers, windowsills, window boxes, and hanging baskets. Even the smallest plot with just a few plants will give you a taste of what growing your own fruits and vegetables is all about.

Community gardens *are ideal for beginners to learn the basics and to experience the pride of growing crops for the first time.*

Greater choice

Commercial growers are motivated by yield, shelf-life, and uniformity, and grow vast monocultures of just a few varieties, giving little choice in the markets. When growing your own, you can set your own priorities when deciding what to plant. There are thousands of different crops and varieties to try, many developed over generations, with qualities better suited to your own tastes.

(above) **Beets are quick to grow** *and require little care or experience. Try varieties you don't see in supermarkets, like ones with striped flesh.*

(above left) **Strawberries are the taste of summer** *and are very easy to grow. Plant them in patio pots or in hanging baskets, and enjoy them utterly fresh.*

You're unlikely to ever see 'Nun's Bellybutton' green beans, 'Fat Lazy Blonde' lettuce, or 'Yellow Stuffer' tomatoes in the supermarket aisles, so why not grow them instead? You can even develop your own strains.

Crops in small spaces

There's no denying that having less space limits the amount of fruit and vegetables you can grow, but by thinking laterally you can still produce enough to supplement your needs, even if you can't grow everything. Instead of planting vegetables that take up lots of space but are cheap to buy, choose more space-efficient crops, such as climbing beans, that make best use of the room you have. Prioritize what you grow, and plant the crops you like to eat—think quality not quantity, and grow varieties that are expensive to buy in the supermarket.

Small spaces can be highly productive; *the trick is make use of every inch available, including the walls and fences. Position containers wherever there is enough room, and train growth vertically.*

Small but perfectly formed

Small spaces are terrific for growing fruits and vegetables since they are usually enclosed by walls or fences, giving them similar growing conditions to traditional, walled gardens—just on a smaller scale. A south- or west-facing bed offers the perfect environment for chili peppers, peaches, eggplant, strawberries, herbs—and any other number of crops that revel in the warmth of the sun. In contrast, north- and east-facing exposures are cooler and shadier, ideal for growing tender lettuces and leafy brassica crops.

Most small plots have a full range of exposures, which means they can provide the complete spectrum of growing environments any kitchen gardener would require. In contrast large plots are often more exposed, lacking shade, shelter from the wind, or a handy water supply. This limits the crops that can be grown to those that will tolerate everything the elements can throw at them.

(left) **Growing bags** *are designed for crops and can be used outside as mini beds. For deep-rooted crops, cut them in half, and stand them upright.*

(below) **Fewer crops means less care***, which is ideal if you are short on time and space. Only grow as much as you can care for to avoid disappointment.*

Urban gardens

Small plots are particularly productive in towns and cities, thanks to the "urban heat island" effect. In essence, large buildings provide shelter from the wind and also absorb heat during the day, which is radiated back at night. This action, along with the heat generated by urban life, raises the local temperature by a useful few degrees. This allows urban growers to extend their growing season in spring and fall, and to benefit from higher summer temperatures than rural counterparts. In practice, it means that long-season crops, such as chili peppers, sweet corn, and winter squash, give a better harvest. It can even make growing exotic crops more successful, such as figs, okra, loquat, and tomatillo.

Less space, less effort

Having a small plot also brings other advantages, besides the crops you can grow. Although off-site gardens can accommodate more plants, they also take a lot more looking after. The novelty of pushing a wheelbarrow to your garden plot or leaving slugs in your car trunk on the journey home from the plot can soon wear thin.

Small gardens are far less daunting, especially for those new to growing their own crops. You can cultivate areas in bite-sized chunks, there's little risk of being overwhelmed with weeds, and you won't be tethered to a watering can all summer. It's also easier to sneak out in your pajamas in the morning to enjoy homegrown fruit for breakfast.

Space for creative thinking

Making the most of a small plot involves being creative with the space you have and the crops you grow—which is part of the fun. Any object that holds sufficient compost and has drainage holes can be used as a planter, so use your imagination. Certain crops grow well planted together, so try different combinations to create plans that are both colorful and productive.

The sky's the limit

Space at ground level is the most limiting factor in small plots because all plants need room to grow. However, a useful way around this is to plant climbing and trailing crops and to train their growth vertically, leaving space at their base for other crops. Climbing green and runner beans, cucumbers, trailing squashes, and cordon tomatoes all produce valuable crops in minimal space. They can either be planted to grow against walls or fences, or at the base of free-standing wigwams, which can even be sited in ornamental beds.

Speedy crops

To make the most of the space you have, choose crops that can either be harvested over a long period or those that mature quickly and can soon be replanted. One large pot sown with cut-and-come-again salad leaves will keep the average family supplied for well over two months. Once cut, these rapid growers will yield again within three weeks. "Baby" vegetable varieties of turnip, cauliflower, beets, carrots, and cabbage are harvested within a couple of months of sowing. Another way to ensure maturity within minimal time is to start plants off under cover in pots and modules, or to purchase plants. The time saved by planting rather than sowing into the final growing locations allows you to squeeze in another crop or two before the growing season ends.

Bountiful varieties

As well as choosing crops that mature quickly or over a long period, look for varieties that are known to give a particularly large crop. If you only have space for a few plants, it's worth making sure the ones you plant are as productive as possible. Many fruit and vegetable varieties have been bred specifically to suit compact gardens, so seek advice when deciding what to plant.

(above) **Tasty young turnips** *can be harvested a few weeks after sowing. Start early, and you can enjoy several crops in the same season.*

(left) **Containers can be planted** *under cover in the spring to give the crops a head start. They can also be moved inside in the fall to grow on longer.*

(far left) **A wigwam of beans** *will crop all summer but only takes up the same amount of space as three or four potato or cabbage plants.*

Tips to make the most of limited space

1 Hanging baskets These offer a space-saving way to grow many different crops, including mixed summer herbs, salad leaves, tumbling tomatoes, and even peppers. They must be kept well watered and fed and given a bright spot. Hang near the kitchen for easy picking.

2 Trailing crops Plants like squashes can be trained along the ground as well as vertically. Use short stakes to train the stems along the edges of beds or paths so they are easy to harvest, and to free up space for planting other crops.

3 Quick spring container crops Make use of vacant planters not yet filled with summer flowers. Early Swiss chard and radishes will be ready to harvest before your tender ornamentals need to be planted outdoors in early summer.

4 Handy mini crops Sow quick crops wherever gaps develop in the garden during the year. Many mature in a matter of weeks so can be sown direct to crop before the end of the season. Also sow between your ornamentals.

5 Wall training Use vertical surfaces to support climbing and trailing crops. Many fruits, including apples, crop very well when trained against walls and fences, freeing up useful bed space.

6 Underplanting Take advantage of the bed space beneath taller crops, like sweet corn, by underplanting. Keep them well-watered. Lettuce will benefit from the light shade, while long squash stems can be trained out toward the sunlight.

Essential tools and equipment

Gardening involves many practical and strenuous techniques, but choosing the right tools for the job will make the tasks easier and more successful. For example, using shears to cut through very thick stems not only hurts your hands, it can also damage the tool itself. Similarly, budget tools made of poor quality materials will wear out more quickly, proving a real false economy. Buy the best you can afford, and also consider good quality second-hand tools.

Growing your own need not be expensive, *many key pieces of equipment can be bought cheaply and reused. Be prepared, and stock up on the essentials at the beginning of the season.*

Digging

A good spade and fork are essential for digging, along with a hand trowel for excavating smaller holes. Assess your physical strength before buying a fork or spade—the smaller blade of a border spade, for example, will allow you to lift a lighter weight of soil than a larger, standard model. Handle designs vary from brand to brand, so choose one that feels comfortable. For repetitive tasks such as digging these are important considerations.

Weeding

A hoe is an extremely useful tool for removing young weed seedlings from among your crops. Long-handled models are ideal or larger beds or if you find bending difficult, while short-handled "onion" hoes are ideal for smaller areas and raised beds. A hand fork will also help you to easily remove weeds, especially those with long taproots, like dandelions.

Propagation

When preparing a seedbed outside, a rake is extremely handy. The fine teeth filter out clods of earth and loosen weeds and stones so that the soil takes on a fine, crumbly texture, perfect for germination. The edge of a hoe can be used to make drills.

Indoor propagation, or sowing into pots, requires a range of containers and seed compost as well as labels, a pencil, and a dibber. If you invest in a heated propagator, you will be able to raise a wider range of crops.

Pruning

A good pair of shears is essential. Cutting and pruning are repetitive tasks, so a well-designed handle grip will be easier on your hands—try out a selection of models before you buy. If your fruit trees need reworking, then loppers and a pruning saw are also invaluable for the more sizable branches. Telescopic loppers with extendable handles are useful if your plants have reached lofty dimensions.

Keep your tools well maintained

It is vital to keep tools clean and in good condition, otherwise the health of your plants might suffer. Clean tools like shears with disinfectant between uses to prevent diseases from passing from one plant to another, and keep them well oiled and tightened up to ensure that they cut as cleanly and efficiently as possible. Apply oil to tools such as spades and forks to prevent them from rusting.

The garden basics

It is best to invest in good-quality tools that will last, so make sure you only buy those you really need—a fork is needed in a community garden but may not be if you are growing in pots on a patio.

1 Fork Excellent for working organic matter into the soil, forks are also useful for lifting crops or moving plants.

2 Spade Ideal for digging over large areas of light soil and moving mulches, a spade is a vital tool for a larger plot.

3 Dutch hoe This versatile tool is ideal for killing annual weeds: it severs the roots so that the plants then die. It is also useful for drawing soil up around crops.

4 Rake This tool is crucial in site preparation: use it to remove rocks and clods of earth, level the soil, and create a fine tilth for sowing seeds.

5 Dibber Used for making holes for sowing or planting, a dibber is also useful for marking out seed drills.

6 Trowel The ideal tool for creating planting holes, a trowel is an essential tool when transplanting your crops.

7 Shears This versatile tool can be used for harvesting crops such as peppers and asparagus as well as for pruning back fruiting bushes.

8 Cloche Useful for warming up the soil for early crops or for providing pest protection, a cloche is an easy way to get your plants off to a good start.

Deciding what to grow

It's inevitable to have an abundance in your fruit and vegetable harvests, but that's what freezers and friends are for. But with a little preparation you can minimize the peaks and valleys to ensure a steady flow of homegrown food. It is a good idea to begin planning your crops the previous fall, when seed companies release their catalogs. While it's not crucial to be extremely organized on a small-scale plot, time spent planning is time well spent. Each crop entry in this book gives sowing times and weeks to maturity. These will vary according to your location but will help you plan your supply of food.

Grow what you like

Make a list of the fruit and vegetables you eat, and then create two columns: "to buy" and "to grow." Although self-sufficiency is a wonderful idea, few people have enough space to actually achieve it, so select crops carefully to maximize space. Try to be fairly picky at this stage—for example, if you only have space for containers, devoting them to early, melt-in-the-mouth new potatoes is sensible; planting them with main potatoes, which will take far longer to mature, may not be the best use of the space. At the top of your "to grow" list should be crops that are expensive to buy or difficult to get, or those that are at their very best eaten fresh. Bulkier crops, or those that are cheap and readily available, should be a low priority.

Consider your space

Once you've established your "to grow" crops, compare your selections with the space you have available, and it should become apparent if certain crops need to migrate into the "to buy" column instead. Calculate how much room you'll need to grow them and which month they'll mature. Consider how well certain crops store. For example, extra chilis to dry or blueberries to freeze is actually a godsend since these crops preserve very well. Winter squash and garlic are easily kept in a dry, frost-free shed or garage. In contrast you may not have space or inclination to store more than a few pumpkins.

Staggering your harvests

It is important to consider how soon you'll be able to eat the produce that you grow, and to sow your seed accordingly. Carry out "successional sowings"—sow a little seed every few weeks rather than all at one time, for a constant supply of fresh crops. Alternatively, swap cultivars with friends and family. These will mature at different rates, and a single sowing of a selection of types can provide a more steady supply and allow you to

Storing surpluses

If you have extra and can't eat your fresh crops fast enough, do not despair. There is a wide range of ways to store surplus crops, but knowing which to use is critical. Not all fruits and vegetables suit every method.

1 Drying Vegetables such as onions and garlic should be dried thoroughly before storing—lay them out on racks in a dry, frost-free place. Herbs and chilis can also be dried. Consider drying slices of other crops such as apples and plums in the oven on a low heat to completely dry them out.

2 Freezing This is a useful method for storing a wide range of crops. To prevent berries from forming a solid lump when you freeze them, lay them out on trays so that none of them are touching. Vegetables will store for longer if they are blanched, quickly immersed in boiling water, before freezing. This is ideal for crops like asparagus and broccoli.

3 Preserving Transforming crops into delicious savory chutneys or relishes and sweet jams and jellies is an ideal way to preserve a wide range of fruits and vegetables, capturing their flavors when they are at their peak.

4 Storing Many fruits and vegetables will keep well if they are simply kept in a cool, well-ventilated, frost-free place. Wrap apples and pears in waxed paper to help maintain their juiciness; keep potatoes in paper sacks so that light cannot reach them.

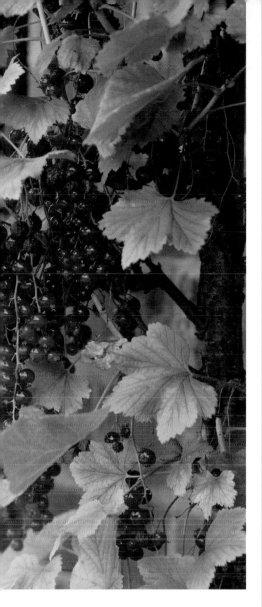

(above) **Red currants** can be used successfully in jams and jellies or frozen for later use, so a surplus need not mean that the fruit has to go to waste.

(above left) **Salad leaves** can be expensive to buy and are ideal for sowing successionally—they will be ready in just a few weeks. Sow a variety of types for a constant supply of delicious, mixed leaves.

try different flavors and textures, too. Another option is to sow some seeds under cover, and some outside. Those that are protected will get a head start. To extend the season, also consider growing crops that mature naturally over a long period.

Choosing the right spot

The microclimates that your garden creates will inevitably suit some crops better than others. For this reason don't rush in, but instead take a little time to identify the different areas within your plot, and then match the crops accordingly. Draw a plan, and mark on it where the sun can and can't reach since this is the primary factor to consider when deciding what crops to grow. When given the right location, you'll find that your fruit, herbs, and vegetables will thrive, yield more heavily, and will also show greater resilience to pests and diseases.

Hot and sunny

South- and west-facing sites capture the most sunshine, so count yourself lucky if you have a fence or wall with this orientation. Many crops, such as fruits and fruiting vegetables, rely on sunlight to maximize their sugar levels, so make the most of these areas. These high-sugar crops often require a long growing season and benefit from additional shelter.

Bright but cool

Soil and container compost dries more quickly in sunnier locations, which will affect different crops in different ways. Container-grown fruit trees, for example, produce bigger and sweeter harvests when exposed to full sunlight, but will shed fruitlets if they become dry during the crucial spring fruit-setting period. To ensure a good crop, position them in the sun, but keep the roots cool and well-watered. Conversely, a potted fig will revel with hot sun on its roots, as do most Mediterranean herbs.

An open, sunny location is ideal for a range of crops, including carrots, leeks, lettuces, and potatoes, as long as they receive adequate water and are not allowed to dry out.

Cold and wind

Many gardens experience regular prolonged freezes and frosts. Sloping sites and valleys in particular are at risk of collecting cold pockets of air, known as "frost pockets," at their lowest points. A wall, fence, or thick evergreen hedge can also harbor cold air if the ground slopes above it. In these cases, choose hardy, robust vegetables, and if you wish to grow fruit, choose late-flowering varieties to avoid the worst of the cold, or wrap plants with fabric during frosty spells. Cold soils are less damaging if they are dry, so add bulky organic matter to these sites to help plants overwinter.

Some garden sites may also be vulnerable to the wind. Wind has two major actions: buffeting foliage and drying out plants. While many herbs would be quite happy in such conditions, leafy spinach or Swiss chard would quickly become ragged. Use screens or other more robust plants to deflect or filter fast-moving air, and plant in large, thick-walled containers to moderate the effects.

Shade and moisture

North- and east-facing sites receive less sunlight but are equally useful in the vegetable garden, providing a cool environment in which many leaf crops thrive, such as cabbages, kale, spinach, and summer salads.

The main advantage of a shadier spot is that it is easier to maintain cool roots, which allows for steady growth with less risk of premature flowering, known as "bolting." Moisture is also lost less quickly from the soil, and crops growing here may require watering less frequently as a result. If however, you find that these cooler pockets are too moist for your crops, add plenty of bulky organic matter to the soil, such as composted bark, to improve drainage. Alternatively, grow them in raised beds filled with free-draining soil or compost.

Rain shadows

One final key area requiring careful management is the base of walls and fences, especially the sides facing

(top) **Plant leafy crops** *such as colorful Swiss chard in partially shaded, north- or east-facing sites. The plants will benefit from this site since too much sun might otherwise scorch its large, lush foliage.*

(above) **Wall-trained fruit trees** *take up very little growing space and can look impressive. Ensure that they are not allowed to dry out when in flower or fruit if they are planted in a "rain shadow."*

away from the prevailing wind. These areas often suffer from "rain shadows," where rainfall cannot reach the soil. If planting here, keep the area well watered during spring and summer, especially if you are growing fruit crops, which are sensitive to even brief dry spells.

If a late cold spell is forecast, *cover vulnerable plants over with horticultural fabric to protect them from frost damage.*

Preparing the soil

Whether you sow your seeds directly in the ground or sow crops under cover first and then plant them out, preparing your soil in advance is crucial. Start by identifying your soil type and pH so you can decide whether you need to make any changes; some crops cope better than others in certain conditions. The best time to dig over your plot is between mid-fall and mid-spring—break up compacted soil, remove any weeds, and work in plenty of organic matter, such as well-rotted garden compost, to improve yields.

Understanding soil types

The type of soil you have plays an important role in how well your crops grow. Most plants have preferred conditions—such as warm, light, well-drained, or cool and moisture-retentive. The soil you have also affects how you manage it for the best results and how easy it is to work with. The first step is to identify the soil type you have and to check it in different parts of the garden.

Sand, silt, and chalk soils

Soils that contain a high proportion of sand drain very freely and lose nutrients quickly, although they warm up rapidly in spring. They are light and easy to dig but need regular watering and feeding throughout the year. Soils rich in silt and chalk particles also drain freely but retain nutrients better, which makes them better suited to growing crops. All three types can be made more moisture- and nutrient-retentive by regularly digging in well-rotted organic matter such as garden compost, manure, leaf mold, or bark chips. This organic matter will act like a sponge to help absorb moisture and fertilizers you apply, while at the same time allowing the soil structure to remain airy and open.

Clay soils

Clay soils have the opposite qualities to sandy types; they are moisture-retentive and fertile, but slow to warm in spring and are heavy to dig. They are also very sticky when wet, often becoming waterlogged, and are prone to baking solid during summer dry spells. Moderate clay soils are good for growing most crops, especially if improved by digging in well-rotted organic matter. If the soil contains a lot of clay and drains very poorly, try growing your crops in raised beds.

Loam soils

This type of soil contains an even mix of sand, silt, and clay, and is a real godsend for growers. It is ideal for most fruit and vegetable crops and needs very little improvement.

How to test your soil

Soil testing kits are commonly available and are a quick, easy way to find out the pH of your soil (from very acidic (1) to very alkaline (14), with 7 being neutral). Simply shake up a sample of your soil with the testing solution, and then judge the color against the kit's pH chart. Perform the test in several places around your garden because the pH may vary greatly, even within one site.

An easy way to check your soil type is to roll some between your fingers. Clay soils can be easily molded into balls due to their clinging, sticky texture. Sandy soils are far more crumbly and will not hold together (see image, left). Loamy soils feel silky and mold quite well. Your soil is likely to be a mixture of all three types, but performing this test will help you to tell which is dominant.

Soil cultivation

A final consideration is whether to dig the soil over extensively or not. There are two schools of thought, known as the "dig" and "no-dig" approaches. The argument for digging is that it breaks up compacted soil, removes pernicious weeds, incorporates soil improvers, and encourages the deep rooting of crops. A winter dig also exposes pests to predators and cold conditions and helps to break up heavy clods of earth. Most garden soils will benefit from an initial dig.

However, there is also an argument for fewer cultivations after the initial dig. This encourages natural fertility to rise and soil structure to stabilize. Weed seeds aren't repeatedly brought to the surface, and worms and other beneficial fauna are undisturbed. Mulches are simply laid on the surface for worms to draw down into the soil.

Ultimately, a combined approach is often best. It may be necessary to dig if compacted areas of soil form or if perennial weeds begin to encroach.

Acid and alkaline soils

Even if your soil is fertile, the crops growing may not be able to absorb all the nutrients they need, which leads to deficiencies (see. p.246). A common cause for this is soil acidity, or pH, which can restrict the availability of certain nutrients to the plants growing there. While it is possible to alter soil pH to suit the crops you'd like to grow, it is a difficult and endless task that is rarely worth the hard work involved.

Instead, check the pH of your soil (see left), and grow those crops that grow best in the conditions you have. Brassicas, for example, crop better in alkaline soil, while blueberries must have acidic conditions. Alternatively, if you want to grow crops that don't suit your soil pH, plant them into raised beds or containers filled with suitable soil or compost.

(top) **Digging in well-rotted organic matter** *helps to improve the structure of your soil as well as the nutrient content. Apply it at least once a year in spring or fall for long-term benefits.*

(above) **Raised beds or containers** *offer the ideal solution to problematic, hard-to-manage soils since they give you the opportunity to start fresh. Fill with a loamy, rich, free-draining soil.*

For a "no-dig" mulch, *lay a thick layer of organic matter such as compost on the soil surface, and simply leave it to be broken down.*

Sowing and planting

Raising plants from seed is an easy and inexpensive way of growing many vegetables and herbs, and it opens the door to a vast array of delicious homegrown food. If you only have limited space, consider which crops can be sown directly outside and which should be started indoors. Don't waste valuable indoor space on crops that thrive when sown outside, such as beets. Instead, save it for crops like sweet peppers that benefit from a longer growing season.

Sowing under cover

Sowing seed under cover allows you to get off to an early start and extend your growing season—seed can be sown indoors at times of year when it would otherwise perish outdoors. This is also especially useful for long-season plants such as eggplant and peppers since it gives them sufficient time to mature and set their fruits. Heated propagators are readily available and are useful for starting off crops over winter. Generally, set a temperature of 54°F (12°C) for hardy crops and 64°F (18°C) for tender ones.

Light levels

If you sow your seed too early, when light levels are low, your seedlings will struggle and produce leggy growth, even if you provide them with additional heat. Early spring is sufficiently early to sow most crops. However, if providing enough light is problematic, consider sowing hardier crops directly outdoors, and buy plug plants of those that require a longer growing season. While plug plants are more costly, they are excellent if you want just a few plants for a small plot, and the variety available is increasing annually.

Pots, trays, and compost

Crops that have large seeds, such as runner beans and squashes, can be sown singly in pots. Module trays are ideal for medium-sized seeds such as cabbage and beets, while small-seeded lettuces and celery should be sown in seed trays—once the seeds germinate, transfer or "prick out" into pots or modules. Use seed compost since it is finely milled to remove lumps and contains few nutrients.

Hardening off

Young plants grown under cover will not have been exposed to the weather or to outside temperatures and will need to be acclimatized to outdoor conditions before being planted out —a process termed "hardening off." Place crops in a shady, sheltered spot outside during the day, and then bring them back indoors at night to gradually make the plants more robust. Do this for seven to ten days,

(above) **Tender plants such as cucumbers** *should be started off under cover since they need a minimum temperature of 68°F (20°C) to germinate.*

(right) **Use the cut-off tops of bottles** *to serve as homemade cloches. These will keep plants warm in cold, frosty weather and will also deter pests.*

depending on the hardiness of your crop. If you are pricking out or planting into another container or growing bag, water this well, and then leave it in a warm spot overnight. The aim of this is to prevent the compost from becoming too cold. This can cause transplant shock.

Direct sowing

If given sufficient protection, hardy crops can be sown directly into the ground, which is good if you do not have indoor space for a propagation area. Some crops, like broccoli, dislike having their roots disturbed so benefit from not being transplanted, and most root crops will thrive if sown direct. Ensure that you prepare the soil in advance—you may need to warm the soil using a cloche or cold frame if the weather is cold.

Plant buying options

If you don't have the space or time to grow plants from seed, there is a range of other options for you to choose from. Plants are available to buy at varying stages of growth and will provide a faster and easier alternative to growing from seed. Remember, however, that the range of varieties is not as great as is available for seeds, and that the process is invariably more expensive.

1 Plug plants Available from garden centers or via mail order, plug plants are crops that are purchased when they are mature enough to plant out. They offer a faster and easier, but more expensive, alternative to growing crops from seed and are ideal if you have a small space and only want a few plants.

2 Tray packs If you are looking to fill a whole row of plants or want to buy in bulk, trays of plants will be more cost-effective than buying individually grown plants. Buy them while they are still relatively young.

3 Pot grown plants Crops can also be purchased at a more advanced stage of growth, grown in individual pots. This method is relatively expensive, but it is a good way to buy crops that need a long growing season, such as bell peppers and sweet corn.

4 Bare-root Plants such as brassica seedlings (shown) are sown in seed beds and then dug up and sold "bare-root." Fruit trees and bushes are also available to buy from fall to spring and should be planted outside right away.

Getting an early start

When growing crops in a limited space you want it to be as productive as possible. While you can't make the plot itself any bigger, you can at least prolong the growing season as much as possible—so that your crops mature sooner and continue later into fall. This involves protecting your plants from spring frosts and fall chills, so you can start them off early and to keep them going as long as possible. This is simple to achieve, especially if you grow hardier crops and those that reach a harvestable size in a matter of weeks.

Sowing under cover

A greenhouse or sunroom offers the ideal conditions to sow seeds early and to grow plants before planting outdoors. They are not essential however, and you can easily start seeds on your windowsills, where they will germinate quickly at room temperatures. Seedlings can also be grown here, but turn them every few days to prevent them from growing toward the light and becoming crooked. Shade hot windows to avoid scorching the young soft growth.

Simple covers

Cold frames and mini-greenhouses offer similar benefits to full-size greenhouses and can be used to raise hardier crops in spring or for later sowings of more tender seeds—remember that plants must be kept well ventilated or they may dry out. They are also ideal for acclimatizing seedlings raised on windowsills to outdoor temperatures. Both are good for smaller plots—they can be taken apart and stored when not in use. Unlike cold frames, mini-greenhouses are often tall enough to grow mature crops, such as tomatoes and peppers.

Garden cloches

Cloches are temporary covers that trap heat and protect plants from cold and can be used to warm the soil before sowing outside and to encourage early growth. They are usually made from glass or rigid plastic, and there are many different types available, including tunnel cloches to cover rows, or dome cloches for single plants. Place them over seeds sown directly outside to promote quick germination or to protect newly planted crops from the cold weather. Alternatively, you can also use them to protect late-sown summer crops during the fall.

Protective fabric

Garden fabric is lightweight, used to protect tender seedlings and plants from frost damage. It is useful for spreading across larger areas, such as whole beds or drills, but can also be wrapped around individual plants. To be effective however, the fabric needs (above) **In late summer,** use cloches to cover more delicate plants like basil to keep them cropping longer, especially as the nights cool down.

(above left) **Starting plants under cover** gives them a valuable head start. Peas and fava beans can be sown in fall to plant out in spring.

to be held away from the leaves using canes or wire hoops. Fabric should also be held firmly in place because it can easily blow away. For extra protection, use several layers but remove them once the risk of frost has passed.

DIY protection

Although you can buy cloche and cold frame kits, it's often just as easy to make your own. That way you can tailor them exactly to your site and the crops you grow. It will also be cheaper, especially if you reuse materials or objects you already have.

1 Windowsill growing Group seedlings together in trays on your windowsill to keep them warm and moist. If you want to provide more light, make a reflector using cardboard and foil. This will encourage seedlings to grow straight and promote stronger stems.

2 Cold frames These are easy to make using old window frames. Use bricks or blocks to build up the sides, or make a simple wooden base, placing the window on top. These can be permanent or temporary features.

3 Simple shelters Small squares of glass, Lucite, or clear plastic make excellent cloches and can be leaned together at the top or propped up on stakes to form more open shelters. Any clear glass will do, such as that from old windows. Be careful with sharp edges, or wear gloves.

4 Bottle cloches Cut-off clear plastic bottles make excellent cloches, especially larger ones, and can be used to protect individual plants. Remove the tops to provide good air flow, and protect the plants growing inside with a light sprinkling of slug pellets. With the base removed, the cloches stack and store easily.

Growing in raised beds

If you have enough space outside, raised beds are excellent for growing fruit, vegetables, and herbs, and can make an attractive addition to the garden. Their raised level allows you to easily and comfortably reach your crops for weeding, maintenance, and harvesting, while the additional height also helps the soil to warm up rapidly in spring, naturally extending the growing season by a precious few weeks. Many raised beds are quick and simple to build, and can be constructed from a variety of materials such as railroad ties or slate tiles.

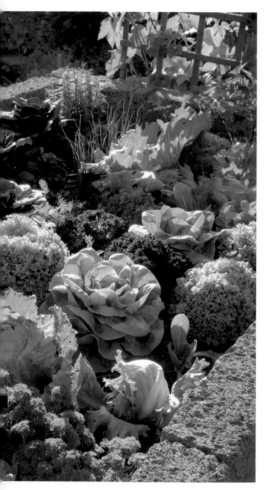

Long-lasting, brick-built structures *can look attractive and will stand the test of time. To give low-growing crops extra shelter from the wind, fill the bed leaving an 8in (20cm) gap at the top.*

The benefits of beds

Growing in raised beds rather than in the open ground allows you greater control over the growing conditions of your crops. When creating a new bed or renovating an old one, you can fill it with fresh, rich soil, but even in subsequent years it will be easy to improve the soil to suit your crops.

It is far easier to control the pH of a contained area of soil, so crops such as brassicas, which require a slightly alkaline environment, can be easily accommodated. The raised height of the bed also makes it easier to dig it over and remove rocks, which is ideal for root crops such as carrots that will suffer in rocky, compacted soil. Organic matter can be applied as necessary, and there will be little waste, unlike on a larger plot, where it may be added to an area that later becomes a path between beds.

The elevated soil level will provide good drainage, so if your ground is usually waterlogged, then this is a great way to provide a space for herbs and other warm-season plants that flourish in a well-aerated plot.

Bed management

However, raised beds are not without their drawbacks: the soil drains more quickly than in a ground-level bed, so they will need watering more often. Ants like free-draining soil, although regular cultivation will keep them from establishing, and snails may like to gather at the bed edges—however, this means that they're easy to find.

Temporary raised beds

An attractive temporary option, although only suitable for crops with shallower root systems, is to surround growing bags or wide containers with an edging frame, made from a material such as wicker, shown here. These raised beds can be "constructed" in different locations year-by-year, and once you have harvested your crops, they can be taken down and packed away to save space.

Different materials and designs

It's simple to create your own raised beds, but there are many kits available if your DIY skills aren't particularly polished. Think creatively when choosing your edging, and invest in good-quality, sturdy, durable materials.

1 DIY kits Ready-prepared kits, available in a variety of materials, can be easily assembled for a neat, stylish effect.

2 Wood Invest in some good-quality lumber, and ensure that it is properly treated to prevent it from rotting. Be creative: decking, for example, makes excellent edging, while chunky pieces of wood give a more modern feel.

3 Metal Raised beds made from metal suit a contemporary design. However, keep the soil well watered—it will be vulnerable to temperature changes.

4 Brick Use new or recycled bricks, blocks, or stone to create sturdy, long-lasting raised beds. These structures could be used to create some informal seating around the growing area, and can suit a English garden design.

5 Recycled materials Think creatively, materials such as used tires can make a striking design statement. Bear in mind that old railroad ties, which were once very popular, ooze tar in hot weather, so are used less widely now.

6 Slate pieces Tiles of slate are very attractive and can be used to edge a shallow bed. They will not support a lot of weight though, so do not overfill.

Growing in containers

Growing crops in pots is second nature to many. As well as providing extra growing space, it offers many benefits, such as easier weeding and the option to move your crops under cover for protection or to extend their cropping season. It can also give you a wider choice of crops to grow since you can choose the soil type, meaning you are not limited to growing only those plants that will thrive in your garden soil. However, feeding and frequent watering are vital, and you may wish to invest in an automatic irrigation system. To help conserve moisture, add water-retaining gel to the compost and mulch the surface to prevent evaporation.

Mix and match *crops in containers of different sizes and colors. Integrate the pots with ornamental plants to add color and interest to the display while the edible plants are developing.*

Choosing the right container

All containers should have drainage holes in the base to allow excess water to drain away, but the material they are made of will determine how quickly they will dry out. Unglazed terra-cotta pots are extremely porous and so will readily lose water through their sides, especially if positioned in a sunny spot. Conversely, thick-walled concrete tubs are very moisture-retentive. Wooden barrels are best lined with plastic to reduce water loss.

Match the container to the crop you'll be growing in it. The shallow roots of radishes and salad leaves, for example, means that container choice for these crops is virtually limitless—from window boxes to old boots and tea pots, you can really have fun with the way you grow them. Just bear in mind the smaller the pot, the more frequently it will need watering. Large crops, such as cabbages and potatoes, will require tubs with a minimum depth and diameter of 12in (30cm).

Fruit in containers

It's crucial to pick a container that is deep and wide enough for long-term fruit crops. Opt for a minimum depth of 12in (30cm) and a width at least 4in (10cm) larger than the existing pot. Repot annually in early to mid-spring when your tree or bush is still young and its growth rate is rapid. As the plant matures, its growth rate slows—check the roots—if they're not yet filling the compost, then don't repot until the following year. When the container is large enough to make repotting unnecessary, simply "top-dress" each spring by replacing the top 4in (10cm) of compost. Stand your pot on "feet" in winter to aid drainage.

Quirky containers

Think creatively when choosing where to sow or plant your crops. Experiment with unexploited growing areas and unusual containers, such as these cress-sown egg shells, which would make a fantastic family project. Plant growers are latching onto the trend for all things small by developing some hugely productive yet very compact varieties, so watch for these.

Different types of containers

With the wide range of container types available, you will easily be able to find one that fits your garden design. Try to make the most of all of your available space—many pots can be fastened onto walls or fences so can be incorporated into even the smallest garden.

1 Hanging baskets Suitable for tumbling crops such as tomatoes and strawberries, hanging baskets can look incredibly striking when planted with a mix of colorful edible and ornamental plants.

2 Terra-cotta pots Available in a range of sizes and shapes, these rustic-looking containers make an lovely addition to a patio and will support a variety of crops.

3 Window boxes Ideal for crops with shallow roots such as salad leaves, window boxes are best sited close to the kitchen for easy access during cooking.

4 Fabric bags The depth of these bags makes them a great choice for potatoes, which can be easily earthed up during growth. They can then be folded up after your crops have been harvested.

5 Wall pouches These attractive, space-saving devices allow you to make the most of an unused vertical surface. They are ideal for herbs or salad leaves but will need frequent watering.

6 Wall planters These containers must be securely fastened since they will need to support the weight of relatively large plants. Keep them well watered, and ensure that fruits are supported.

Watering and feeding

Keeping your fruit and vegetable plants well-watered and fed is essential for a good harvest, especially in smaller plots where every plant matters. Regular care also promotes strong, healthy growth, which is better able to fend off pests and diseases. Crops in pots and raised beds are almost totally reliant on you, so keep a watering can handy.

How and when to water

Growing fruits, herbs, and vegetables closely together in a small space, especially in containers, limits the amount of root space these plants have. This high concentration of roots needs continual access to moisture if it is to grow well. The ideal would be to install a drip irrigation system set at a level that ensures your soil or compost is evenly and consistently moist, but this is a luxury. Watering cans and garden hoses are more the norm; a thorough soak of beds every few days will ensure water penetrates to the deepest of roots, not just those near the surface. (Pots may require a daily drench.) Do this in the evening or morning, not during the heat of the day, to reduce evaporation. Keep all plants well-watered when they are in flower or setting fruit. Dry spells then will cause flowers and young fruits to wither, reducing the harvest.

Make the most of moisture

To help your soil retain moisture better, especially if it is light, regularly dig in well-rotted organic matter, which acts like a sponge. If you grow

(above) **Mulching plants** *helps to retain moisture in the soil by preventing evaporation. Organic mulches will also feed your plants.*

(left) **Automatic micro-irrigation** *is a worthwhile investment if you grow lots of crops in containers but have limited time to water them.*

(far left) **Young plants** *are especially vulnerable to drying out. Water them regularly, at least until they are planted out and fully established.*

crops in containers, add water-retaining granules before planting. Set up water barrels in your garden to collect rainwater, and consider recycling some household water, such as that which has been used to wash and prepare vegetables and salads. If you are going on vacation, group potted crops together in a shady spot, and stand them in trays—or ask a neighbor to water while you are away. Doing this is actually better than an automatic watering system, because crops can be harvested at the same time to ensure repeated cropping. (It also serves as a great reward for the temporary waterer.)

Feeding your crops

Growing crops takes a lot of nutrients from the soil or compost, which can become exhausted, so it is essential to replenish them regularly. There are three main nutrients that plants need most: nitrogen for leaf growth, phosphorus for healthy roots, and potassium (potash) for flowers and fruits. In addition, they also require small amounts of "trace" elements for overall health, including magnesium, iron, and boron. When feeding your crops, choose a feed that meets your crops' needs. Root crops benefit from fertilizer high in phosphorus to encourage root growth; leaf crops require feeds rich in nitrogen; and fruiting crops, such as tomatoes, require lots of potash. The wrong type of fertilizer can encourage the wrong type of plant growth. Soil type will affect how often you should feed—sandy soils lose nutrients quickly; clay holds on to them.

Fertilizer types

There are two types of garden fertilizer to use: natural feeds based on organic plant and animal matter, and artificial ones made from chemicals. Both can be applied in various ways, and each offers its own advantages. Most are allocated an "N:P:K" value, which is the general ratio of nitrogen (N), phosphorus (P), and potassium (K) within a fertilizer to help you choose the right feed for your crop. Whichever you use, avoid overfeeding in the hope of bigger harvests since you are more likely to damage plant roots.

1 Granular fertilizers This type of fertilizer breaks down slowly in the soil and provides plants with long-term nutrition, often lasting all season. They are easy to handle and apply and are available as natural or artificial feeds.

2 Liquid fertilizers These are quick-acting feeds, ideal for giving crops a boost. Natural and artificial types are available, sold as soluble powders or liquid concentrates. Dilute them according to the instructions given.

3 Compound fertilizers Rather than supplying a balanced feed, these chemical or natural fertilizers are used to supply specific nutrients, such as iron sulphate to increase iron in the soil, or bone meal to add phosphorus.

4 Well-rotted organic matter This is used to add natural nutrients to the soil as well as to improve its structure. There are many types to use, such as garden compost and horse manure.

Planning your plot

Getting started

A three-square-yard plot is a good size for most first-time fruit and vegetable growers and provides ample space for a useful selection of crops, yet is small enough to look after easily. To illustrate this, we created, planted, and harvested the plot featured throughout this chapter in a single growing season, showing what you can achieve. To help you get started and decide what to grow, follow the planting guides (pp.44–49) for different summer combinations to suit different needs: easy-to-grow, the family plot, and a plan for gourmet crops. Although these plans are for a 10x10ft (3x3m) square plot, you can adapt them to whatever space you have, whether it's a smaller bed or a collection of pots and growing bags on the patio.

Preparing your plot

Before sowing or planting, the most important task is to prepare the area first between the fall and early spring (see pp.20–21). Exactly what this will involve depends on your soil and site, but it's worth spending time now to ensure a good harvest and to prevent problems later. Provide the best conditions you can by enriching the soil with nutrients and by resolving problems such as poor drainage, perennial weeds, or areas of compaction.

If you are growing in containers or growing bags, place them in the sunniest location possible before sowing or planting (see pp.28–29).

Dig the soil well, *breaking up large clumps and removing any weed roots. Avoid walking on newly dug areas.*

Add well-rotted organic matter, *such as garden compost, to the soil to improve fertility and moisture retention.*

Rake the surface *to leave it fine and level, which is ideal for sowing seeds directly. Remove any weed seedlings.*

Use plastic sheeting *to help control weeds if you are unable to sow seeds right away.*

Our planting plan

This combination of vegetables is aimed at beginners, growing their own crops for the first time. It includes reliable crops that are quick to grow and can be picked over several weeks. Speedy salad leaves and herbs can be picked a few weeks after sowing, either as cut-and-come-again leaves or as whole plants. The beans will last through summer, and the potatoes and kale will provide a welcome harvest in the fall.

TOP ROW: ■ sweet corn x 9 ■ summer squash x 1 ■ runner beans x 8 ■ green beans x 6 ■ main potatoes x 4

MIDDLE ROW: ■ dwarf bush tomatoes x 5 ■ cucumbers x 3 ■ kale x 4 ■ zucchini x 2

BOTTOM ROW: ■ beets x 20 ■ carrots x 40 ■ radishes x 40 ■ Swiss chard x 8 ■ kohlrabi x 12 ■ Asian greens x 20 ■ lettuces x 20 ■ cilantro x 6 ■ parsley x 4

Warm the soil with cloches *so your seeds germinate more quickly. Use them to protect young plants.*

Insert garden stakes *to mark out your planting plan, indicate where to sow, and to support plants.*

OTHER JOBS TO DO

- Weed regularly to keep weeds from competing with your seedlings.
- Fork in granular fertilizer before sowing seeds directly.
- Keep the soil free from plant debris, which can harbor diseases.
- Start sowing seeds under cover to plant out in spring.
- Pre-germinate early potatoes (see p.146) to give them a head start.

Planting the bed

Once the soil is prepared, you can turn your attention to sowing and planting. Hard frosts are likely in early spring, making it too soon to plant tender crops that could be damaged. Instead, sow hardier vegetables now, such as carrots, peas, beets, and radishes, directly in the soil. These will germinate more quickly in soil that has been warmed first with cloches and plastic sheeting. To encourage stronger growth, protect the seedlings with cloches, and thin them as they develop to ensure good air flow and to prevent competition between the young plants.

Frosts become fewer and less severe in late spring, when you can start to acclimatize tender crops sown under cover or purchased, such as sweet corn, green and runner beans, tomatoes, and zucchini. This involves putting seedlings outside during the day and bringing them in at night for about ten days. Plant out in early summer when the risk of frost has passed.

Plants grow rapidly as the weather warms, *making this a busy time on your plot. Keep on top of maintenance at this stage to ensure your plants get the best start. Weak or dead plants can easily be replaced if replanted soon.*

Green and runner beans *climb up their supports once established. Tie in any young, wayward shoots.*

Water seedlings well *when planting out to encourage deep rooting, making them more resilient.*

Some hardy seeds *can be sown directly in spring. Prepare your soil well first, and keep it evenly moist.*

Thin direct-sown crops *as soon as they develop so that the remaining plants grow unhindered.*

Biodegradable pots *mean less root disturbance when planting out. Keep them moist to help them rot away.*

Keep garden fabric handy *in case the weather turns cold. Cloches can also be used.*

OTHER EARLY-SEASON JOBS

- Be vigilant against slugs and snails—use pellets around seedlings.
- Encourage germination by temporarily covering drills with newspaper.
- Sink upturned bottles next to squashes for easy watering.
- Hoe between crops to keep on top of weed control.

Tending the crops

Growth rates will increase as temperatures rise in early summer, so it's important to keep on top of crop developments. Quick-maturing crops such as radishes, salad leaves, and herbs may begin to provide you with early harvests, while fruits and vegetables that take longer to mature will benefit from continued care and maintenance—tie in tomatoes and cucumbers to their stakes, and remove any yellowing leaves from plants.

Earthing up potatoes will ensure that the developing tubers don't become exposed to any light, which would turn them green and inedible. Keeping on top of weeds will discourage unwanted competition, while erecting insect-proof barriers will prevent carrot root flies from attacking and boring holes in crops. Be sure to keep up with these jobs now, and the results will pay dividends.

Regularly tie in *developing cucumber stems to their supports using soft twine. They grow quickly.*

Radish sowings *will mature in as little as five weeks. Pick them young before they become woody.*

Keep carrots well weeded *since competition from unwanted growth can cause reduced yields.*

Erect insect netting *24in (60cm) high around your carrots to prevent carrot flies from laying their eggs.*

To ensure strong roots *that will sustain plenty of pods, keep green and runner beans well watered.*

Regularly earth up *soil around your developing potato plants to keep light from reaching the tubers.*

Check plants *for signs of pests and diseases. Remove any diseased growth, and control pests promptly.*

Salad crops *will be developing quickly, so harvest leaves from individual plants as needed.*

Young growth *is a magnet for slugs and snails. Make sure appropriate controls are in place, such as pellets.*

Remove yellowing foliage *from plants such as kale, kohlrabi, and zucchini to ensure good hygiene.*

OTHER MID-SEASON JOBS

- Thin out Swiss chard plants, using the thinnings as baby salad leaves.
- Attach individual tomato plants to a stout bamboo stake.
- Regularly harvest basil and cilantro to encourage further growth.
- Feed fruiting vegetables weekly with liquid tomato fertilizer.

Plenty to pick

Mid- to late summer is the most productive time on the plot, when spring sowings and plantings are ready to harvest. Pick crops such as green beans, zucchini, salad leaves, and herbs regularly since their individual pods, fruits, and leaves mature in succession, giving you a continuous harvest. Other crops, such as carrots and beets, yield one harvest, and once picked, the area they occupied can be reused. Making further sowings or plantings at this time will ensure that your plot's productivity doesn't fizzle out, and if watered well, new crops will quickly establish.

Remember that certain long-season crops, such as sweet corn, tomatoes, and runner beans, will begin to mature in late summer. Make sure you look after them well to encourage good harvests into the fall.

Train wayward squash stems *since they'll be putting on plenty of strong stem growth now.*

Cucumbers reach their peak *over a few days. Check regularly and cut them as soon as they are ready.*

Sow seeds direct *in bare patches of soil for a continuous supply. Keep the drills well watered in hot spells.*

Pull up individual carrots *as soon as they reach a harvestable size, selecting the largest roots first.*

Harvest zucchini regularly *or they will soon grow too large. Check plants every few days.*

Pull up whole lettuce plants *or leave the cut stalk in the ground to resprout fresh loose leaves.*

Keep sweet corn well watered *after the silks and tassels emerge to encourage the greatest yields.*

OTHER PEAK-SEASON JOBS

- Pull up baby beets regularly.
- Check for pests and diseases.
- Water crops thoroughly.
- Apply liquid feeds routinely.

Ending the season

Now is the time for late crops to come into their own. Sweet corn, winter squashes, and tomatoes require ample growing time and sunshine to reach their sweetest and will reach their best in the fall. Main potatoes are also ready for harvesting, since their skins will have formed, preparing them for storage.

Bare patches will become more common as spent crops are pulled up. Sow these with quick-growing microgreens or hardy salad leaves for a late crop, or start preparing the area for next year—cover it with mulch to prevent weed growth, or leave it bare to the elements so that frost can penetrate and expose pests. Your compost heap will be getting full now as crops are cleared. Turn the contents once or twice during the fall, moving material on the outside to the center.

Focus your watering *on crops that are still maturing, such as late pumpkins and salad leaves.*

Cut winter squashes *before the first frost, and lay them in a sunny location so that the skins harden.*

Mulch bare soil *with organic matter, which will break down in time for spring planting.*

Squeeze in late sowings *of hardy crops, such as salad leaves, which can be covered with cloches.*

Green and runner beans *will keep on producing until the first frost if the beans are picked regularly.*

Gently pull back *the outer leaves of corncobs to check and see if the kernels are mature enough to pick.*

Leave main potato tubers *on the soil surface for a few hours to dry before placing them in storage.*

Zucchini plants *will be coming to the end of their life now—make a final harvest, then compost them.*

Harvest the leaves *and seed pods of cilantro. Dry the seeds, and freeze any surplus leaves until required.*

Pull up spent crops, *and place on the compost heap. Chop them into pieces to speed up decomposition.*

OTHER LATE-SEASON JOBS

- Continue to harvest Swiss chard through the winter.
- Cover over any new sowings with bell or tunnel cloches.
- Stop watering tomato plants to encourage the fruit to ripen.
- Store surplus root crops in a frost-free shed or garage.

The easy-to-grow plot

If you are new to growing your own food, this mix of vegetables, along with strawberries, will provide a steady supply for your kitchen. Many crops are ideal for beginners, either because they are easy to care for, suffer from few pest and disease problems, or yield reliable harvests with little input. By growing just one or two different crops per square yard, you can easily get a handle on their cultivation. As your confidence and experience grow, try adding more of the crops listed below to the overall plan, and tailor the plot to supply your own specific needs.

Growing in containers

Low-maintenance vegetables are ideal for containers, window boxes, and even hanging baskets. You can also grow a wall of summer strawberries by planting one per 8in (20cm) pot and fixing each to a fence or trellis in a sunny spot. Shallow-rooted salad crops are perfect for smaller containers, while onions and green beans need pots with a minimum depth of 10in (25cm). Choose large tubs or even sacks for potatoes and zucchini.

Alternative easy-to-grow crops

Tomatoes
pages 54–57

Garlic
pages 162–163

Runner beans
pages 70–71

Sweet corn
pages 166–169

Fava beans
pages 76–77

Winter squashes
pages 86–89

Carrots
pages 138–139

Turnips
pages 140–141

Easy-to-grow mix

This combination of crops will provide you with all the basics, giving quick results and high yields if grown on well-prepared, fertile soil. The large patch of strawberries will ensure a bumper crop throughout the summer months; easy-to-grow green beans will crop reliably right through the fall; and just two zucchini plants will supply more than you can eat. Sow fast-growing radishes in regular batches for a steady supply, sowing your next crop as soon as the previous row has been cleared.

TOP ROW: ■ main potatoes x 4 ■ new potatoes x 6 ■ onions x 60

MIDDLE ROW: ■ spinach x 16 ■ beets x 30 ■ zucchini x 2 ■ green beans x 12

BOTTOM ROW: ■ radishes x 40 ■ lettuce x 8 ■ radishes x 40 ■ strawberries x 12

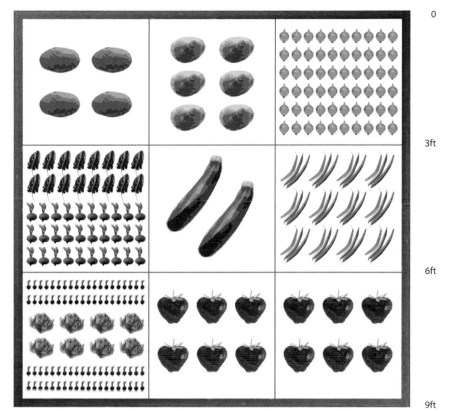

0

3ft

6ft

9ft

0   3ft   6ft

Swiss chard
pages 124–125

Asian greens
pages 120–121

Fall raspberries
pages 202–203

Lettuce
pages 112–115

Shallots
pages 156–157

Plums
pages 218–219

Also consider growing:
■ Chili peppers (pp.60–63)
■ Endive (pp.128–129)
■ Kohlrabi (pp.170–171)
■ Rhubarb (pp.186–187)
■ Cilantro (pp.190–191)
■ Parsley (pp.190–191)
■ Mint (pp.192–195)
■ Chives (pp.192–195)
■ Cabbage (pp.94–99)
■ Black currants (pp.208–209)
■ Blueberries (pp.212–213)
■ Plums (pp.218–219)

The family plot

There are plenty of delicious fruits and vegetables on the family shopping list that can easily be grown in the garden: a 10x10ft (3x3m) plot can provide you with a range of fresh crops, and many will grow in containers too, if space is tight. Consider giving each family member responsibility for a specific section or crop since this will encourage friendly rivalry that may result in a better-maintained garden. Sharing the growing experience and passing tips and techniques down through the generations will ensure that growing fruit and vegetables becomes second nature to all involved.

Growing in containers

If you don't have a lot of space, or you simply enjoy growing in containers, choose large pots, and fill them with high-yielding family favorites. Baby parsnips and carrots can be sown in deep containers, while lettuce and beets will thrive in shallow pots. Blueberries, strawberries, and apples are also ideal. Ensure that crops such as green beans, tomatoes, squashes, zucchini, and sweet corn are given a warm, sunny spot to encourage their pods and fruits to develop.

Alternative family crops

Peas
pages 68–69

Cabbages
pages 94–99

Pumpkins
pages 90–91

Cucumbers
pages 80–81

Radishes
pages 134–135

Brussels sprouts
pages 106–107

Swiss chard
pages 124–125

Kohlrabi
pages 170–171

Family mix

Designed for maximum productivity, this planting design includes popular crops that will be ready to harvest in summer, fall, and early winter. Make full use of the space by underplanting a triangle of slower-growing sweet corn with a fast-growing squash, which will cover the ground under the sweet corn. Winter crops like broccoli and purple-sprouting broccoli occupy the ground for a long period and so are planted together where they won't be disturbed.

TOP ROW: ■ early potatoes x 6 ■ beets x 30 ■ lettuce x 8 ■ bush tomatoes x 4

MIDDLE ROW: ■ broccoli x 8 ■ sprouting broccoli x 2 ■ squash x 1 ■ sweet corn x 9 ■ green beans x 12

BOTTOM ROW: ■ carrots x 45 ■ parsnips x 8 ■ onions x 30 ■ leeks x 10 ■ zucchini x 2

0

3ft

6ft

9ft

0   3ft   6ft

Chicory
pages 126–127

Peppers
pages 58–59

Strawberries
pages 200–201

Annual herbs
pages 190–191

Eggplant
pages 64–65

Red currants
pages 206–207

Also consider growing:

■ Chili peppers (pp.60–63)
■ Runner beans (pp.70–71)
■ Fava beans (pp.76–77)
■ Cut-and-come-again salads (pp.116–117)
■ Spinach (pp.122–123)
■ Turnips (pp.140–141)
■ Garlic (pp.162–163)
■ Rhubarb (pp.186–187)
■ Raspberries (pp.202–203)
■ Blueberries (pp.212–213)
■ Apples (pp.214–215)
■ Cherries (pp.220–221)

The gourmet plot

The vegetable and fruit world is a diverse one, and exciting for adventurous cooks. Many crops, such as globe artichokes and chicory, or unusual varieties of fruit and vegetables like purple carrots or red gooseberries, add excitement and interest to the garden, so why not embrace them—they're not likely to be found in many stores. These crops are also colorful characters, allowing you to create an eye-catching garden as well as a highly productive one. The saying that you "eat with your eyes as well as your mouth" has never been more appropriate.

Growing in containers

This plot features a mixture of textures and colors, meaning you can create movable combinations of pick-and-mix crops. Unusual salad leaves, herbs, edible flowers, and the feathery foliage of fennel and asparagus are just a few contrasting examples. Some bush fruits and perennial vegetables are included and require loam-based compost to boost health and longevity. Thirsty crops, like fennel and celery root, will need regular watering.

Alternative gourmet crops

Kale 'Black Tuscan'

Carrot 'Purple Haze'
page 138

Cabbage 'Siberia'

Tomato 'Tigerella'
page 56

Sprouting broccoli 'Claret'
page 104

Watercress
pages 130–131

Kohlrabi 'Kolibri'
page 170

Swiss chard 'Ruby'

Gourmet mix

The aim here is to fill your plot, no matter how large or small, with produce that is expensive to buy or rarely seen in your local supermarket. Asparagus and red currants are luxury crops that are relatively easy to grow. Fava beans, picked young and sweet, are a revelation compared with any you can buy in the store; and rows of fresh Asian greens will supply enough leaves and stems for your stir-fries and salads all summer.

TOP ROW: ■ salad potatoes x 6
■ fava beans x 20 ■ asparagus x 4

MIDDLE ROW: ■ celery root x 9
■ strawberries x 8 ■ red currant x 1
■ Florence fennel x 10 ■ garlic x 14

BOTTOM ROW: ■ squash x 1
■ chicory x 6 ■ shallots x 8
■ loose-leaf lettuce x 8 ■ Asian
greens x 10 ■ loose-leaf lettuce x 8
■ Asian greens x 10

0

3ft

6ft

9ft

0   3ft   6ft

Also consider growing:
■ Pepper 'Yellow Stuffer'
■ Chili pepper 'Ancho'
■ Pea 'Purple Podded'
■ Green bean 'Lingua di Fuoco'
■ Winter squash 'Uchiki Kuri' (p.88)
■ Pumpkin 'Rouge Vif d'Etampes' (p.90)
■ Jerusalem artichokes (pp.184–185)
■ Cilantro (pp.190–191)
■ Gooseberry 'Lancashire Lad' (p.210)
■ Gage 'Coe's Golden Drop'

Beet 'Chioggia Pink'
page 136

Peppermint
pages 194–195

Peach 'Garden Lady'
page 222

Globe artichokes
pages 182–183

Calabrese broccoli 'Romanesco'
page 102

Blueberries
pages 212–213

GROW YOUR OWN Vegetables

Fruiting crops

Although commonly regarded as vegetables, these crops are actually fruits because this is the part of the plant you eat, unlike root or leaf crops. They are among the most exciting vegetables to grow, coming in a range of shapes, sizes, and colors to suit all tastes. Requiring a sunny, warm spot and high-potash feed, tomatoes, peppers, chili peppers, and eggplant will reward you with produce that is sweet (and in some cases hot) as well as delicious. Many varieties have been bred to be compact and heavy cropping, so they are perfect for those who don't want their vegetables to take up too much space in the garden.

STEP-BY-STEP Tomatoes

Tomatoes are easy to grow under cover or outside in a sunny spot and produce a reliable harvest all summer. There are many varieties to choose from, producing fruit in a wide array of colors, flavors, and sizes. These fall into two main types: cordon tomatoes that are usually trained up tall stakes or strings, and bush varieties that are grown more freely. There are also dwarf varieties to grow in containers and tumbling tomatoes for hanging baskets.

	SPRING	SUMMER	FALL	WINTER
SOW				
HARVEST				

TIME TO HARVEST: 16–18 WEEKS

SUITABLE FOR: BEDS, CONTAINERS, AND GROWING BAGS – UNDER COVER OR OUTSIDE

0   3ft   6ft   9ft

11 plants

9FT (3M) ROWS
Plant 12in (30cm) apart, depending on variety

GROWING BAGS
3 plants in each

1 Sowing seeds

Sow tomatoes under cover in mid-spring. Fill a pot or tray with compost, water well, then sow the seeds on top, spacing them about ½in (1cm) apart. Cover lightly with compost, and place the tray in a heated propagator set at 72°F (18°C) for a week or two, or until they germinate. Place the seedlings into individual pots when they develop their first pair of leaves. Grow them under cover for a few weeks until ready to plant into their final growing positions.

Sowing seeds individually *into modules removes the need to separate them as seedlings. This minimizes root disturbance of young plants.*

Grow the seedlings *until roots appear at the base of the modules. They can then be potted into larger pots or planted outside if conditions allow.*

To conserve moisture, *make the planting holes in your growing bags just large enough to plant in, and leave room so you can water easily.*

Support tomato plants *as they grow, especially those trained as cordons. Vertical strings are very practical for indoor crops and are very flexible.*

2 Growing indoors

Tomatoes crop best when grown under cover in greenhouses or growing frames and can be planted into beds, growing bags, or containers. They need a bright spot, shaded from hot sun, with good airflow. They should be watered daily in warm spells and fed regularly. Cordon types, trained as a single stem with the sideshoots removed, are best for growing this way; they require less space than bush types.

TIP *Hang sticky yellow traps near indoor crops to control whitefly (see p.238).*

3 Growing outside

To grow tomatoes outside, choose a sunny site, and prepare the soil by digging in well-rotted organic matter. Alternatively, plant into growing bags or containers. Water plants during dry times, and regularly feed with tomato fertilizer. Bush tomatoes have more room to spread outside and should be supported with several stakes per plant.

Plant tomatoes outside *at the same depth as they were in their pots, and firm them in gently.*

Insert stakes *near the plants after planting. Outdoor cordons require only a single support.*

Tie in the tomato stems *as they grow to help support the developing trusses of fruit.*

Use your fingers to pinch off *sideshoots as soon as they appear on cordon tomatoes. Use a sharp knife to remove older, thicker shoots.*

Tomato plants are especially thirsty *when they are in flower or fruit. It is important to keep plants in growing bags constantly moist.*

4 Training

Cordon tomatoes are grown as single stems trained up a stake or string. Regularly check your plants for sideshoots in the leaf joints, and pinch them off. The sideshoots on bush-types can be left to grow. Once cordon plants have formed four or five flower trusses, cut out the tops to stop further growth.

5 Routine care

Water all plants regularly (possibly daily for under cover crops), and feed them every week with a high potash tomato fertilizer once the first flowers appear. Avoid letting plants dry out, which can cause the fruit to split and may lead to the nutrient disorder, blossom end rot (see p.247).

6 Harvesting

Tomatoes ripen from midsummer onward; for the best flavor, wait until each fruit is evenly colored. Smaller tomatoes ripen quickly, but larger fruits, like those from beefsteak types, can take several days. Picked tomatoes keep for a few days, but if you can't use them soon, cook and freeze the surplus. Underripe fruits will ripen indoors if kept in the sun near a banana.

To harvest fruit, *place your thumb on the stalk "knuckle," and bend the tomato upward.*

Tomatoes

1 'Totem' This dwarf bush variety should be planted in a growing bag or window box and won't need pinching off. The cherry-sized red fruits are produced in abundance.

2 'Tumbling Tom Yellow' This compact, cascading bush tomato is ideal for growing in sunny hanging baskets. Pick the cherry-sized, golden fruits throughout the summer.

3 'Tumbler' This cascading bush tomato is an excellent choice to grow in hanging baskets, window boxes, and containers. It is particularly well suited to smaller gardens.

4 'Marmande' This beefsteak variety bears large, deep red fruits with few seeds. Grow this cordon-type outdoors; support it with a stake, and remove any sideshoots.

5 'Sungold' One of the sweetest-tasting, this hybrid bears cherry-sized, deep-orange fruits. It is suitable for growing indoors or out and should be trained as a cordon.

6 'Gardener's Delight' A well-known cherry variety, it bears long trusses of sweet, red fruits. It can be grown under cover or outside and should be trained as a cordon.

7 'Sweet Olive' A hybrid "baby plum" tomato, it yields oblong-shaped red fruits, each about 1½in (4cm) long. It is suitable for growing inside or out, but should be staked for support.

8 'Moneymaker' A traditional cordon variety that can be grown indoors or out, it bears red, medium-sized tomatoes. Remove sideshoots, and train the stem up a cane or vertical strings.

9 'Tigerella' This unusual, early variety bears medium-sized, red fruits with distinctive yellow stripes. It can be grown under cover or outside and should be trained as a single cordon.

Other varieties
'Gartenperle'
'Roma VF'
'Ferline'
'Green Sausage'
'Yellow Stuffer'
'Black Russian'

STEP-BY-STEP Peppers

Ideal for growing in containers, just two or three plants will supply you with plenty of sweet, delicious fruits, particularly if they are grown under cover. There are many different varieties to choose from, with fruits in a range of shapes and colors—including purple, orange, and black. Either harvest while the fruits are green to encourage others to form, or leave them to color up and mature so they develop their full sweet flavor.

	SPRING	SUMMER	FALL	WINTER
SOW				
HARVEST				

TIME TO HARVEST: 20–26 WEEKS

SUITABLE FOR: BEDS, CONTAINERS, AND GROWING BAGS – UNDER COVER OR OUTSIDE

8 plants

9FT (3M) ROWS
Plant out 16in (40cm) apart

GROWING BAGS
3 plants in each

1 Getting started

Peppers are tender plants that require a long growing season, so it's important to sow them under cover early in the year to give them time to mature and produce fruit. Plants will grow well in large containers as long as you provide them with fertile compost and enough space to develop.

'California Wonder' *bears large, squarish, glossy red fruits with a very sweet flavor.*

'Marconi' *fruits are long, thin, and tapered. They mature to a rich, glossy red color.*

'Gourmet' *is a compact plant that bears good yields of sweet, bright orange peppers.*

'Gypsy' *peppers are borne prolifically. The compact fruits are fleshy and very flavorful.*

Seed can be sown *individually in smaller pots. Cover each seed with a thin layer of soil, and place in a heated propagator.*

Plant strong seedlings *into 3½in (9cm) pots, and continue to grow them under cover. Keep the young plants well watered.*

Once the plants' roots *fill their pots, they can be planted on again. Choose a large pot so the pepper has space to grow.*

2 Sowing seeds

Fill pots with seed compost, firm gently, water well, and allow to drain. Sow seeds ½in (1cm) apart on the top, pressing them gently into the surface. Cover with a ¼in (5mm) layer of compost, water lightly, and place on a sunny windowsill. Once germinated and large enough to handle, remove from the propagator, and place the seedlings into individual pots. When plants reach 8in (20cm) in height, start feeding them regularly with a liquid tomato fertilizer.

TIP *At about 12in (30cm) tall, pinch off the growing tips to promote bushy growth.*

3 Planting out

If you plan to position peppers outside, harden them off in early summer by placing them outside during the day and inside at night for two weeks. Plant in a sunny, sheltered site, spacing plants 16in (40cm) apart in each direction, or into containers of multi-purpose compost with a minimum diameter of 12in (30cm). Water well.

Pepper plants will be ready to transplant *in early summer. Only plant them out once all risk of frost has passed, in a warm, sheltered site.*

Firm the plants in well *since they will become heavy over time. Water thoroughly, and keep the plants moist during all stages of growth.*

Insert a stout bamboo stake *24in (60cm) in height next to each plant, and tie it in. The large fruits become heavy as they develop.*

When the first fruits appear, *feed the plants every two weeks. Feeding and regular watering will deter the fruit skins from splitting.*

4 Growing indoors

Peppers can also be grown on a sunny windowsill indoors or in a bright spot under cover. You will need to hand pollinate indoor flowers. Simply insert a cotton swab or soft paintbrush into the center of each flower once it is fully open, then transfer the attached pollen to a similarly open bloom.

5 Routine care

Keep plants well watered, and feed regularly with a high potash liquid fertilizer such as tomato feed to encourage flowers and fruit to form. Often plants will produce one large fruit before then developing others; it is best to pick this while green so that subsequent fruits are given the chance to mature.

6 Harvesting

Individual fruit will begin to color up from green, through to either yellow, orange, red, or purple, depending on the variety. Either harvest them while green, or wait for them to mature, when their flavor becomes sweeter. Cut individual fruit off with a pair of shears instead of pulling them, because this can damage the plant. Cover outdoor plants with a cloche in the fall to help speed up ripening.

Cut the peppers *leaving a small portion of stem attached—this will help them to last longer.*

STEP-BY-STEP Chili peppers

These tiny peppers add real color to the plot and are very easy to grow. All they need is a bright, sunny location, and they will crop well in the smallest garden, even on a windowsill. Available in red, green, yellow, orange, and purple, and with a huge array of "heats"—from mild to atomic—it's easy to select a variety to suit your taste. Many are also excellent for drying, meaning that one plant can provide you with a whole year's supply of chilis.

	SPRING	SUMMER	FALL	WINTER
SOW				
HARVEST				

TIME TO HARVEST: 24–28 WEEKS

SUITABLE FOR: BEDS, CONTAINERS, AND GROWING BAGS—UNDER COVER OR OUTSIDE

11 plants

9FT (3M) ROWS
Plant out 12in (30cm) apart

GROWING BAGS
3 plants in each

Chili seeds *are quite large and easy to handle. Sow ¼in (5mm) deep, and if sowing into trays, space the seeds roughly ¾in (2cm) apart.*

Thin the seedlings *as they grow to one per pot. If using biodegradable pots (as above), the plants can be planted out in them; the pot will soon rot away.*

1 Sowing under cover

Chili peppers need a long growing season and should be sown under cover in early spring. Fill small pots or seed trays with seed compost, water well, and allow to drain. Sow the seed, water again, and place the trays or pots in a heated propagator set at 68–75°F (20–24°C). Once seedlings appear after a week or two, continue to grow them under cover in a warm location.

TIP *You can place sowings in a cupboard if you check them daily.*

2 Growing on

Grow the seedlings under cover in a bright location, keeping them no cooler than 64°F (18°C), even at night. Pot module-raised plants into 4in (10cm) pots as soon as their roots fill the cells. When seedlings reach 4in (10cm) tall, start feeding them using a high-potash liquid fertilizer, such as tomato feed. To encourage plenty of fruiting stems, pinch off the plants when 8in (20cm) tall, unless they branch out naturally.

Pot on plants *as they grow to prevent them from becoming pot-bound, which will check their growth. Use a multipurpose compost.*

Grow under cover *until frost has passed and plants can be planted out. Pot indoor crops into their final containers once large enough.*

3 Planting out

If you plan to grow your chili plants outside, begin hardening them off in early summer. Once they are ready they can be potted up into containers or a growing bag, or planted into free-draining soil in a sunny spot. If you are growing your plants on under cover, ensure that you pot them into containers at least 10in (25cm) wide.

Plant chilis out *at the same depth as they were in their pots, and water them in well. Protect them from slugs with a scattering of pellets.*

Support the plants *by inserting a sturdy stake next to each one, and tie it in with soft string. Use several stakes to support large-fruited varieties.*

Keep plants well watered *all summer to encourage a good crop. Dry spells can result in lower yields and smaller, hotter chilis.*

Chilis crop over many weeks, *and surplus fruit can be frozen as well as dried. Be careful not to touch your eyes after handling them.*

4 Routine care

Water plants regularly during the growing season, especially those under cover or in containers, and feed often with a liquid tomato fertilizer. If the weather is cool or windy, or if the plants are growing under cover, hand-pollinate the flowers using a soft brush or cotton swab to encourage fruit to set.

5 Harvesting

Chilis mature over several weeks and can be harvested as soon as they are large enough, whether still green or fully colored. At the end of the season, outdoor plants can either be covered with cloches or pulled from the soil and hung in a warm dry spot for any remaining fruits to ripen.

Drying the peppers

Chilis can be dried green or fully ripe, although you'll need varieties with thin skins—fleshier types tend to decay. Lay the fruits out under cover on wire racks in a warm, dry, well-ventilated spot. Fruits can also be strung together and hung up. Chilis dry in about a week and can be stored on strings or in jars.

Chili peppers

1 'Apache' This compact variety is ideal for patio containers and window boxes since it only reaches 18in (45cm) tall. The red fruits have a medium heat and grow to 1½in (4cm) long.

2 'Alma Paprika' A mild-tasting variety, this chili is suitable for cooler areas. The rounded fruit grow to 2in (5cm) long and can be sliced and used in salads. The fruits are best used fresh.

3 'Hungarian Hot Wax' This is a good choice for cooler areas, producing large, pointed, mild-tasting fruits. They ripen from pale yellow to red and can be harvested once large enough.

4 'Prairie Fire' This is a prolific variety and gives a steady crop of small, brightly colored fruits throughout summer—they are very hot. Suitable for containers and for drying.

5 'Aji Amarillo' Bearing long, slender fruits that are particularly hot-tasting, this variety needs a warm location to grow well and does best under cover. The fruit can be picked green or red.

6 'Padron' This chili produces a good crop of 2in (5cm) long fruits over several weeks that can be picked when mild and green, or left to ripen fully and heat up. It is suitable for drying.

7 Cayenne This is a type of chili, rather than a distinct variety, and bears long curling fruit, up to 12in (30cm) long. It has thin skin, making it ideal for drying, and a hot, fiery flavor.

8 'Cherry Bomb' Producing masses of tiny, berrylike fruit that are very hot, this chili is compact and suitable for pots. It is also attractive enough to grow as an ornamental.

9 'Demon Red' This variety gives a large crop of small red fruit that are thin-skinned and very hot. It is a compact plant, suitable for containers, and grows well in cooler areas.

Other varieties
'Heatwave'
'Hot Mexican'
'Inferno'
'Ring of Fire'
'Tabasco'

STEP-BY-STEP Eggplant

Eggplant ideally need a warm, sheltered spot, but the introduction of modern hybrids and grafted plants means that they can crop well in cooler climates. A plant can produce from four and eight fruits—they do best in well-enriched soil and when given a sunny site in a greenhouse. There are many different types of eggplant available, from the classic large-fruited, purple-skinned varieties to tiny, green- or white-skinned types used in Asian cooking.

	SPRING	SUMMER	FALL	WINTER
SOW				
HARVEST				

TIME TO HARVEST: 24–28 WEEKS

SUITABLE FOR: BEDS, CONTAINERS, AND GROWING BAGS, UNDER COVER OR OUTSIDE

0   3ft   6ft   9ft

11 plants

9FT (3M) ROWS
Plant 12in (30cm) apart

GROWING BAGS
3 plants in each

1 Getting started

Eggplant are commonly raised from seed, but they can also be bought as young plants in spring. Grafted plants crop very heavily and consist of a named fruiting variety grafted onto the vigorous root system of another. These plants are available from mail order seed suppliers and nurseries.

'Moneymaker' *is a reliable, large-fruited variety to grow under cover or outside.*

'Calliope' *produces a good yield of small rounded fruit. It is a good choice for pots.*

'Black Enorma' *is grown for its very large, dark, glossy fruit. It crops heavily and reliably.*

White-fruiting *plants are not widely sold but gave rise to the common name, eggplant.*

Fill small pots or modules *with seed compost. Firm it in gently, water well, and leave it to drain before sowing.*

Sow one seed *in each pot, and put them in a warm propagator. Germination takes about a week, but check the pots every day.*

Remove from the propagator *and keep growing the seedlings. They don't need separating, just repot them as they grow.*

2 Sowing under cover

Start seed under cover in early spring. Fill small pots with seed compost, firm gently, water well, and allow to drain. Sow seeds on the surface, spacing them ¾in (2cm) apart (or sow individually—see left), and lightly press them into the surface using a pencil or dibber. Cover the seed with a little more compost, water them in, and place the pots in a heated propagator. Once seedlings are large enough to handle, place them into individual 4in (10cm) pots of multi-purpose compost, and grow them under cover. Feed regularly with a balanced liquid fertilizer to encourage healthy growth.

3 Growing indoors

When roots appear through the base of the pots, repot the plants individually into containers at least 12in (30cm) wide, filled with multi-purpose compost. If you have several plants, plant three in each standard-sized growing bag. Grow them in a bright sunny location under cover, such as in a greenhouse or mini greenhouse.

Root disturbance checks growth, *so keep the root ball intact when potting plants. Also avoid letting young plants become pot-bound.*

Outdoor plants should be hardened off *fully before being planted out. Gradually acclimatize them to outdoor conditions over a few weeks.*

Eggplant fruits become heavy *as they develop. Support fruiting plants with stakes and string to prevent the stems from snapping.*

4 Growing outside

Once all risk of frost has passed, plant eggplant out in a sunny, sheltered spot. Plant directly into the soil, or grow outside in containers. Support all plants with stakes, and pinch off the main shoot when they reach 12in (30cm) tall to promote bushier growth.

5 Routine care

Keep plants well watered, and as soon as the first flowers appear, switch from a general purpose liquid feed to one high in potash to encourage fruiting. The flowers require pollination, so open greenhouse doors on sunny days if growing plants under cover.

6 Harvesting

Harvest fruits as soon as they are large enough. The skins should still be shiny; if they are dull then the eggplant are overripe. Pick regularly to encourage fruiting, and remove small fruits at the end of the season to help those that remain to develop fully.

 TIP *Eggplant don't keep well, so use them shortly after picking.*

Cut ripe eggplant *from the plants using shears. The stems can be tough and woody.*

Podded crops

Harvested while still young and eaten within the hour, the taste of peas and beans is absolutely sublime. One of the secrets to a good harvest is encouraging a strong root system to ensure the continued production of flowers and pods—a cool, moist root zone is ideal. Continual picking also encourages a prolonged harvest of peas and beans, giving a steady supply of tender pods throughout summer. The ability of some crops, such as peas and beans, to absorb nitrogen from the air and lock it into the soil also increases soil fertility.

STEP-BY-STEP Peas

All vegetables taste better when picked fresh, but that is especially so with peas, which are almost like a different crop from store-bought pods. Peas are very easy to grow, with dwarf and climbing types, and are ideal for smaller plots. Sown little and often, you can enjoy fresh peas from late spring to mid-fall. As well as traditional podded peas, try growing premium types like sugar snaps and snow peas, which are expensive to sow.

	SPRING	SUMMER	FALL	WINTER
SOW				
HARVEST				

TIME TO HARVEST: 12–14 WEEKS

SUITABLE FOR: BEDS AND CONTAINERS

60 plants

9FT (3M) ROWS
Sow or plant out 2in (5cm) apart

CONTAINERS
20 plants in each

1 Getting started

Peas are raised from seed and come in two forms, those with smooth or wrinkly seeds. Smooth-seeded varieties are hardier and are suitable for sowing early. Those with wrinkly seeds are sweeter tasting and are best sown in late spring and summer. Check the packet before deciding which to plant.

'Oregon Sugar Pod' *is a sugar snap variety that should be harvested as whole pods when young.*

'Douce Provence' *bears a good harvest of traditional podded peas on dwarf plants.*

'Meteor' *produces a generous crop of sweet-tasting peas on compact plants. It is good in pots.*

'Feltham First' *is a dwarf, early-cropping variety, suitable for growing in containers.*

In small pots, *sow three seeds in each, but don't thin them; in "growing tubes," sow seeds singly. Seeds should be sown 2in (5cm) deep.*

Keep seedlings cool and well watered *until planted out to encourage a strong root system. Their growth can be stunted by poor care, reducing yield.*

2 Sowing under cover

Peas can be sown in spring to plant out when the weather warms. Alternatively, for an earlier crop, they can also be sown in fall and kept under cover to plant out as larger plants in spring. Sow into cardboard "growing tubes" or deep pots filled with seed compost. Water the seeds in, and they will germinate without additional heat within two weeks. Grow them on, harden them off, and plant out when the plants reach about 8in (20cm) tall.

TIP *Make your own "growing tubes" using old newspaper or rolls of cardboard.*

3 Sowing outside

When the soil starts to warm up in spring, make a drill 4in (10cm) wide and 2in (5cm) deep. Water it well, then space seeds 2in (5cm) apart along its length. Cover the seeds with soil, firm in gently, and water. If you are sowing in summer, water the soil well in the two days beforehand, and sow seed deeper than normal, at 3in (8cm).

Pea seeds need warm soil, *around 50°F (10°C), in order to germinate and may fail to grow or rot if it is too cold or wet. Space the seed evenly.*

Thin any seedlings *growing closer than 2in (5cm) apart. These plants can be cropped as tasty pea sprouts rather than composted.*

Insert stakes or pea sticks *next to the seedlings for support, or stretch a length of pea netting along the length of the row.*

Water pea plants thoroughly, *especially when the flowers appear, since this well help the developing pods to swell more quickly*

4 Providing support

Most peas are climbing plants and need support as they grow. Just after sowing or planting outside, insert twiggy sticks along the row, tall enough to suit the variety you are growing (check the packet). You can also use pea netting or chicken wire held upright using sturdy stakes.

5 Routine care

Keep the plants well watered throughout summer, especially when in flower or pod. Pigeons love pea foliage and pods and can quickly strip plants bare. If they are a problem in your area, cover young plants with fine netting, held taut to prevent birds from becoming snagged. Check for gaps.

6 Harvesting

Tender young peas should be ready to harvest from early summer onward. Pick them as they mature, and eat them as soon as possible to enjoy them at their sweetest. If your plants produce a glut, it is better to pick and freeze them regularly, since peas store particularly well this way. Leave a few pods to dry on the plants and turn yellow at the end of summer if you want to collect your own seed.

If picked regularly, *plants will crop for several weeks. Check plants every few days.*

STEP-BY-STEP Runner beans

This is one of the most productive crops you can grow and will supply a ready harvest of tender pods throughout summer; the more you pick, the more will grow. Most runner beans are climbing plants and take up little bed space, making them a good choice for smaller plots. The easiest way to grow them is up a wigwam of poles, which can easily be incorporated into flowering borders. This also makes efficient use of your vertical growing spaces.

	SPRING	SUMMER	FALL	WINTER
SOW				
HARVEST				

TIME TO HARVEST: 12–16 WEEKS

SUITABLE FOR: BEDS AND CONTAINERS

15 plants

9FT (3M) ROWS
Sow direct or plant out 8in (20cm) apart

CONTAINERS
4 plants in each

1 Getting started

For larger crops it's cheaper to grow your own plants from seed, sowing them under cover or directly outside. Runner beans are also sold as plants in spring, which is ideal if you only want a few. As well as climbing varieties, there are also dwarf bush-types that are ideal for growing in patio containers.

'Desiree' *is a tasty and productive variety that gives a prolonged harvest during summer.*

'White Lady' *has white flowers that are less attractive to birds, which may eat them.*

'Lady Di' *produces long, stringless pods during summer. It is a reliable variety for beginners.*

'Polestar' *is a stringless variety, bearing large pods, 10in (25cm) long, throughout summer.*

Prepare the soil by *digging in well-rotted organic matter before sowing—this is ideal for beans, which prefer rich, moist soil.*

Insert poles *either in two rows to join at the top, which can then be linked as a row, or in circles of four or five to create wigwams.*

Wait until the soil is warm *enough before sowing directly. It needs to be at least 54°F (12°C) for them to germinate.*

2 Sowing outside

Runner beans are tender plants and should only be sown outside once the risk of frost has passed. Before sowing, prepare the soil well by digging a trench or large circle (for wigwams) in spring, and fill it with well-rotted organic matter, such as compost or manure. Insert poles where the plants are to grow, and sow one or two seeds at the base of each, 2in (5cm) deep. Cover the seeds with soil, firm in gently, and water well. The seeds will take a couple of weeks to germinate, after which they should be thinned to the healthiest one per pole. Protect the seedlings from slugs with a light sprinkling of pellets.

3 Sowing inside

In cooler areas, start seeds off under cover—seed will germinate earlier and more reliably. Sow the seeds individually into pots or "growing tubes" filled with seed compost, and water them well. Grow them on under cover in a bright spot for a few weeks. Plant out once risk of frost has passed. Keep them well watered.

Sow the seeds *2in (5cm) deep, and water well. It's worth sowing more than you need in case some fail to come up.*

Harden off the seedlings *by standing them outside during the day and bringing them in at night for about two weeks.*

Plant out seedlings *at the base of your poles, one per support. Water the plants in well, and twist the stem up the pole.*

Mulch plants *with plenty of well-rotted manure or garden compost. This will help to keep the root area moist and encourage the best crop.*

Runner bean roots *grow deep into the soil. Ensure you give your plants a good soaking so the water penetrates right down to them.*

4 Mulching

Runner beans are hungry and thirsty plants. To help conserve moisture and to help feed your crop, mulch the plants in summer with well-rotted organic matter, such as garden compost. This is particularly worthwhile for crops growing in containers.

5 Routine care

Plants must be kept well watered once the flowers appear in order to produce beans; dry spells can cause the flowers or beans to wither and fall. Pinch off the growing tips when the stems reach the top of the poles to promote new cropping sideshoots.

6 Harvesting

Pick the pods as soon as they are large enough, and check plants every two or three days; regular picking promotes a prolonged harvest. Beans left to grow for too long become tough, so pick regularly when they are young and tender, and freeze any extra.

| TIP | *If you are going away in summer, ask neighbors to pick the beans for you.* |

To save your own seed, *leave a few pods to develop fully on the plants at the end of summer.*

STEP-BY-STEP Green beans

Otherwise known as snap beans, green beans are an easy crop for beginners and can be harvested for their plump pods or for the beans themselves. They are also a good choice for smaller lots, with climbing varieties that can be trained up space-saving rows of wigwams and dwarf varieties that can be grown in containers. If you have access to a warm greenhouse, you can even grow them under cover for an extra-early spring crop.

	SPRING	SUMMER	FALL	WINTER
SOW				
HARVEST				

TIME TO HARVEST: 12–16 WEEKS

SUITABLE FOR: BEDS, CONTAINERS, AND GROWING BAGS

12 plants

9FT (3M) ROWS
Sow or plant out 10in (25cm) apart

CONTAINERS
4 plants in each

1 Sowing outside

The simplest way to grow green beans is to sow seed in the soil in late spring. Prepare the site by digging in well-rotted organic matter such as garden compost (this can also be done in the fall), and remove any weeds. Firm the soil, and rake it level. Insert stakes where climbing plants are to grow, 10in (25cm) apart, and sow two seeds at the base of each, 2in (5cm) deep. Thin the seedlings to one per stake.

Green beans are hungry plants *and need moist soil, rich in organic matter, to crop well.*

Sow seed directly *only once the soil has warmed up in spring. Use cloches to hasten this process.*

2 Sowing under cover

For an early start in cooler areas, sow seed under cover, 1¼in (3cm) deep, two per pot or "growing tube" filled with seed compost. Keep them moist, and germination will take about one weeks at 59–64°F (15–18°C).

Paper "growing tubes" *are easy to make and ideal for bean plants, accommodating their deep roots.*

Seedlings grow quickly, *so don't sow them too early—they can't be planted out until after the last frost.*

3 Growing on

Grow the seedlings on under cover in a bright location until the risk of frost has passed. As they grow, thin those plants sown in pots to leave the strongest seedling per pot. Once the plants reach 3in (8cm) tall, harden them off by standing them outside during the day and bringing them in at night. Any seedlings sown directly outside should be kept well watered and protected from slugs. Use bottle cloches to encourage strong growth.

Seedlings become tangled *unless they are thinned early. The roots will also be hard to separate.*

4 Planting out

Plant out indoor-raised seedlings of climbing types at the base of their stakes, water in well, and gently twine the main stem around its stake. If space is limited, insert the stakes after planting. Dwarf beans can also be planted in large containers (offering at least 10in (25cm) of space per plant), or plant three beans to a growing bag.

Carefully ease pot-raised beans *from their pots. Plants raised in "growing tubes" are planted tube-and-all; the paper tube will quickly rot away.*

Plant at the same depth *as the plants were in their pots, firm gently, and water well. Twine the young stem around the stake after planting.*

Insert a row of poles *at least 8ft (2.5m) tall for climbing varieties, pushing them 12in (30cm) into the soil. Tie in the young stems using soft string.*

Weeds attract pests *and slow down growth, so keep them under control. Remove weeds between plants by hand, or carefully use a hoe.*

5 Providing support

Climbing beans are self-clinging once established and will wrap themselves around their supports, although new growth and the occasional wayward stem may need tying in. Dwarf varieties are bushy and do not require additional support or tying in.

6 Routine care

Once the plants start to flower, keep them well watered, and feed regularly with a balanced liquid fertilizer. Dry spells may cause the flowers and young beans to drop. Protect young plants from slugs and snails with a light scattering of pellets.

7 Harvesting

Tender young pods can be picked as soon as they are large enough. Check plants every few days to pick them at their best; picking often also encourages a larger crop. If growing them for the bean seeds, leave the pods on the plant until fully mature.

TIP *Leave a few pods to mature fully at the end of the season to collect the seeds.*

Pinch the young pods *from the stem using your fingers before they become old and tough.*

Green beans

1 'Selma Zebra' An heirloom climbing variety, it matures early, bearing green pods that are heavily streaked. The distinctive purple color disappears during cooking.

2 'Borlotto' This dwarf variety produces flat pods that are heavily speckled with red. The beans can be used fresh or dried. Support the plants to keep the pods off the soil.

3 'Rocquencourt' A dwarf variety that freely bears vivid yellow pods. It is cold-tolerant and matures quickly, so is ideal for early and late sowings if given protection.

4 'Purple Teepee' This dwarf variety bears pods that are held above the foliage, making harvesting easier. Early and profuse, the stringless pods turn deep green when cooked.

5 'The Prince' Widely grown, this is a productive dwarf variety. The uniform green pods are borne steadily over a long season, which is unusual for a dwarf variety.

6 'Speedy' Incredibly quick to mature, this variety only takes approximately 60 days to produce green pods on stocky, dwarf plants. It is a good choice for early or late crops.

7 'Cobra' This climbing bean bears a long succession of tender, stringless, green pods. It also produces attractive purple flowers, making it a good choice to grow in an ornamental bed.

8 'Amethyst' Ideal for patio pots, this dwarf variety is especially compact. The purple pods are slender and stringless and are available for a long harvesting period.

9 'Delinel' This popular dwarf, green-podded variety bears tender pods that are totally stringless and have an excellent flavor. It is suitable for containers if watered well.

Other varieties
'Cornetti Meraviglia di Venezia'
'Yin Yang'
'Barlotto Lingua di Fuoco'
'Cannellino'
'Neckargold'

STEP-BY-STEP Fava beans

These small, tender beans are a must-grow crop, and store-bought pods don't compare to those picked fresh from the plant. They are one of the first vegetables to harvest in spring, which makes them a good choice for small plots since they can soon be replaced with other summer crops. If space is limited, they can also be grown in containers. As well as the mature beans, the young tips and pods are also edible, so make the most of their versatility.

	SPRING	SUMMER	FALL	WINTER
SOW				
HARVEST				

TIME TO HARVEST: 12–28 WEEKS

SUITABLE FOR: BEDS AND CONTAINERS

9FT (3M) ROWS
Sow direct or plant out 10in (25cm) apart

12 plants

CONTAINERS
16 plants in each

1 Getting started

Fava beans are usually raised from seed, although you may see young plants for sale in spring. They can be grown in most soil types, although those sown directly outside in the fall need good drainage to prevent them from rotting in the cold and wet. Check the packets for varieties suitable for fall sowing.

'The Sutton' *can be sown in fall or spring and crops early on sturdy dwarf plants.*

'Super Aquadulce' *gives an early crop of flavorful beans. Sow fall or spring.*

'Stereo' *is best sown in spring and can be picked as whole young pods or as mature beans.*

'Jubilee Hysor' *bears large pods, each packed with 6–8 beans. Sow in fall or spring.*

2 Sow inside

In cooler areas seeds can also be started off under cover in the fall or spring to plant out later, but don't give them too much warmth. Fava beans have long taproots, so sow the seeds individually into taller pots or "growing tubes." Germination takes a week; grow them in a cool, light spot, keeping them frost-free.

TIP *Plants grown in blocks help hold each other up.*

Tall "growing tubes," *which you can buy or make, are ideal for sowing beans under cover.*

3 Sowing outside

Fava beans can be sown directly into the soil during the fall or early spring. Fork the soil over first to remove any weeds and large lumps, and either sow into drills or into a grid pattern of individual holes, 10in (25cm) apart.

Fava beans *absorb nitrogen from the air and fix it in the soil. They don't require additional feeding.*

Sow the seed *2in (5cm) deep directly into beds or pots. Cover with soil, firm gently, and water in well.*

4 Planting out

Once indoor-sown plants show strong growth, harden them off for a week or two to acclimatize them to outdoor temperatures. Dig over the site thoroughly to remove weeds and break up lumps, and plant out 10in (25cm) apart each way. If planted in blocks, additional support is not necessary, except on more exposed sites.

Harden off plants *before planting them out in fall or spring. Place them outside in the day, bringing them in at night.*

Seedlings raised *in "growing tubes" can be planted still in the tube—the roots will penetrate through; the tube will rot away.*

Protect seedlings *with fabric if hard frosts are due right after planting. Direct-sown plants don't require protection.*

Young plants *should be well watered at first but soon develop a deep taproot. On lighter soils, mulch plants with compost to retain moisture.*

Pinching off tips *encourages the bean pods to develop and also provides an early crop of tasty leaves, which are delicious when steamed.*

5 Routine care

Fava beans require little care once they are growing strongly and need only watering in summer when plants are flowering. Plants should be kept well weeded until they establish. Those grown in blocks crowd out most weeds anyway, but check occasionally.

6 Pinching off

When the first flowers begin to set pods, pinch off the soft growing tip of each plant. This causes the plants to focus on developing pods rather than leafy growth and also deters blackfly (see p.240), which feed on the shoots during late spring and summer.

7 Harvesting

Crops sown in fall are ready to harvest in late spring. These early crops are best harvested before the developing beans create visible swellings in the pods. All fava beans are best picked while young, so pick and freeze any you can't use right away. After harvesting, cut the plants to the ground, but leave the roots in the soil to break down. They will release their stored nitrogen for the next crop to use.

Fava beans *are best eaten fresh but keep well in their pods in the refrigerator for a few days.*

Cucurbits

This group of plants, which includes zucchini, summer and winter squashes, pumpkins, and cucumbers, is one of the most generous, especially summer varieties that produce crop after crop of melt-in-your-mouth, colorful fruits. Pumpkins and winter squash are invaluable for storing, allowing you to savor their sweet, nutty flesh throughout the fall and winter (and beyond in many cases). The fruits of some varieties can be gargantuan, too. Vigorous growth and a hungry appetite demand fertile soil and ample moisture, with plenty of warmth to speed up fruit development. Get these conditions right, and the rewards will be huge.

STEP-BY-STEP Cucumbers

These summer salad stalwarts are easy to grow in any garden, and although some varieties require a greenhouse to crop well, "ridge" varieties are perfectly happy outside. These can be left to sprawl over the ground, or where space is limited, they can be trained up sturdy stakes, making good use of your vertical surfaces. Small-fruited "snacking" cucumbers are particularly productive and convenient, with fruit just large enough for a lunch box.

	SPRING	SUMMER	FALL	WINTER
SOW				
HARVEST				

TIME TO HARVEST: 16–20 WEEKS

SUITABLE FOR: BEDS, CONTAINERS, AND GROWING BAGS, UNDER COVER OR OUTSIDE

0   3ft   6ft   9ft

11 plants

9FT (3M) ROWS
Plant 12in (30cm) apart

GROWING BAGS
3 plants in each

1 Getting started

Cucumbers can be raised from seed, which is ideal if you want several plants. They can also be bought as seedlings in spring, which may be a better choice if you only want a few. Cucumbers are productive, and depending on variety, just two or three plants will satisfy most families all summer.

'Burpless Tasty' *is an outdoor variety that freely produces long, glossy green fruit.*

'Passandra' *grows indoors and gives a large crop of small, single-serving fruits.*

'Masterpiece' *is an outdoor "ridge" variety. The fruits have small prickles on their skins.*

'Crystal Apple' *bears a good crop of small, round, juicy fruits. It is easy to grow outside.*

Cucumber seed can be expensive. *Sow one seed per pot, and keep them warm, 72–77°F (22-25°C), to encourage good germination.*

Check the seed regularly *until they germinate, which should take a week or two. Remove them from the propagator, and grow them indoors.*

2 Sowing seeds

Cucumber seeds should be started off under cover. Plants need a long growing season to fruit well and are very sensitive to the cold. Hybrid seeds may be more expensive, but they result in more vigorous, productive plants so are worth the extra expense. Fill 4in (10cm) diameter pots with seed compost, water well, and allow to drain. Sow one seed per pot, ¾in (2cm) deep, water lightly, and place them in a heated propagator until they germinate.

TIP *Cucumbers require constantly high temperatures, so don't sow too early.*

3 Planting out

Once they are large enough, plant cucumbers out in early summer —enrich the soil thoroughly in advance. Outdoor "ridge" varieties can be planted directly into the soil in a sunny spot and left to trail across the surface or can be trained up stakes. Greenhouse types can be planted one per 12in (30cm) pot, or three per standard-size growing bag.

Outdoor varieties *should be hardened off for a few weeks before planting to acclimatize them to outdoor conditions.*

Insert stakes to train *plants upward where space is limited. This also keeps the fruit clean and away from crawling pests.*

Growing bags are ideal *for greenhouse crops, but they can also be used outside. Allow the bag to warm up before planting.*

Female flowers *have an embryonic fruit behind the petals. These must be pollinated unless the variety is "all female." Check the label to be sure.*

Swelling cucumbers *become heavy, so make sure the stems are attached to their supports, especially mature plants with several fruits.*

4 Pollination

Outdoor varieties have both male and female flowers; the latter must be pollinated to set fruit. Many modern greenhouse varieties are "all female" and must not be pollinated—they will bear bitter-tasting fruits if they are. Grow these well away from varieties that produce male flowers.

5 Routine care

Keep plants well watered, and regularly apply tomato fertilizer, as directed on the packet. Indoor plants thrive in high humidity, which you can achieve by watering the ground around plants. This also helps deter red spider mite and powdery mildew (see p.240 and p.244), which are both common.

6 Harvesting

As soon as individual fruits are big enough, cut them from the plants using shears. Cucumbers grow quickly, and their quality declines if they are left too long on the plant. To enjoy them at their best, check plants daily, and harvest them as soon as they are ready. The fruit can be stored in the fridge until needed, if necessary. If you expect a surplus, very young fruits can be harvested as gherkins for pickling.

Some cucumbers *are smooth-skinned, others have small prickles, but they taste the same.*

STEP-BY-STEP Zucchini

Zucchini are notoriously productive, and just two or three plants are all you need to be self-sufficient in them throughout the summer. They require a rich soil and are extremely easy to grow in containers and growing bags, as well as in the ground. There are many varieties to choose from, with green or yellow fruits that can be either round or elongated. Leave them to mature, and your zucchini will develop into larger squashes, ideal for fall stews.

	SPRING	SUMMER	FALL	WINTER
SOW				
HARVEST				

TIME TO HARVEST: 14 WEEKS

SUITABLE FOR: BEDS, CONTAINERS, AND GROWING BAGS—UNDER COVER OR OUTSIDE

0   3ft   6ft   9ft

4 plants

9FT (3M) ROWS
Plant 36in (90cm) apart

GROWING BAGS
2 plants in each

1 Getting started

Zucchini are very easy to raise from seed, which is the best choice if you want to grow a particular variety. Alternatively, young plants are widely available to buy in the spring. Zucchini crops very quickly, so consider yellow-fruited varieties since the fruits are easier to spot among the dense foliage.

'Zucchini' *crops earlier than most varieties and bears green fruit, best cut at 6in (15cm) long.*

'Defender' *is resistant to cucumber mosaic virus (see p.242) and crops very heavily.*

'Jemmer' *produces attractive yellow fruits that stand out clearly among the dense leaves.*

'Parador' *fruits are a striking bright yellow, and keep their color well when cooked.*

Sow seeds *into 4in (10cm) wide pots part-filled with compost. Place the seeds on their sides to discourage decay, then cover with more compost.*

Direct sow seeds in pairs *1¼in (3cm) deep, 36in (90cm) apart, in early summer. Water well, cover with mini cloches, then thin each pair to one seedling.*

2 Sowing seeds

Zucchini are tender plants, and it is useful to sow seeds under cover to give them a head start for when the frosts pass. Sow seed singly in pots, 1in (2.5cm) deep, and place them in a heated propagator until germinated. Seed can also be sown directly outside during early summer, and provide a useful second flush of crops after indoor-raised plants. Choose a sunny and sheltered site, and improve the soil with organic matter before sowing.

TIP	*Young plants are prone to slug attack; protect your plants using pellets.*

3 Growing on

Grow the plants on under cover at a temperature of 64°F (18°C). Keep well watered, and begin feeding them with a balanced liquid fertilizer after two weeks. Plants will grow quickly and may need repotting if roots appear at the base of the pots. Harden them off, and plant out in beds or growing bags (see left), or one per 12in (30cm) pot.

Seedlings sown early *may need to be repotted if they outgrow their original pots before the frost has passed.*

Plants sown in later spring *can be hardened off as soon as the risk of frost has passed to acclimatize them to life outside.*

After planting out *you can cover plants with cloches or cut-off clear plastic bottles to help plants establish quickly.*

Mature plants *develop a broad canopy of leaves. A funnel (see below) makes watering easier; mark its position with a short stake.*

Powdery mildew *(see p.244) can develop on the foliage and weaken plants. Remove heavily affected leaves, and water more regularly.*

4 Watering

Zucchini are quick growing and fruiting, and should be kept well-watered throughout summer. To make this easier, create a well around individual plants for water to collect in, or plunge a funnel (an upturned bottle with the base cut off works well) next to each plant for direct watering.

5 Routine care

Young plants need weeding until established when their dense canopy of leaves will smother other competing plants. Most zucchini form a large rosette of leaves, but some newer varieties have a trailing style and can be trained up stakes. On older plants, regularly remove any yellowing leaves.

6 Harvesting

Using a sharp knife, harvest traditional zucchini when they measure between 3–6in (8–15cm) long; round-fruited varieties should be picked when 3–5in (7–12cm) across. Check over the plants daily—the fruit develop very quickly in summer. Alternatively, leave the fruits on one or two plants to develop fully. These plants will then give a smaller crop of thick-skinned squashes to harvest in late summer.

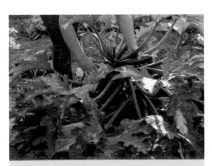

Keep harvesting young fruits—*if they are allowed to grow on, fewer fruit will be produced.*

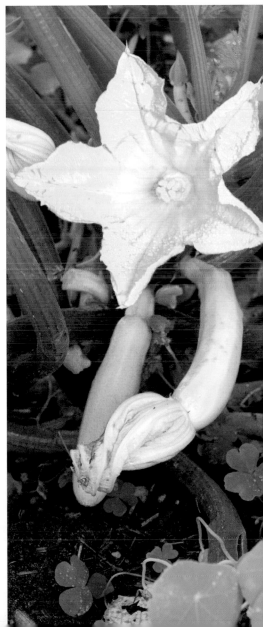

STEP-BY-STEP Summer squashes

A close relative of zucchini, summer squash are very easy to grow, and some can be trained upward, making them ideal for smaller plots. They come in a wide selection of shapes and sizes, including scallop-edged "patty pans" and crook-necked, vase-shaped varieties. All are extremely free-fruiting. The fruits are either harvested when small and thin-skinned to eat whole or can be allowed to grow large enough to stuff and roast for a hearty dinner.

	SPRING	SUMMER	FALL	WINTER
SOW				
HARVEST				

TIME TO HARVEST: 18–20 WEEKS

SUITABLE FOR: BEDS, CONTAINERS, AND GROWING BAGS

2–3 plants

9FT (3M) ROWS
Plant 3–5ft (1–1.5m) apart, depending on variety

GROWING BAGS
2 plants in each

1 Getting started

Only a few varieties of summer squash are commonly sold as young plants, so they are best raised from seed. The plants crop heavily, and two or three will give a good supply of fruit all summer, so don't grow more than you need. The fruits can be harvested while young to help keep on top of any summer surplus.

Patty pan *is a type of squash, not a variety, and can be yellow, green, or white in color.*

'Sunburst' *can be picked as young fruit or left to grow on. It crops freely if harvested often.*

'Tromboncino' *is best harvested when 12in (30cm) long, but can reach 3ft (1m) if left to grow on.*

'Rolet' *gives a good crop of baseball-sized fruits that have sweet-tasting flesh.*

Sow seed under cover *into 4in (10cm) wide pots, ¾in (2cm) deep, and cover with compost. Water them, and place the pots in a propagator.*

To sow direct, *first prepare a seedbed, and sow the seeds ¾in (2cm) deep, 36in (90cm) apart. Position each seed on its side to help prevent it from rotting.*

2 Sowing seeds

For an early start, sow seeds under cover into individual pots, and place them in a heated propagator until they germinate. Once the seedlings emerge, grow them under cover at 64°F (18°C) in a bright spot. After about two weeks, start feeding weekly with liquid fertilizer. Seeds can also be sown directly into the soil in early summer. Sow seed in pairs, water them in, and cover with a cloche or cut-off plastic bottles. Thin each pair to leave the stronger.

TIP *Summer squash prefer rich soil, so dig in organic matter well before planting.*

3 Growing on

Grow plants under cover until the risk of frost has passed, then harden them off to grow outside. Plant them out 3–5ft (1–1.5m) apart, and water in well. To make watering easier, bury an upturned bottle with the base cut off next to each plant to act as a funnel. Plants can also be grown one per 12in (30cm) container.

Harden off seedlings *for a few weeks before planting out, placing them outside during the day, but bringing them back under cover at night.*

Trailing summer squash varieties *can be planted beneath taller crops, such as sweet corn or tomatoes, or near rows of climbing beans.*

Mulch to help maintain moisture *if plants are allowed to dry out or are watered irregularly, the skins of the fruits may split.*

Train trailing squash stems *along the edges of beds or paths so the fruits are easy to pick. This will also free up bed space for other crops.*

4 Routine care

Summer squashes are vigorous plants and should be watered well and regularly fed with tomato fertilizer. To help conserve soil moisture, mulch around plants with a thick layer of compost or similar organic material. The mulch will gradually break down, steadily releasing nutrients to the plants.

5 Training

Most varieties are trailing plants and can be left to creep across the soil. To make harvesting easier, gradually remove the lower leaves as they grow to provide access to the fruit. If space is limited, the stems can also be looped into circles on the ground or trained vertically up cane wigwams.

6 Harvesting

Squashes produce separate male and female flowers on the same plant, but it is only the females that fruit. The flowers wither as soon as they are pollinated, and the fruit begins to develop. Young, tender squash will be ready to harvest after four to seven days, depending on the weather. They can be left to grow longer for larger fruit that are ideal for stuffing and roasting.

Squash that develop a thick skin *before harvesting will keep longer in storage.*

STEP-BY-STEP Winter squashes

Winter squash are available in a huge range of shapes and colors and provide a delicious feast in late fall and winter, especially when roasted or in soups. Easy to grow, they can be left to trail across the ground and make good use of the space between your other crops. They can also be grown in containers, with the stems trained to make a feature of the decorative fruit. If you have space, the crop stores and lasts well into the winter months.

	SPRING	SUMMER	FALL	WINTER
SOW				
HARVEST				

TIME TO HARVEST: 18–20 WEEKS

SUITABLE FOR: BEDS AND CONTAINERS

9FT (3M) ROWS
Sow or plant 3–5ft (1–1.5m) apart
2–3 plants

CONTAINERS
1 plant in each

1 Sowing under cover

Winter squash are frost sensitive but can be sown under cover in spring to be planted out when any danger of frost has passed. Fill 4in (10cm) pots with seed compost, water them well, and then leave them to drain. Sow one seed per pot at a depth of 1¼in (3cm). Place the pots in a heated propagator set at 59–64°F (15–18°C) for a week or two. Once the seedlings emerge, grow them in a warm, bright location.

Sow the seeds on their edge, thin-side down, so moisture doesn't collect on the top of the seed when it is watered, running the risk of decay.

Winter squash seedlings grow quickly but can only be planted out after the frost has passed, so don't sow them too early. Pot them on if necessary.

Direct-sow seed at the base of a sturdy support if you plan to train your squash plants as climbers. Seed can also be sown beneath tall crops.

Thin surplus seedlings to leave the strongest. If you have unwanted gaps, carefully move spare plants to where they are needed. Water in well.

2 Sowing outside

Sow seeds direct in late spring. First, prepare the soil by digging in plenty of well-rotted manure or compost, and remove weeds. Then firm and rake level. For an earlier crop, warm the soil first with cloches. Sow seeds in pairs, 1¼in (3cm) deep and 3ft (1m) apart, water well, and cover with a bottle cloche. Once each group of seedlings emerges, thin to leave only the strongest. Protect plants from slugs and snails.

TIP	Cut the base off clear plastic bottles to make your own mini cloches.

3 Planting out

Plants sown under cover can be planted out into their final positions in early summer. Before doing so, harden them off first to acclimatize them to outdoor conditions. Place them outside during the day, but bring them back in each night for two weeks. Plant out at 3ft (1m) apart, and water them in well. Protect young plants from slugs.

Water the plants well *before planting them out to help their roots establish successfully.*

Plant out at the same depth *as the plants were in their pots, and firm them in gently.*

Water in well, *and keep plants moist until they are growing well, especially on lighter soils.*

Mulch plants with well-rotted compost *to help retain moisture, especially on lighter soils. The mulch will break down, feeding your plants.*

Trailing stems *can be looped around stakes to form circles or trained up supports. Both methods will contain the plants' spread in smaller gardens.*

4 Routine care

Plants require plenty of water during the summer months, so to make watering easier, bury an upturned plastic bottle with the base removed next to each plant (see p.91). Also feed plants well by regularly applying a general-purpose liquid fertilizer, as directed by the instructions.

5 Training

Winter squash are either bushy or trailing. Bush-types form neat clumps of leaves, while trailing plants send out long, winding stems. These can be trained into loops if space is limited, or allowed to ramble among other plants. You can also train smaller-fruited varieties up trellis work or stakes.

6 Harvesting

In mid-fall the leaves will start to die back, and the fruits should be coloring up well. These need to be harvested before the first frost. Cut them from the plant, leaving a short length of stem attached to act as a handle. Leave the fruits in a warm, sunny spot for two weeks to harden the skins—a windowsill is ideal. The fruits can then be stored until needed.

Colorful fruits *can be used as a temporary seasonal decoration until needed in the kitchen.*

Winter squashes

1 'Sweet Dumpling' This trailing variety bears slightly ribbed, white-skinned fruits with green vertical stripes. Each fruit grows 5–6in (12–15cm) in diameter with yellow flesh.

2 'Uchiki Kuri' Also known as the "onion squash," this trailing variety bears delicious fruit with intense orange flesh. Expect to harvest five or six fruits per plant.

3 'Queensland Blue' This heirloom Australian variety bears heavily-ribbed gray-blue fruits. They reach 10in (25cm) in diameter and have intensely nutty, orange flesh.

4 'Butternut' These classically shaped squashes are borne on trailing plants. With deep orange flesh and few seeds, they are ideal for roasting or stuffing. They also store well.

5 'Cream of the Crop' This variety produces large acorn-shaped fruits with cream skins and nutty-flavored, golden flesh. The compact plants will yield three or four fruits each.

6 Turk's Turban A trailing type with sweet flesh, it bears unusually shaped orange fruit with bold green and white stripes. The fruits grow to 8–10in (20–25cm) in diameter.

7 'Crown Prince' This trailing plant bears round, squat, gray-blue fruit, 8–10in (20–25cm) in diameter. The deep orange flesh has a very good nutty flavor when cooked.

8 'Harlequin' With its highly colored fruit, this is an attractive variety to grow where space is limited and plants need to look good and produce a good harvest.

9 Vegetable spaghetti When steamed, the mild-tasting flesh of this trailing crop separates into spaghettilike strands. Expect three or four large fruits per plant.

Other varieties
'Blue Hubbard'
'Butternut Harrier'
'Celebration'
'Sunshine'

STEP-BY-STEP Pumpkins

Mammoth pumpkins take up a lot of space in the garden, but there are plenty of varieties with smaller fruit that are ideal where space is limited—some can even be planted in containers. Pumpkins are reliable and easy to grow. They just need a good supply of water and fertile soil, with some protection against slugs and snails. Although best known for carving at Halloween, the fruit has tasty sweet flesh and stores well into winter.

	SPRING	SUMMER	FALL	WINTER
SOW				
HARVEST				

TIME TO HARVEST: 18–22 WEEKS

SUITABLE FOR: BEDS AND CONTAINERS

2–3 plants

9FT (3M) ROWS
Plant 3–5ft (1–1.5m) apart, depending on variety

CONTAINERS
1 plant in each

1 Getting started

Pumpkins may be sold as plants in spring, but they are usually grown from seed, and there are many varieties to choose from. If you want large fruit for carving, pick a suitable variety, and thin the fruit to one or two per plant. For edible fruit, pick your variety, and let each plant develop four or five fruit each.

'Atlantic Giant' is one of the largest fruiting varieties and can be eaten if picked early.

'Jack be Little' bears small, brightly colored fruit that are tasty as well as decorative.

'Rouge Vif d'Etampes' is an heirloom variety, with large fruit, good for eating or decoration.

'Baby Bear' is a compact variety with thin-skinned fruit, each the size of a soccer ball.

Sow seed individually ¾in (2cm) deep into 4in (10cm) wide pots, and place them in a warm propagator set at 68–77°F (20–25°C).

Check the seeds daily until they germinate, which takes between one and two weeks. Remove the pots from the propagator, and grow them under cover.

2 Sowing under cover

Pumpkins need a long growing season to develop full-size fruit. Start them off under cover in spring, especially in cold areas, and then harden them off and plant outside when the frosts have passed. Part-fill small pots with seed compost, sow one seed per pot, water well, and allow to drain. Place pots in a heated propagator, and keep the compost moist. When seeds germinate, grow seedlings under cover for a few weeks in a bright spot.

TIP Sow the seeds on their sides to keep them from decaying in the compost.

3 Sowing outside

In late spring seeds can also be sown directly into the soil. Well before sowing, improve the soil with well-rotted organic matter such as garden compost, then sow the seeds 1¼in (3cm) deep and 3ft (1m) apart. Water them well, and cover with a cloche or a large, cut-off clear plastic bottle. Keep well-watered as they grow.

Sow outdoor seed *in groups of two or three in case any fail to grow. You can then thin to the strongest seedling as they start to develop.*

Carefully transplant *stronger spare seedlings if they are needed elsewhere in the bed. Lift them with a trowel, and water well once planted.*

Mulching plants *with well-rotted organic matter such as garden compost will help retain moisture in summer. It will also feed your plants.*

Where space is limited, *train pumpkin plants vertically, using old nets to support the swelling fruit. Tie the stems in as they grow.*

4 Routine care

Pumpkins are hungry plants and will benefit from regular feeding with a liquid general-purpose fertilizer. Young plants need weeding until they establish fully. To keep the fruit clean and off the soil, place a short plank of wood under each one.

5 Training

Most pumpkins have trailing stems and can be left to ramble over the ground among other plants. Where space is limited, tie the stems to stakes set out in a circle and pushed into the soil. Small-fruited varieties can also be trained up sturdy supports.

6 Harvesting

In mid-fall your fruits will be ready for harvest. Cut them with a short length of stalk attached to prevent the stem from rotting back into the fruit, and to provide a handy carrying handle. Unless you plan to use them right away, dry or "cure" the skins by leaving them in a sunny spot outside for at least a week. If rain is predicted, move them to a bright location under cover. The fruit will store well for months.

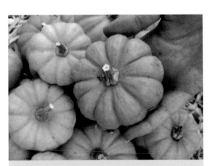

Small pumpkins *can be cooked whole; larger fruits should be cut into manageable pieces.*

Brassicas

Delicious and versatile, brassicas are a must for any vegetable garden. Robust crops like sprouting broccoli, Brussels sprouts, and kale provide vitamin-rich green vegetables in the middle of winter when crops are scarce, while cabbages and cauliflower have been bred for harvesting all year round. Calabrese, more commonly known as broccoli, also offers tender summer-season crops. Provide brassicas with fertile, well drained soil, and cover plants to prevent damage from pests such as cabbage white butterfly caterpillars, and you can enjoy a range of tasty, nutritious green vegetables every month of the year.

STEP-BY-STEP Summer and fall cabbages

Whether you eat cabbage as part of a midweek dinner or use them in more exotic dishes like stir-fries, they are an essential vegetable. They can be grown throughout the year (also see p.104), with summer and fall varieties producing a large, reliable harvest if kept well-watered and covered with nets. Once harvested, the stumps can be left in the ground to resprout, giving a second crop of loose leaves and making best use of your plot.

	SPRING	SUMMER	FALL	WINTER
SOW				
HARVEST				

TIME TO HARVEST: 18–24 WEEKS

SUITABLE FOR: BEDS

8 plants

9FT (3M) ROWS
Plant out to between 14–16in (35–40cm) apart

Sow the seeds thinly, *and check them daily until seedlings emerge. They don't need additional heat.*

Thin seedlings *as they develop in their trays; those left can be pulled and placed into small pots.*

1 Sowing under cover

For an early harvest, sow summer varieties under cover in the spring. Fill trays with seed compost, water well, allow to drain, then sow the seed ¾in (2cm) deep. When the seedlings appear, thin them out to leave the strongest, then plant the remaining ones into individual small pots. Grow the young plants on indoors in a bright spot for a few weeks longer.

TIP	*Cabbages, like most brassicas, are prone to club root (see p.242).*

2 Sowing outside

Although cabbage can be sown under cover, the main season crop is sown outside directly into the soil. A few weeks before sowing, turn over the soil, remove any weeds, firm it, and then rake the surface level. Create a drill ¾in (2cm) deep, water it well, and then sow the seeds thinly along the base. Cover over with soil, firm gently, and water lightly. When the seedlings have a few leaves, thin them out, leaving the strongest. Water regularly, and protect plants from slugs and snails.

Carefully tip seeds, *directly from the packet or use your fingers to sow them in pinches.*

Thin the seedlings *to their final spacings, or transplant them once they reach 6in (15cm) tall.*

3 Planting out

Once large enough, move the young plants, whether raised indoors or out, to their final positions. Prepare the area first by turning it, removing weeds, and applying some high-nitrogen granular fertilizer. Water the young plants well, and lift them from the seedbed or from their trays or pots, and plant them 16in (40cm) apart.

Transplant young plants carefully *to help minimize root loss or disturbance, which can check growth. Water plants well after planting.*

Young plants are vulnerable to attack *from many different pests, including aphids (above, see p.240). Check for damage and infestations.*

Water well, *directing the spray at the base of the plants. On lighter soils, mulch around plants to help retain moisture or lay pieces of cardboard.*

Cover with fine netting *to prevent cabbage white butterflies from laying eggs on your plants. Use stakes to hold it clear of the leaves.*

4 Routine care

Keep beds weeded until plants are well established, by which time their foliage will suppress weeds. Water regularly, especially during hot or dry spells, and apply a balanced liquid feed, following package directions, to promote strong, leafy growth.

5 Protecting plants

Put aluminum foil around each plant to deter cabbage root fly (see p.240). At the same time, cover plants with fine netting to protect against cabbage white caterpillars (see p.238) and pigeons. Keep the netting pulled taut, and check regularly for holes.

6 Harvesting

The plants are ready to harvest from late summer onward, once they have fully-formed, leafy heads. To harvest, either cut through the tough stalk with a sharp knife, or lift the roots using a fork. Mature plants can be left in the ground for a few weeks until needed but will gradually deteriorate. Trim off the outer, tougher leaves, and use only the tender heart; cut heads can be stored in a fridge for about a week.

Harvest young cabbages, *picking every other one in a row, to allow others space to fully mature.*

Summer cabbages

1 'Greyhound' This reliable, fast-maturing variety forms loose, leafy heads with few tough stalks. If sown in spring, the first heads can be harvested in early summer.

2 'Derby Day' An early summer variety, this cabbage produces rounded heads, tightly packed with tender leaves. It is the earliest "ball" cabbage to mature during the season.

3 'Hotspur' Forming large tasty heads that are ready to harvest from late summer onward, this variety has a short stem and few tough stalks, meaning there is little waste when cooking.

4 'Red Jewel' This variety produces dense, round heads, tightly packed with dark red leaves that retain their color well when cooked. It is good for storing and also keeps well in the soil.

5 'Duncan' This quick-maturing variety forms loose, pointed heads. It is a versatile choice that can be sown in spring to harvest in fall, or sown in fall to crop in spring.

6 'Marner Early Red' Forming large heads of reddish leaves that are ready to harvest from mid-fall, this cabbage keeps its color when cooked and can be finely sliced and used raw.

7 'Stonehead' These mid-size, compact plants can be grown closely together, making the best use of smaller plots. The heads will last well in the soil during fall until needed.

8 'Kalibos' This heirloom variety develops small, pointed heads, packed with deep red leaves. It can be used raw in salads if chopped finely, or eat it lightly boiled instead.

9 'Hispi' This cabbage is very quick to mature and can also be sown in fall to harvest in spring. It forms neat, pointed heads of tasty leaves and is a good choice for smaller gardens.

Other varieties
'Elisa'
'Kilaton'
'Primo'
'Redcap'
'Ruby Ball'
'Surprise'

STEP-BY-STEP Winter and spring cabbages

From deep green, crinkle-leaf savoys to pointed, dense-hearted spring cabbages, these hardy brassicas are invaluable during the leaner months of the year. Spring-cropping plants can be packed tightly together, making efficient use of small plots. They also give a useful secondary crop of loose leaves in spring if the cut stumps are left to grow back. Always cover your crops with netting to protect them from pests like pigeons and caterpillars.

	SPRING	SUMMER	FALL	WINTER
SOW				
HARVEST				

TIME TO HARVEST: 26–28 WEEKS

SUITABLE FOR: BEDS

7–11 plants

9FT (3M) ROWS
Plant out 12–20in (30–50cm) apart, depending on variety

1 Getting started

The best way to raise cabbages is from seed, sown either under cover in late spring, or inside or outdoors in summer for both winter and spring cabbages. Alternatively, if you are planning to grow just a few crops, you can buy young plants in summer, which is an easier but more costly option.

'Tundra' *is a winter variety that can be left in the ground for several weeks until needed.*

'Jewel' *produces loose heads of smooth leaves that keep well in the soil through winter.*

'January King' *can be cropped in fall as young heads, or left to mature through winter.*

'Tarvoy' *is a slow maturing, winter savoy cabbage with sweet-tasting, crinkled leaves.*

Cabbage seeds are reliable, *but sow two to a cell, just in case one fails. They are large and easy to handle, allowing you to sow them accurately.*

Grow the seedlings *in a bright location under cover for two or three weeks until they can be planted out into beds. Keep them cool but frost-free.*

2 Sowing under cover

Raising plants under cover helps reduce the effects of club root disease on your plants (see p.242). Fill seed trays with seed compost, water well, and allow to drain. Make holes ½in (1cm) deep in each cell, sow one seed in each, then thin to leave the strongest seedling once they emerge. Grow the seedlings under cover until 6in (15cm) tall. Prepare them for outdoor conditions by moving them outside during the day, then back in at night.

> **TIP** *Acclimatize plants to outdoor temperatures for about two weeks.*

3 Sowing outside

These cabbages can be sown outside in summer when the soil is warm. Prepare a seedbed by digging over the soil, removing weeds, and raking it level. Make drills, ¾in (2cm) deep, water the base well, then thinly sow the seed. Fill the drill with soil, firm gently, and lightly water again. The seeds will germinate in a week or two.

Prepare the soil before planting *out your seedlings. Digging in some well-rotted organic matter will help encourage plenty of leafy growth.*

Make drills long enough *to suit the size of your plot. To retain moisture during dry spells, cover with newspaper until the seeds germinate.*

Young cabbage plants *are ready to plant out when they are about 6in (15cm) tall. If much larger or smaller, they may be slow to establish.*

Cabbages develop a crown of leaves, *so aim the water directly at the base to ensure it reaches the roots. Use a watering can with a long spout.*

4 Planting out

Winter cabbages are planted out in summer, spring cabbage in fall. Prepare the site by digging it over to remove weeds, and fork in some high-nitrogen granular fertilizer. Plant out or transplant winter cabbages 20in (50cm) apart, spring-types 12in (30cm).

5 Routine care

Water plants regularly, especially during dry spells. To encourage strong growth before winter, apply high-nitrogen liquid feed in late summer as directed by the packet. Weed the beds regularly, and remove any yellowing leaves from the plants.

6 Harvesting

Using a sharp knife to cut through the stalk, harvest during winter and spring when individual heads are large enough to use. Mature plants can be left in the ground for a few weeks until needed but may deteriorate the longer they are left. Leave the stumps of spring cabbages in the soil, and make a cross in the cut end. This will encourage them to produce a crop of loose leaves, which you can harvest a few weeks later.

Loose spring leaves *make a useful bonus crop after the cabbage heads have been harvested.*

STEP-BY-STEP Cauliflower

It is possible to grow and harvest delicious fresh cauliflower all year round since there is a wide range of varieties to choose from. As well as conventional white-headed types you can also grow cauliflower with striking purple, orange, or green heads. Space the plants widely so that the heads can grow to full size, or plant them densely to produce "mini" cauliflower. They can produce very high yields if given enough food and water.

	SPRING	SUMMER	FALL	WINTER
SOW				
HARVEST				

TIME TO HARVEST: 20–26 WEEKS

SUITABLE FOR: BEDS AND CONTAINERS

5–6 plants

9FT (3M) ROWS
Plant 24–28in (60–70cm) apart

CONTAINERS
8 plants in each

1 Getting started
Cauliflower that mature from fall to spring are sown when conditions are warm, and sowing direct into warm soils in mid-autumn is very successful. On the other hand, summer-maturing varieties are sown from mid- to late spring, and in such cases sowing in seed trays under cover is the best method.

'Snowball' is sown in spring for an fall harvest; the medium-sized heads keep well.

'Violet Queen' bears purple heads in late summer that turn green when cooked.

'Walcheren Winter Pilgrim' is a hardy variety that is ready to harvest in spring.

'Mayflower' is an early variety that can be sown in mid-winter to harvest from midsummer.

2 Sowing under cover
Fill seed trays or pots with compost, water well, and allow to drain. Make a hole ½in (1cm) deep in each cell, and sow two seeds into it. Firm over with compost, and water in. Once emerged, thin to leave the stronger seedling.

Summer and fall varieties should be sown in midwinter, and then placed in a propagator.

Keep seedlings well watered. Cauliflower are thirsty plants and require a lot of water at all stages.

3 Sow outside
For winter and spring cauliflower, sow the seed direct in late spring. Prepare a seedbed by turning over the ground, incorporating plenty of organic matter. Then excavate a short drill, ¾in (2cm) deep. Water the base thoroughly, sow your seeds, and then cover with soil to level, and water in lightly. To prevent a build-up of soil diseases, ensure that you do not plant cauliflower where other brassica crops have grown in the past three years.

Sow seed thinly along the drill—once the seedlings develop, they can be thinned if necessary.

4 Planting out

Harden off tray-raised seedlings when they are 15cm (6in) tall. Place them outdoors during the day and inside at night for a week. Once seedbed-raised plants reach this height, water them well, and then lift gently from the soil. Summer varieties should be spaced 24in (60cm) apart each way; winter types 28in (70cm).

Hardened-off cauliflower *should be planted promptly. You risk encouraging the plants to bolt if they become too large.*

Plant both tray-grown *and seedbed-raised seedlings in soil that has had a high nitrogen granular feed incorporated.*

Firm the plants in well, *the heads will become very heavy as they grow and will need to be well supported.*

Ensure that netting *reaches the ground, leaving no gaps for pests to crawl underneath— peg the netting down, or bury it in the soil.*

Covering the cauliflower head *with its leaves will prevent white varieties from yellowing in the sun. Fix the leaves in place using garden string.*

5 Protecting plants

Water in your transplants, and fit aluminum foil around the base of each. Place netting with a maximum mesh diameter of ½in (1cm) around plants. This will deter cabbage white butterflies and pigeons. Hoe between young plants—established cauliflower will smother any competing plants.

6 Routine care

It's especially important to keep cauliflower well watered during the summer months to obtain a good-sized curd. As these develop, bend a few leaves in over the head—this protects summer varieties from being "burnt" by the sun and offers winter types some frost protection.

7 Harvesting

As soon as the curds reach a harvestable size, cut them from the plant. The heads are best eaten fresh but can be stored in the fridge for a few days; they will keep better if you cut them with a few leaves attached. Blanch and freeze surplus heads.

| TIP | *Grow in pots for "mini" 2½in (6cm) wide curds. Space 6in (15cm) apart.* |

Make sure you harvest *cauliflower while the heads are still tight, when they are at their best.*

STEP-BY-STEP Calabrese broccoli

It's well worth growing your own broccoli because homegrown crops are much more tender and flavorful than store-bought. The plants produce one main central head and then numerous smaller sideshoots, which prolong the harvest period; the florets also freeze well, so any surplus can be preserved for later. Don't worry if you don't have space to start plants off indoors since direct sowings outdoors in summer perform extremely well.

	SPRING	SUMMER	FALL	WINTER
SOW				
HARVEST				

TIME TO HARVEST: 12–16 WEEKS

SUITABLE FOR: BEDS

15 plants

9FT (3M) ROWS
Plant out 8in (20cm) apart

1 Getting started

Broccoli prefers rich, well-drained soil, so dig in plenty of organic matter such as well-rotted manure or compost in the season before planting. Ensure that no other members of the brassica family have been planted in the same location in the past three years to help prevent the build-up of soil diseases.

'Romanesco' *has lime-green curds that are both highly ornamental and full of flavor.*

'Fiesta' *produces large, well-rounded heads and a good crop of secondary sideshoots.*

'Corvet' *is a high-yielding variety that is renowned for its large, gray-green heads.*

'Belstar' *keeps well once cut and is worth growing for its tasty blue-green heads.*

Calabrese broccoli can winter *in a frost-free greenhouse for harvests in the early spring. Sow in pots in the late summer or the early fall.*

Seedlings will need to be thinned *to one per pot or module as they develop. Close spacing will encourage the plants to produce smaller shoots.*

2 Sowing seeds

Calabrese broccoli can be sown under cover in pots or large trays to transplant later. Fill the container with seed compost, firm gently, water well, and make two holes per pot or module, ½in (1cm) deep. Drop a seed into each hole, cover with compost, and water lightly. Once emerged, thin to leave the stronger seedling. Alternatively, seed can be sown directly into the final position outside. Create a seedbed, mark out rows 12in (30cm) apart, and sow a cluster of three seeds every 8in (20cm), into holes ¾in (2cm) deep. Thin the seedlings to the strongest, and protect them from slugs by using pellets.

3 Planting out

Once indoor-sown plants are 6in (15cm) tall, harden them off and plant out 8in (20cm) apart, in rows 12in (30cm) apart—do not let them become root-bound since this can cause the premature formation of small heads. Keep the plants well watered and well weeded. Place aluminum foil around each plant to deter cabbage root fly.

Divide up your plot *using bamboo poles and string—this will help you work out your plant spacings and will also act as a support for netting.*

Young plants *should be hardened off and planted out as soon as possible in spring. They cope best with being moved if the weather is not too warm.*

Tall varieties may need staking *if earthing up does not provide sufficient support. Tie the plants in to sturdy bamboo poles as necessary.*

Mealy cabbage aphids *target brassica crops and can swarm plants, disfiguring the leaves. Aim to protect crops from an early age.*

4 Routine care

As the heads of the plants begin to develop, draw soil around the base of the stems to stabilize them—this is called "earthing up." At this point a granular high-nitrogen fertilizer can be applied to boost the main head size and to encourage the production of sideshoots for subsequent harvests.

5 Protecting plants

Erect a frame of netting over your plants to deter birds—especially pigeons—and cabbage white butterflies. Ensure the net is fine, with a maximum mesh diameter of ½in (1cm) to stop the adult butterflies from reaching your plants. It is important to keep the netting taut so that birds don't get tangled in it.

6 Harvesting

The first cutting can be expected approximately 3–4 months after sowing, depending on the variety and time of year. Cut the main head off first, and then, once the smaller sideshoots appear, harvest these. The younger leaves of broccoli can also be eaten.

TIP	*Broccoli plants can be spaced 6in (15cm) apart for a crop of small heads.*

Use a knife *to cut the heads whole before the flower buds open. This encourages a second crop.*

STEP-BY-STEP Sprouting broccoli

This hardy crop is one of the most eagerly awaited in winter and spring and bears a profusion of tender stems tipped with tasty white or purple florets when few other crops are available. Traditional varieties become large plants that mature slowly and are best suited to bigger gardens. If you enjoy broccoli but have a smaller plot, there are now summer varieties that can be harvested within weeks of sowing, freeing up space for other crops.

	SPRING	SUMMER	FALL	WINTER
SOW				
HARVEST				

TIME TO HARVEST: 16–36 WEEKS

SUITABLE FOR: BEDS

0   3ft   6ft   9ft

6 plants

9FT (3M) ROWS
Plant out 24in (60cm) apart

1 Getting started

Traditional broccoli is easy to raise from seed or can be bought as young plants, plugs, or as bare-root transplants in spring. Summer-maturing broccoli is less widely available and is best raised from seed. Sow in batches from late winter to mid-spring, and harvest florets in early summer to mid-fall.

'Claret' *is a reliable variety that produces succulent heads from mid-spring onward.*

'Purple Sprouting' *is very hardy and bears an abundance of dark shoots in early spring.*

'White Star' *crops in late spring, producing attractive white heads that can be eaten raw.*

'Bordeaux' *matures in summer from a spring sowing, giving a quick crop of tasty florets.*

Sowing into seed trays *means the seedlings don't need to be picked out, reducing root disturbance. They can also be sown in trays.*

Thin the seedlings, *leaving only the strongest one per module. If you have gaps, carefully replant stronger thinned seedlings into vacant cells.*

2 Sowing under cover

Broccoli is hardy, and most varieties need a long growing season; give crops a head start by sowing under cover in spring. Fill module trays with seed compost, water well, then leave to drain. Make one hole per cell, ¾in (2cm) deep, and sow two seeds in each. Cover with compost, and water in lightly. The seeds won't need additional heat and will germinate within two weeks. Grow the seedlings under cover until they are planted out.

TIP *Raising plants under cover reduces the effects of club root disease (see p.242).*

3 Sowing outdoors

Seed can either be sown into seedbeds with the seedlings transplanted when large enough or directly in their final growing positions. For seedbed sowing, dig the soil over, and rake it fine and level, then sow into drills ¾in (2cm) deep. Alternatively, sow pinches of seeds at 24in (60cm) intervals, and thin to the strongest per spot.

To sow longer rows, *carefully pour the seeds directly from the packet, tapping the top so they drop out at regular intervals.*

Sowing direct in clusters *takes away the need to transplant your seedlings and means less root disturbance for the crop.*

Place aluminum foil snugly *around the base of each plant soon after planting to stop cabbage root flies from laying their eggs at soil level.*

Net plants from pigeons *and cabbage white butterflies. Keep the netting taut to avoid snaring birds, and check it regularly for gaps.*

4 Planting out

Harden off indoor-raised plants before planting out, and water seedbeds well so outdoor-grown plants are easy to lift. Prepare the soil by forking in granular high-nitrogen fertilizer, as per the instructions on the seed packet. Plant out seedlings 24in (60cm) apart, and water well.

5 Routine care

Water and weed plants regularly to ensure steady growth and, as the plants become taller, earth soil up around the base of their stems to help stabilize them. If your garden is in an exposed area, you might want to insert a sturdy stake at the base of each plant for support during fall storms.

6 Harvesting

Once plants mature in winter and spring and begin to develop their florets, look them over daily to ensure you harvest the heads while still tightly closed. Cut them with a length of stem attached, roughly 4in (10cm)—this and the leaves are extremely tender to eat. Continual picking promotes new sideshoots to grow, leading to a longer harvest. The florets are best eaten soon after picking but can also be frozen.

Tender florets *should be picked before the tiny flower buds open. Cut them with a sharp knife.*

STEP-BY-STEP Brussels sprouts

A winter plot would be incomplete without Brussels sprouts, so choose from varieties that will crop from mid-fall right through until early spring. Individual "buttons" develop over a long period, meaning that two or three plants can provide a steady supply over the winter months. In addition to the tasty sprouts, a further treat is the sprout "top"—a loose rosette of leaves that has a deliciously mild flavor, high in quality if not quantity.

	SPRING	SUMMER	FALL	WINTER
SOW				
HARVEST				

TIME TO HARVEST: 30–36 WEEKS

SUITABLE FOR: BEDS

0   3ft   6ft   9ft

6 plants

9FT (3M) ROWS
Thin out or plant to 24in (60cm) apart

1 Getting started

Brussels sprouts are worth raising from seed to give you a large crop, although they can also be bought as plants in spring. Prepare your site by digging in plenty of well-rotted manure or compost during the season before planting. Brussels sprouts prefer a pH of at least 6.8, so apply lime to the soil if necessary.

'Bosworth' *is a popular variety—its firm, even, sweet sprouts should be harvested in early winter.*

'Red Delicious' *keeps its color well during cooking; harvest the sprouts in winter.*

'Trafalgar' *bears heavy crops of reliable, firm, flavorful sprouts from midwinter to early spring.*

'Maximus' *is a high-yielding variety, bearing sweet green sprouts over a long season.*

Sprinkle the seed evenly *along the base of a short drill, with a plan to transplant them later. This makes the best use of limited space.*

If you are sowing under cover, *sow the seed into holes spaced 2in (5cm) apart. Pull the seedlings out when they are strong enough to handle it.*

2 Sowing seeds

To sow seed in the ground, turn over the soil to remove any weeds, firm it well, and rake it level. Either sow a short drill, ¾in (2cm) deep, from which seedlings will be moved to their final position, or sow clusters of seed at 24x24in (60x60cm) apart—this allows you to thin each cluster to the strongest seedling, minimizing root disturbance. You can also start plants off in modules under cover. Fill a module tray with seed compost, firm gently, and water well. Sow two seeds per cell, ¾in (2cm) deep, and cover with compost. Water lightly, and, once germinated, thin out to leave the strongest seedling per module.

3 Planting out

Once tray-grown plants reach 4–5in (10–12cm) in height, harden them off to prepare them for outside. Prepare seedbed-raised sprouts for transplanting by watering the bed thoroughly. Turn over the soil to ready it for planting, rake it level, and firm well. Space the seedlings 24x24in (60x60cm) apart, and water in well.

Transplant *the healthiest of your seedlings once they have reached 4–5in (10–12cm) tall and have four or five true leaves.*

Ensure that the seedlings *are planted 24in (60cm) apart so that the plants remain well ventilated. Plant Brussels sprouts in firmly.*

Use brassica collars *to deter cabbage root fly, which is a common brassica pest that can cause the young plants to die.*

Bird netting *should be pulled taut to prevent birds from becoming snagged. Regularly check for gaps at the base where birds could sneak in.*

Older leaves *near the base of the stems naturally yellow and die; it is not a sign of poor health. They should snap off easily.*

4 Protecting plants

Fit brassica collars around the base of each seedling to prevent attack from cabbage root fly (see p.240), and erect a frame of netting over plants to deter pigeons and cabbage white butterflies. Brussels sprouts can grow to around 32in (80cm) in height, so ensure the frame is tall enough.

5 Routine care

Keep the top-heavy plants stable by earthing up soil around their bases, or steady them with stakes. The lower leaves will yellow as they age and should be picked off to encourage good air flow around the developing buttons. Keep plants well watered and fed using a high-nitrogen liquid fertilizer.

6 Harvesting

Harvest sprouts when large enough by firmly twisting them off; older cultivars mature from the bottom of the stem upward. Newer hybrids mature more evenly and can be cut as whole stems; stand them indoors in water in the cool to harvest as needed.

> **TIP** *Harvest the delicious leafy "top" before picking the sprouts themselves.*

Sprouts taste especially sweet *from late winter, once they have been frosted a few times.*

STEP-BY-STEP Kale

Packed with vitamins, kale is a very robust plant and stands extremely well over the winter, providing a generous harvest in otherwise lean times. The plants are highly ornamental and are also less prone to the common pests and diseases that affect others in the brassica family. Leaves should be harvested little and often to ensure they remain tender; two or three plants can provide pickings if used as cut-and-come-again crops.

	SPRING	SUMMER	FALL	WINTER
SOW				
HARVEST				

TIME TO HARVEST: 24–28 WEEKS

SUITABLE FOR: BEDS

7 plants

9FT (3M) ROWS
Plant out 20in (50cm) apart

1 Getting started

Kale plants prefer a rich, well-drained, firm soil and must be given sufficient space to develop. There is a good variety to choose from: there are crinkled and savoy-leaf types, dwarf forms, and some types with striking purple stems. All are highly ornamental and look great in a border.

'Cavolo Nero' *has a rich flavor and its dark green, savoyed leaves are tender when cooked.*

'Nero di Toscana' *is a traditional "black" kale, with flavorful, dark green savoyed leaves.*

'Redbor' *makes an attractive border plant thanks to its purple-stemmed frilly leaves.*

'Starbor' *has heavily frilled leaves that are best harvested while young and tender.*

Seeds can also be sown into pots—*use a dibber or pencil to make holes in the compost. Sow two seeds into each planting hole.*

Sow clusters of two or three seeds *in a grid pattern, then thin the seedlings to the strongest. Protect the young plants against slugs using pellets.*

2 Sowing seeds

Crops can be sown under cover in mid-spring. Fill seed trays with seed compost, water well, allow to drain, and then make holes, ½in (1cm) deep in each cell. Drop two seeds in each cell, cover with compost, and water in lightly. Thin to leave the stronger seedling in each cell, and grow on under cover. Kale can also be sown outside. Dig over a seedbed, removing any weeds, and work in some high nitrogen granular fertilizer. Firm the soil gently, and rake it level. You can either sow a short drill to transplant later, or sow two or three seeds at their final spacings: 20x20in (50x50cm) apart.

3 Planting out

Plant out or transplant the kale seedlings at 20x20in (50x50cm) spacing during summer. Water plants in well, and place cabbage root fly collars around the base of each plant. These small discs prevent the adult female fly from laying her eggs next to the stem at soil level (see p.240). Hoe between plants regularly to keep weeds at bay.

Once the seedlings' roots *fill their module cells or pots, begin hardening them off, ready for transplanting outside.*

Seedlings should be *firmed in well when they are planted; the soil will help to support the eventual weight of the plants.*

Kale plants *can become quite large, so it is vital to plant them with enough space to develop: around 20in (50cm) is ideal.*

Keep plants well weeded, *especially when they are young and vulnerable to competition. Pull out weeds by hand where possible.*

Cabbage white butterflies *(see p.238) lay tiny yellow eggs on the underside of leaves. Grow the plants under fine mesh netting to deter attacks.*

4 Protecting plants

Keep seedlings fed and well watered to help them recover from flea beetle attack, which can check their growth. If cabbage white butterflies (see p.238) or pigeons are a problem, use poles to erect some taut netting over the plants—use a maximum mesh size of ½x½in (1x1cm). Check for gaps.

5 Routine care

As plants continue to grow they can become quite top-heavy and tall—some cultivars can reach up to 3ft (1m) high—so you might find it necessary to stake the plants individually using stout poles or sticks. Remove and compost any older leaves that begin to turn yellow.

6 Harvesting

The inner leaves of each rosette are the most tender, and the outer ones tougher. Harvest the leaves when they are large enough, but keep in mind that removing all the young leaves will weaken plants. Pick from the plants every few days to ensure a steady supply.

TIP *Pull up plants and compost them once they develop flowers in spring.*

Kale develops one main rosette *of leaves, and then occasionally offsets of smaller rosettes.*

Salads and leaves

Some crops don't require a lot of
time, attention, or space—welcome
to the world of salads and leaves.
This is a hugely diverse group that
extends from tiny seedlings picked
days after germination and cut-and-
come-again crops that harvest
repeatedly to robust Swiss chard
that will crop throughout winter.
Flavors vary significantly too, from
crisp, buttery mildness through to
a hot, peppery bite. Some of these
crops can be grown in no more than
a patio container or hanging basket,
which means that room can be
found for them in any garden.

STEP-BY-STEP Lettuces

Fast-growing and attractive, lettuces are ideal for filling a pot or window box if you don't have space elsewhere. Choose from dense-headed "hearting" types and frilly loose-leaf varieties—they can be harvested as cut-and-come-again crops (see pp.122–123), or the plants can be allowed to develop to full size and cut whole. You never need to be short of this excellent salad staple, since sowing under cover allows you to harvest fresh leaves all year round.

	SPRING	SUMMER	AUTUMN	WINTER
SOW				
HARVEST				

TIME TO HARVEST: 6–8 WEEKS

SUITABLE FOR: BEDS, CONTAINERS, AND GROWING BAGS

9–20 plants

9FT (3M) ROWS
Plant 6–14in (15–35cm) apart

GROWING BAGS
4 plants in each

1 Sowing under cover

Early sowings can first be made under cover between late winter and early spring to be planted outside once weather conditions are suitable. Fill modules or trays with seed compost, firm gently, water well, and allow to drain. Make a ½in (1cm) deep hole in each pot or module cell, and drop two seeds into each. Alternatively, sow seed in larger trays at the same depth. Cover the seeds over with compost, then water in lightly. Place in a warm, light place.

Sow two or three seeds *per pot or module, and then once they emerge, thin them out, leaving the strongest to grow on for planting out.*

Sow seed thinly *in larger seed trays, and then pick the seedlings out once they develop. Plant them into individual pots or modules for growing on.*

Lettuce seed *can prove difficult to germinate, so sow seed in clusters in case some fail to germinate, every 4in (10cm) along the drill.*

As seedlings develop, *thin to leave the strongest per cluster, then later to 12in (30cm) between plants. The thinnings can be eaten.*

2 Sowing outside

Outdoor sowings of summer varieties can be made from early spring until midsummer; winter-hardy lettuces should be sown in late summer. Dig over the soil to remove any weeds, firm it gently, and rake it level. Create drills ½in (1cm) deep and 12in (30cm) apart, and sow seeds in clusters of four or five every 4in (10cm). Cover the seeds over with soil, and water lightly. Protect the seedlings against slugs.

TIP *Leave cut stumps in the soil—they will form a second crop of smaller leaves.*

3 Planting out

Once indoor-raised seedlings are large enough to handle, gradually harden them off by placing them outside during the day and inside at night for seven to ten days. Prepare the soil by turning it over to remove any weeds. Plant the seedlings out 12in (30cm) apart, and cover them with a cloche or cold frame in cool weather.

Module-raised seedlings *are ready to be hardened off and planted out once their roots fill their cell. Water them well before planting out.*

Firm the soil in well *around the heads after planting. Ensure that the lettuces have adequate room by spacing the rows 12in (30cm) apart.*

Regularly weed lettuces *used as a cut-and-come-again crop to avoid harvesting unwanted growth by mistake. Weed by hand or with a hoe.*

Lay a sand or grit *ring around the plants to keep slugs away. Check it regularly to ensure that the line has not been broken.*

4 Routine care

Keep plants well watered in warm weather so that they bulk up quickly—ensure that they do not dry out in the last weeks before harvesting, because this can cause them to bolt. Weeding between rows regularly will also be helpful since it reduces competition for light, nutrients, and moisture.

5 Protecting plants

Slugs and snails (see p.240) are the most common pests, especially during periods of warm, wet weather. Lay bait traps or organic pellets for them, or use grit to create a barrier around your crops. Aphids can also be problematic, so check out plants regularly for signs of damage.

6 Harvesting

Cut individual leaves from loose-leaf lettuces when they mature, or harvest them all at once. Varieties that form a dense head of leaves, or "heart," can be cut whole once mature. Sow seeds little and often for a regular supply of fresh leaves. Although some types will mature faster than others, a good rule of thumb is to sow a new batch when the previous one is ready to be planted out or thinned for a second time.

Harvest lettuces whole *as soon as they are big enough, leaving loose-leaf crops to grow on.*

Lettuces

1 'Pinocchio' This semi-Romaine lettuce has upright leaves and sweet, yellow hearts. It is cold tolerant so is good for early sowings. Its compact style makes it ideal for containers.

2 'Tom Thumb' A butter variety, it produces tender green leaves, which are sweet with little bitterness. Compact, it is useful for window boxes or containers.

3 'Freckles' This Romaine lettuce is unusual because its deep green, glossy leaves are splashed with burgundy. The upright plants have sturdy growth and are slow to bolt.

4 'Winter Density' Widely-grown, this gem lettuce is popular for its hardiness and its dense hearts. It also has good heat tolerance and is ideal for early or late crops.

5 'Sioux' An iceberg-type, its crisp, green leaves flush an attractive red as they mature, especially in sunny sites. It has good mildew resistance; sow it repeatedly in summer.

6 'Lollo Rosso' Well-known, this loose-leaf variety has red-flushed, crinkled leaves that can be harvested as needed. Alternatively, whole heads can also be cut.

7 'Mottistone' This variety has wavy-edged leaves that are mid-green and flecked with burgundy. The leaves can be harvested individually, or crop the loose heads whole.

8 'Little Gem' A popular semi-Romaine variety, it produces small, dense hearts and is ideal for sowing in containers. It is slow to bolt in the summer and is cold resistant.

9 'Nymans' An eye-catching, semi-Romaine lettuce with glossy burgundy leaves and a yellow heart, it can be harvested as a baby leaf. It is slow to bolt and has good mildew resistance.

Other varieties
'Arctic King'
'Red Salad Bowl'
'Cocarde'
'Lobjoits Green'
'Marvel of Four Seasons'

STEP-BY-STEP Cut-and-come-again salad

This term describes a method of growing salad leaves, rather than an actual vegetable, and is extremely quick and productive. It is ideal for containers and allows you to make use of bare patches for short periods, making it a good choice for smaller plots. Useful crops can even be raised on windowsills. Often these salad leaves are sold in blends, such as a hot and spicy mix, or stir-fry mix, but you can make up your own mixtures to suit your taste.

	SPRING	SUMMER	FALL	WINTER
SOW				
HARVEST				

TIME TO HARVEST: 4–6 WEEKS

SUITABLE FOR: BEDS, GROWING BAGS, AND CONTAINERS—UNDER COVER OR OUTSIDE

30 plants

9FT (3M) ROWS
Sow and thin to 4in (10cm) apart

GROWING BAGS
12 plants in each

1 Getting started

These salad plants are raised from seed and can be sown in batches through the year. Lettuce is commonly used, but most salad crops can be grown this way. They are mainly grown outside in summer, but you can also grow smaller crops under cover, even on the windowsill to harvest in the spring or fall.

Corn salad *is a useful leaf crop to grow during winter. It is very hardy and crops regularly.*

Lettuce *crops reliably as young leaves, and there are many good varieties to grow.*

Land cress *has a spicy flavor. It is a good choice to grow under cover for an early crop.*

Arugula *has a peppery flavor and combines well with milder-tasting leaves like lettuce.*

Sow the seed *according to the spacings given on the packet. Some salads are sown deeper or more thickly than others.*

Pick leaves individually *as soon as they are large enough to use. The plants will continue growing and produce more.*

Cutting the plants off *checks their growth, and they will take a week or two to recover. Water them well to promote regrowth.*

2 Under cover crops

If you don't have outdoor space, or just want an extra early or late harvest, grow plants under cover. Use growing bags or fill pots or seed trays with compost, water well, and leave to drain. Sow seeds on the surface, and cover lightly with compost. Keep moist until the seeds come up in a week or so, then harvest the leaves once large enough, leaving the bases to regrow. Expect two or three similar harvests before the plants run out of steam.

TIP *Feed indoor crops with balanced liquid fertilizer to encourage new growth.*

3 Sowing outside

For larger crops, sow direct into the soil in summer. First turn it over to remove weeds, firm it gently, then rake it level. Mark out drills ½–¾in (1–2cm) deep, and water the base well. Sow the seeds, cover with soil, then water again. If sowing in warm weather, temporarily cover the soil with sheets of newspaper to help retain moisture.

Sow into drills *to help you tell any weeds apart from your crop. On smaller plots, you can also sow directly into containers or growing bags.*

Crops in containers or growing bags *will dry out more quickly than those grown directly in the soil and will need more regular watering.*

Plants picked for individual leaves *will continue to grow until they wear out. They are longer lived than plants harvested to the base.*

4 Routine care

Seedlings will emerge in a few days (if your drills are covered with newspaper, check underneath every day, and remove as soon as the seeds germinate). Keep the rows well weeded, and water regularly to promote quick growth. Protect your plants against slugs with a light sprinkling of pellets.

5 Harvesting

These salad crops can be ready for harvest in as little as three weeks in the height of summer. You can either pick individual leaves as they become large enough to eat, or you can cut back whole rows using scissors. Use the salad leaves fresh, and only pick them when you intend to use them.

Growing on

Salad plants that are cut to the base should be given time to recover and encouraged back into growth. Water them well, adding a diluted liquid fertilizer to the water, and they should be ready to harvest again within two weeks. The plants will wear out after a few crops, so sow new batches to provide healthy replacements.

STEP-BY-STEP Microgreens

This tasty, trendy crop is often featured on fine restaurant menus and is amazingly easy to grow. Harvested as tiny seedlings, the plants are ready to crop in little more than a week. There are dozens of vegetables that can be grown this way, and you can sow them together for different flavor combinations. You don't need a garden or any outdoor space; they grow well in pots on bright windowsills and can even be sown on damp cotton wool.

	SPRING	SUMMER	FALL	WINTER
SOW				
HARVEST				

TIME TO HARVEST: 7–10 DAYS

SUITABLE FOR: BEDS AND CONTAINERS, UNDER COVER OR OUTSIDE

3,000 plants

9FT (3M) ROWS
Sow and thin to ½in (1cm) apart

CONTAINERS
300 plants in each

1 Getting started

Microgreens are raised from seed, and there are many types. Ready-mixed combinations are available, or you can mix your own. Most of the vegetables grown as microgreens are the same as those you sow for conventional crops, they are just harvested as seedlings instead. If you have spare seeds left over from sowing garden crops, try sowing them as microgreens rather than storing them until next year.

Basil *Like many culinary herbs, the young seedlings have a rich, sweet taste.*

Beets *Although normally grown as a root crop, the tasty leaves are also edible.*

Cabbage *All brassica seedlings are edible, and have a delicious nutty flavor.*

Cilantro *Full-grown plants often bolt, so use it as a fresh-tasting seedling instead.*

Swiss chard *These soft-leaf seedlings have a delicate, earthy flavor, good for salads.*

Celery *Enjoy the delicious taste of this late-season stem crop throughout the year.*

Lettuce *Use the tasty seedlings as a garnish, or as an alternative to traditional cress.*

Bok choy *This useful crop can be harvested at almost any stage, including as seedlings.*

Chives *These tender leaves have a sweeter flavor than full-grown plants. Use as garnish.*

Pea shoots *These have the familiar pea flavor and are ideal in salads and stir-fries.*

2 Sowing under cover

Fill seed trays with moist compost, and sow the seeds on top. Cover them lightly with more compost, and water lightly. The seeds will germinate in a few days and should be grown in a bright location until large enough to harvest. Seeds can also be sown uncovered on trays of moist paper towels or cotton wool.

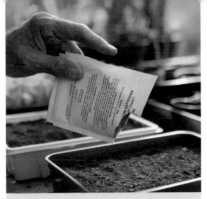

Sow seeds thickly *to give a good crop, and sow more every few days for a constant supply. Keep them handy on your kitchen windowsill.*

Seed can be sown outside *directly in the soil, although you can also sow small batches in containers, growing bags, or even window boxes.*

If you have trouble differentiating weed *seedlings from your crop, sow in drills rather than blocks to make them easier to spot.*

3 Sowing outside

Before sowing outside, prepare the area by weeding it well, and rake the soil level and fine. Water the soil, sow the seed ¼in (5mm) deep in blocks or rows, cover lightly, and water again. Protect plants from slug damage with a light sprinkling of pellets.

4 Routine care

Crops grown under cover need little care other than watering them once or twice until harvested. If sown outside, weed seedlings may also come up among your microgreens. Remove weeds early to prevent harvesting them by mistake.

5 Harvesting

Depending on the temperature and light levels, seedlings can be ready for harvest in as little as a week. Ensure they are kept well-watered during this period. Pinch off individual leaves with your fingers, or cut whole clumps of seedlings with scissors.

TIP	*Use cut seedlings before they have a chance to wilt, within the hour ideally.*

Harvest microgreens *when the seedlings develop their first pair of "true" leaves.*

STEP-BY-STEP Asian greens

The majority of Asian greens are leafy brassicas that work well in stir-fries or for use in salads. There is a plethora of crops in this group, and even bok choy, just one member, ranges from large, tall types grown for their crunchy stems, to those that remain squat, with disclike leaves. Asian greens are ideal for filling summer gaps in the vegetable garden since they benefit from a mid- to late summer sowing and will grow extremely quickly.

	SPRING	SUMMER	FALL	WINTER
SOW				
HARVEST				

TIME TO HARVEST: 6–8 WEEKS

SUITABLE FOR: BEDS, CONTAINERS, AND GROWING BAGS

15–20 plants

9FT (3M) ROWS
Plant 4–8in (10–20cm) apart

GROWING BAGS
5 plants in each

1 Getting started

It is important not to sow Asian greens too early in the year because the cold temperatures and increasing length of days make these crops very prone to bolting (quickly running to seed)—waiting until midsummer will discourage this. High temperatures and dry spells can also cause plants to bolt in summer.

Bok Choy *has large rounded leaves with excellent flavor, good eaten raw or cooked.*

'Red Giant' *mustard leaves are red-flushed with a mild, peppery, flavor. Good in salads.*

Mizuna *has mild-flavored, serrated leaves that look attractive in salads or as a garnish.*

Spinach mustard *has spoon-shaped leaves that are ideal for cutting young for use in salads.*

2 Sow inside

From midsummer onward and at routine intervals, fill trays or modules with seed compost, firm gently, water thoroughly, and then allow it to drain. Sow the seeds lightly across the surface, and cover with compost to a depth of ½in (1cm). Firm the surface again, and water in lightly. The seeds don't require extra heat and will germinate in about a week. When large enough, harden them off and transplant outside.

Plan your sowings *so that you do not end up with a glut—sow a fresh batch every two weeks.*

3 Sowing outside

Oriental greens do well sown directly. Dig over the site, remove all weeds, and apply high-nitrogen feed. Firm the soil, and then rake level, before marking out ½in (1cm) deep drills 6–12in (15–30cm) apart, depending on the crop.

Water the drill, *then sow seeds ¾in (2cm) apart. Cover with soil, and firm with the back of your rake.*

Seedlings *will need thinning as they appear—gently pull them so they are 4–8in (10–20cm) apart.*

4 Planting out

Prepare the soil well: dig it over to remove any weeds, and apply high-nitrogen fertilizer. Once the indoor-grown seedlings are large enough to handle, harden them off by placing them outdoors during the day and bringing them indoors at night for two weeks. Some greens can become quite large, so check the spacing before planting.

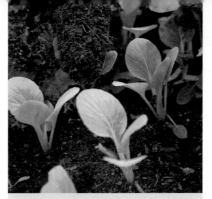

These are quick-growing crops *and can be grown in the gaps left when other vegetables are harvested, making good use of the space.*

Asian greens are thirsty plants *and will dislike competition for moisture from weeds, so remove any that appear nearby by hand.*

These are ideal crops *for cut-and-come-again leaves, especially when sown in repeated batches. They can be cropped for many weeks.*

5 Routine care

Asian greens are prone to brassica pests, such as cabbage root fly (see p.240) and flea beetle, so deter them by covering rows with a fine insect-proof mesh. Keep plants weed-free, and water frequently to encourage quick growth. Doing this will also help prevent them from suddenly bolting.

6 Pick young leaves

When large enough to eat, either snip individual leaves or shoots from your crops, or cut back whole plants. Asian crops grow quickly so it's best to sow small batches frequently during the summer. Sowing seed every two weeks will give you multiple harvests all summer rather than one big crop.

7 Harvesting

Alternatively, allow plants to mature to their full size, gradually thinning the seedlings or transplants out as the season progresses. Cut individual heads whole at the base when a good size, or, for broccoli-type plants, pick individual shoots as they appear.

TIP	*In hot sites, sow seed slightly deeper, and keep the soil moist at all times.*

Whole plants, *such as bok choy, can be cut off at the base once the heads mature.*

STEP-BY-STEP Spinach

Delicious harvested young and used in salads or allowed to mature for cooking, spinach is an easy-to-grow crop that will quickly yield armfuls of large, tender leaves. Sow seed in short drills, little and often, and you are guaranteed a constant supply all summer if you water it well. Spinach matures in six weeks, making it a good crop for small plots—it can soon be replaced. It can also be used for a quick crop in temporary gaps and spaces.

	SPRING	SUMMER	FALL	WINTER
SOW				
HARVEST				

TIME TO HARVEST: 6–12 WEEKS

SUITABLE FOR: BEDS AND CONTAINERS

0   3ft   6ft   9ft

20–45 plants

9FT (3M) ROWS
Plant 3–6in (7–15cm) apart

0   16in

CONTAINERS
7–9 plants in each

1 Getting started

This versatile crop will tolerate cool weather and a shady site and will also grow in containers—even a small patch devoted to it will be extremely productive. Spinach needs very rich, well-drained soil, so dig in organic matter such as well-rotted manure or compost the season before growing.

'Bordeaux' *is both attractive and tasty. It has dark green leaves and bright red stems.*

'Medania' *produces high yields of large, succulent, dark green leaves. It is slow to bolt.*

'Toscane' *is a bolt-resistant cultivar that bears high yields of thick, tender leaves.*

'Tetona' *leaves are smooth and dark green. They resist mildew and are ideal for early crops.*

Sow directly outdoors *from mid- to late spring onward. The last batches can be sown as late as mid-fall if plants are covered with cloches.*

Once seedlings are large enough *to handle, thin them out, leaving the strongest to grow every 3–6in (7–15cm) along the drill.*

2 Sowing outside

Spinach is sown directly, either into the soil or in containers and window boxes, so there is no need to raise plants in seed trays or modules. Direct sowing makes plants less prone to bolting, which can be a problem. Turn over the soil, firm gently, and rake level. Mark out drills ¾in (2cm) deep and 8in (20cm) apart, and water the base thoroughly. Sprinkle seeds roughly ½in (1cm) apart along the drill, cover with soil, firm gently, and water in well.

TIP *Sow in batches every few weeks if you want a constant supply of leaves.*

3 Watering

Annual spinach is a very thirsty, fast-growing crop, so in order to sustain it, ensure that your plants are watered generously and regularly—this may mean watering them as frequently as once a day in very hot, dry weather. Regular weeding is also important since it will also help eliminate any competition for moisture, light, and space.

Ensure plants are kept well watered; *annual spinach can quickly run to seed, or "bolt," if it experiences a check in growth.*

Remove any weeds *close to the plants by hand to avoid damaging the leaves. Use a hoe to remove any weeds between the rows.*

Birds may target young plants, *so net rows as a precaution. Slugs can also be a problem, so apply a light sprinkling of pellets.*

Use a pair of scissors *to harvest the young, tender leaves as a cut and come again crop. Cut the outer leaves first, and work inward.*

4 Routine care

Net plants to deter birds. Downy mildew can be problematic, but resistant varieties are available. Crops will benefit from either a top dressing of a high-nitrogen granular fertilizer such as pelleted poultry manure, or regular doses of a high-nitrogen liquid feed.

5 Cutting salad leaves

Annual spinach can be harvested as a salad leaf while still small; cut individual leaves from plants as and when they become large enough. These can also be cooked as a milder-tasting, more tender leaf than those picked from mature plants.

6 Harvesting

If you prefer to allow your plants to grow larger, leave them until about 10–12 weeks after sowing, and then cut all leaves off about 1in (2.5cm) above the base, discarding any yellowing ones. If the harvested row is well fed and watered, you should get a smaller flush of leaves in two weeks, which can be harvested again. It is then best to discard the plants. Alternatively, dig the plants up whole, and strip the leaves.

Cut leaves as soon as they are ready, *and use them promptly to prevent them from spoiling.*

STEP-BY-STEP Swiss chard

This crop is a hardier vegetable compared to annual spinach (see pp.128–129) and offers the same benefits, although it can also be sown late to crop in fall and winter. It is very easy to grow and is a useful crop for small gardens since its colorful stems allow it to double-up as an ornamental in beds and pots. The foliage can be harvested when needed, either as young tender leaves for salads, or as mature leaves and crisp stems to steam.

	SPRING	SUMMER	FALL	WINTER
SOW				
HARVEST				

TIME TO HARVEST: 6–16 WEEKS

SUITABLE FOR: BEDS AND CONTAINERS

11 plants

9FT (3M) ROWS
Plant or thin to 4–12in (10–30cm) apart

CONTAINERS
8 plants in each

1 Getting started

Swiss chard is often sold as young plants in spring and sometimes also as a winter bedding plant. It is very easy to grow from seed however, which is the best way to raise several plants, especially to crop as baby leaves. This crop is also known as "spinach beet" and "leaf beet," but they are all the same.

'Bright Lights' *is a colorful mix of red- and yellow-stemmed plants. It is good for containers.*

'Bright Yellow' *can be harvested as baby leaves or left for its mature yellow stems.*

'Lucullus' *produces thick white stems that are delicious lightly steamed or braised.*

'Rhubarb Chard' *is grown for its purple-tinted green leaves and dark red stems.*

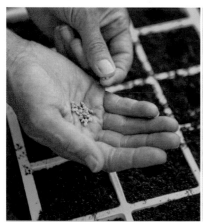

Swiss chard seeds *are large and easy to handle. Sowing into modules rather than pots or trays does away with the need to pick them out later.*

Plant out the young seedlings *into prepared soil, 4in (10cm) apart, and water well. Protect them from slugs and snails with a thin scattering of pellets.*

2 Sowing under cover

Although hardy, Swiss chard can be sown under cover to produce an earlier crop. Fill modular trays with seed compost, firm gently, and water well. Using a dibber or pencil, make holes 1in (2.5cm) deep per cell, drop one or two seeds into each, then cover with compost, and water well. The seed won't require heat and should germinate in a week or two. Thin the seedlings to one per module, and grow them under cover in a bright, frost-free place for a few weeks until large enough to handle. Harden them off for a couple of weeks to acclimatize them to outdoor conditions, then plant them out, 12in (30cm) apart.

3 Sowing outside

Seeds can also be sown directly where they are to grow and will give a later crop. Prepare the soil by digging it over, and work in some granular, high-nitrogen fertilizer. Rake the soil to a fine tilth, and make drills 1in (2.5cm) deep, 12in (30cm) apart. Water the base well, sow seeds 2in (5cm) apart, then cover over with soil.

Space the seed carefully *to sow no more than you need. Unused seeds can be stored for later sowings if kept somewhere cool and dry.*

Don't leave the seedlings too long *before you thin them out. They will become harder to pull, and it will cause greater root disturbance.*

Swiss chard should always be kept moist *– if growing on a lighter soil, mulch around plants with some well-rotted organic matter in summer.*

4 Thinning out

Direct-sown seedlings should be initially thinned to 4in (10cm) apart, then again to a final spacing of 12in (30cm) as the plants mature. Make use of the thinnings as early-season salad leaves. Water the rows after thinning to settle in the soil.

5 Routine care

Water the plants well, and feed regularly with a liquid high-nitrogen fertilizer to promote leafy growth. Keep them well-weeded to prevent competition. For harvestable new leaves in the winter, cover plants with a plastic or fabric tunnel cloche.

6 Harvesting

Plants can be harvested when up to 4in (10cm) tall for salad leaves. Either pick them individually, or cut off whole plants near the base (they will grow back). If you want to cook the leaves like spinach, let them reach full size, and cut them off as needed.

TIP *White-stemmed varieties are the hardiest for overwintering.*

When cutting for use in salad leaves, *leave the base of the plant in the soil to grow back.*

STEP-BY-STEP Chicory

These robust leaves are an asset to any plot: they are highly ornamental and take up relatively little space. They can be cooked or eaten raw and have a slightly bitter but pleasant taste, which can be moderated by blanching. Witloof varieties can also be forced in winter to produce "chicons"—a unique crop of fleshy shoots packed with mild-tasting leaves. All varieties are easy to grow, and most are very hardy; they are suitable for containers.

	SPRING	SUMMER	FALL	WINTER
SOW				
HARVEST				

TIME TO HARVEST: 14–16 WEEKS

SUITABLE FOR: BEDS AND CONTAINERS

8–12 plants

9FT (3M) ROWS
Plant or thin to 10–16in (25–40cm) apart

CONTAINERS
3 plants in each

1 Getting started

There are three types of chicory: Witloof or Belgian types, which have a deep root and elongated, white heads—this type can be forced to produce "chicons;" red chicory, or radicchio, forms a heart, much like a lettuce; finally there are sugarloaf types, which have a loose head of green leaves.

'Treviso Precoce Mesola' *is a radicchio-type with attractive, white-ribbed, red leaves.*

'Palla Rossa' *is a radicchio-type with bitter-tasting red leaves. Good in salads.*

'Variegata di Castelfranco' *is a late radicchio-type, with striking speckled leaves.*

'Pan di Zucchero' *is a sugarloaf-type, ideal for growing as a cut-and-come-again crop.*

Seed can be sown in trays, *although you will need to pick out the seedlings once they are large enough to handle.*

Water the seeds *using a can with a fine rose fitted to prevent washing the seeds to the edges of the tray or into clusters.*

Pick out the seedlings *as soon as they are large enough to handle, planting them on into small pots or individual modules.*

2 Sowing seeds

Very early sowings can be started off under cover. This is also a useful technique for fall and winter sowings for either cut-and-come-again leaves or for spring-maturing crops. Fill trays or modules with compost, water well, and allow to drain. Make holes in each cell, ½in (1cm) deep—or every 2in (5cm)—and then sow one seed in each. Cover with a little more compost, and water in lightly—germination rates are usually very high.

TIP *Sow Witloof chicory between spring and summer for forcing in the fall.*

3 Sow and plant out

To sow direct, dig over the site, and remove any weeds. Create drills ½in (1cm) deep, water well, then sow seeds thinly along them. Cover with soil, and water in. If you have raised seedlings under cover, these can be planted outside as soon as their roots fill the individual cells. Plant at 10–16in (25–40cm) spacings. Water in well.

Seed will do well if sown direct, *as long as the soil has warmed up enough—the plants are liable to bolt if they are sown too early.*

Thin out the seedlings *as they emerge, leaving the strongest 10–16in (25–40cm) apart. The thinnings can be used in salads.*

Keeping plants well watered *will deter them from bolting. Chicory roots grow deeply into the soil, so make sure plants get a good soaking.*

Chicory leaves *can be harvested as cut and come-again crops—snip them from the plant as needed. Alternatively, lift the whole plant at once.*

4 Routine care

Keep plants well watered as they develop, and weed regularly. The plants don't have high nutritional requirements, but plants grown on sandy or alkaline soils, or those in pots, may benefit from a dose of general purpose liquid fertilizer every two weeks.

5 Harvesting

Harvest the leaves once plants reach a good size. For a second harvest, leave the stump in the ground, cut a cross in the top, and remove any remaining leaves. Within a few weeks new, smaller shoots will appear—cover these with a pot to blanch them.

Forcing "chicons"

In winter, Witloof chicory can be forced into producing "chicons." Lift mature roots in mid-fall, removing the leaves, and plant them in a deep pot or box of compost. Water well, then place an upturned pot over the top to block out the light. Keep it in a warm spot. Cut the "chicons" after two or three weeks, at 4–6in (10–15cm) tall.

STEP-BY-STEP Endive

A robust, hardy grower, endive is prone to fewer pests and diseases than other salad crops, which makes it a good choice for those new to gardening. It makes an attractive addition to any vegetable plot, with a slightly bitter taste that many people find refreshing; the bitterness can be moderated by blanching the central heart to create a milder flavor. This salad leaf is similar to chicory in both its cultivation and taste (see pp.126–127).

	SPRING	SUMMER	FALL	WINTER
SOW				
HARVEST				

TIME TO HARVEST: 10–12 WEEKS

SUITABLE FOR: BEDS, CONTAINERS, AND GROWING BAGS

8–12 plants

9FT (3M) ROWS
Plant 10–16in (25–40cm) apart

GROWING BAGS
5 plants in each

1 Getting started

There are two main types of endive, "curly" or "frisée" and "Batavian" or "escarole." Curly endive has narrow leaves and a flat appearance, while Batavian is often hardier, broad-leaf, and the plants tend to grow more upright. Both types prefer rich, well-drained soil in a sunny or partly-shaded location.

'Frenzy' *is a compact, self-blanching type with very fine, curly leaves borne on dense heads.*

'Glory' *produces deeply cut, curly leaves that are especially tender when young.*

'Kentucky' *leaves are finely cut and good for blanching. It is a reliable curly-leaf variety.*

'Natacha' *is a Batavian type, with broad, tender leaves. It has good resistance to bolting.*

To prevent a glut of crops, *sow seed little and often, every few weeks so that you are guaranteed a steady supply.*

Harden the seedlings off *by placing the trays outside during the day and bringing them under cover at night for two weeks.*

Plant the seedlings *out 10–16in (25–40cm) apart, depending on how large you intend your plants to be.*

2 Sowing under cover

Seed can be sown in modules or seed trays under cover in spring. Fill the tray with seed compost, firm gently, water thoroughly, and stand it somewhere to drain. Sow seed ½in (1cm) deep. Make holes in the center of every cell using a dibber or pencil, and then drop one seed into each. Firm over with a little compost, and water in lightly. Seedlings should emerge in about one week. Continue to grow them under cover until strong roots have developed.

TIP	*Harvest as a cut-and-come-again crop: sow thickly in drills and cut as needed.*

3 Sowing outside

Endive can be sown directly into the ground, in growing bags, or in large containers of multipurpose compost. Turn over the soil to remove any weeds, and apply a general-purpose fertilizer to light soils. Create drills ½in (1cm) deep, water well, and then sow your seeds thinly along it. Cover over, firm gently, and water in lightly.

Sow seeds directly outdoors *only once the soil has warmed up in early summer. Exposure to cold temperatures can cause the plants to bolt.*

Once seedlings are well established, *thin them out carefully by hand, leaving a strong seedling to grow every 10–16in (25–40cm).*

Keeping plants well watered *while they are developing will help reduce the risk of bolting; spray with a hose, or use a can with a fine rose.*

Keep the plants well weeded, *especially when they are developing, to reduce the competition for light, nutrients, and water.*

4 Watering

Keep the area well-watered for the first few weeks after transplanting or sowing to encourage a strong root system to develop. Once established, endive is quite drought-tolerant, although it will need watering during very dry conditions.

5 Routine care

Regularly weed between plants until they become large enough to smother any competing growth. Weed by hand to avoid damaging the seedlings; weed between the rows using a hoe. Cover plants with fabric if the weather turns cold to prevent them from bolting.

6 Harvesting

Endive has a bitter flavor that can be lessened by blanching. Some varieties are described as "self-blanching," but others need help. The simplest method is to place a plate over the center of the plant to block out light—first make sure the foliage is dry. Blanching takes about two to three weeks. Cut the leaves once plants reach a suitable size, and leave the stump in the ground to resprout for a later crop.

As soon as plants are blanched, *harvest all the leaves at once using a sharp knife.*

STEP-BY-STEP Watercress

Watercress has steadily become a must-have ingredient in salads, adding crisp texture and a fresh, peppery kick. It can also be enjoyed on its own, as well as in many other summer dishes. Although it usually grows in streams and running water, it doesn't have to, and can easily be grown in containers—providing it is kept well watered. Watercress grows quickly, and if harvested regularly, a few pots will easily meet your needs throughout summer.

	SPRING	SUMMER	FALL	WINTER
SOW				
HARVEST				

TIME TO HARVEST: 8–18 WEEKS

SUITABLE FOR: GROWING BAGS AND CONTAINERS

GROWING BAGS
Plant or thin to 4in (10cm) apart
10 plants

CONTAINERS
16 plants in each

1 Sowing under cover

Watercress is hardy but can be started off under cover. Fill individual pots with seed compost, firm gently, and water well. Sow seeds thinly on the surface, cover with compost ¼in (5mm) deep, and water lightly. Keep the pots on a bright windowsill or in a warm greenhouse, standing in saucers of water, 2in (5cm) deep. Thin the seedlings to leave the strongest, and grow them outside, repotting into containers at least 12in (30cm) wide.

Seed can be sown *into small pots that can be thinned for small crops or potted on.*

Keep the compost moist *at all times. The seeds won't need additional heat to germinate.*

Seedlings grow quickly *once they germinate. Grow them in a bright location under cover.*

An old sink is ideal for growing watercress: *sow seed across the surface and cover with compost, or sow into shallow drills. Water well.*

Thin seedlings as they grow, *and keep them well-watered at all times. Protect the young plants from slugs with a light sprinkling of pellets.*

2 Sowing outside

After the risk of frost has passed, fill containers at least 12in (30cm) wide with multipurpose compost. Sow seed across the surface, ¼in (5mm) deep, and water in. Stand the pots outside in a sunny location in trays of water 2in (5cm) deep, and keep them topped up at all times. The seeds will germinate in about two weeks. Thin them to 4in (10cm) apart, leaving the strongest. Sow batches regularly.

TIP *Use the thinned seedlings as an early crop, treating them as microgreens.*

3 Taking cuttings

Instead of sowing seed, you can also easily raise your own plants from rooting cuttings. Buy watercress from a supermarket, stand a few stems in water, and leave them on a windowsill. The stems will develop roots after 10–14 days, when they can then be potted into a shallow tray of moist compost. Grow them under cover, and harvest.

Stand the cuttings *in a bright location, and change the water every few days to keep it fresh. Remove leaves or stems that turn yellow.*

Watercress grows quickly, *but the plants soon need replacing after a few harvests. Sow more seeds every few weeks for a steady supply.*

Check over plants *every few days, and harvest the young shoots. Take only a few stems per plant, and allow them to grow back.*

4 Routine care

Feed the plants with a high-nitrogen liquid fertilizer to encourage a large crop, and keep them well-weeded to prevent harvesting weeds by mistake. Plants will start to deteriorate after a few harvests and should be replaced; sow a fresh batch.

5 Harvesting

Start harvesting the plants once they have grown to 4–6in (10–15cm) in height. Pinch off the main stems to encourage new sideshoots and to prevent the plants from becoming straggly. Pick from each plant lightly so that they don't become overcropped.

Growing land cress

An alternative to watercress is land cress, which has similar tasting leaves and can be used in the same way. It is easier to grow than watercress because it doesn't require such wet growing conditions. It can be sown directly into the soil or grown in large containers. Plants are hardy and can be cropped through winter.

Root crops

This is an important group of vegetables in the kitchen, producing delicious, energy-packed roots—such as potatoes, parsnips, and rutabagas—that can be stored throughout the winter months. It is a very useful group in the garden too and includes quick-growing roots like radishes and turnips, which can be sown, harvested, and sown again in the same time it takes many other crops to reach maturity. In smaller plots sweet-tasting baby roots, harvested just weeks after sowing, give a worthwhile crop even in containers and are usually expensive to buy.

STEP-BY-STEP Radishes

In the height of summer quick-growing radishes can be ready to harvest in as little as five weeks, which makes these tasty plants extremely handy for filling gaps in small plots. The roots are available in a range of colors and sizes and make an attractive addition to salads. The leaves and seed pods of some varieties can also be eaten. Where space is very limited, they can also be sown directly into patio containers and window boxes.

	SPRING	SUMMER	FALL	WINTER
SOW				
HARVEST				

TIME TO HARVEST: 5–8 WEEKS

SUITABLE FOR: BEDS AND CONTAINERS

60 plants

9FT (3M) ROWS
Sow or thin to 2in (5cm) apart

CONTAINERS
32 plants in each

1 Getting started

Radishes are adaptable plants and will grow in most soils and sites, even in partial shade. Because radishes mature very quickly, it is important to sow seed little and often if you want to obtain regular supplies and avoid a glut. Sow a new batch once your existing plants have reached 3in (8cm) in height.

'Cherry Belle' *is a fast-growing variety. The round, cherry-red roots are ideal in salads.*

'French Breakfast' *has fast-growing, white-tipped, elongated roots with a sweet flavor.*

'Scarlet Globe' *is an easy-to-grow variety that produces attractive, round, bright red roots.*

'Sparkler' *is a reliable variety, known for its round red roots, which have a peppery flavor.*

When sowing in larger module trays *you can simply create ½in (1cm) deep planting holes with your finger, and drop the seed in.*

If the clusters of seedlings *are overcrowded or congested, thin them out, leaving just five or six plants to grow on in each module.*

2 Sowing under cover

Radishes are hardy plants but can also be sown under cover in early spring to give an earlier start in colder areas. Fill module trays with compost to within ½in (1cm) from the top, gently firm it down, water well, then leave it to drain. Sow seed thinly on the surface in small clusters, and cover with compost. Radish seed doesn't need additional heat to grow, and comes up within a few days. Harden off, and plant the modules out when the frost is gone.

TIP *Grow radishes alongside slower growing crops, such as parsnips.*

3 Sowing outside

Radishes mature quickly when sown directly in the ground, which is also the easiest way to grow them because the seedlings don't require planting out. Before sowing, prepare the soil by turning it over to remove weeds, firm it gently, then rake to a fine tilth. Avoid sowing where brassicas have been grown recently.

Mark out drills that are about ¾in (2cm) deep. Radishes are relatively small plants, so the rows can be spaced as close as 4in (10cm) apart.

Water each drill thoroughly, then sow seeds ½in (1cm) apart. Cover them with soil, firming it up with the back of your rake. Water in lightly.

Once the plants are large enough to handle, thin them out to 2in (5cm) spacing. The thinned seedlings can be used as a peppery salad leaf.

Flea beetles create ragged holes in the leaves and can kill seedlings. The best way to deter them is to cover crops with fine mesh netting.

4 Routine care

Thin the seedlings as they grow, and keep them well watered. Radishes are a quick-growing crop and so will compete well with weeds. However, weeds can still harbor pests and diseases, so it is important to regularly weed your beds.

5 Protecting plants

Radishes are vulnerable to flea beetle damage, especially in hot and dry weather, and are at risk from slugs and snails. Keep plants well watered to offset any damage, and cover with fine insect netting, which will also deter cabbage root fly (see p.240).

6 Harvesting

Pull up the roots as soon as they reach a harvestable size. Do not leave them in the ground too long, however, as summer radishes can become very spicy and pithy if they are left to overmature, and some plants are prone to bolting. Pick the radishes daily, checking along the row to find the largest roots. This will allow you to consume your harvest while each radish is young and tender.

Sow radish seed in batches, and pull the roots carefully from the ground as required.

STEP-BY-STEP Beets

One of the most popular crops in the vegetable plot, beet plants are highly productive, trouble-free, and great for small gardens—they also grow well in containers. Beets are very versatile and can be harvested as baby roots a few weeks after sowing or left to reach full size, ideal for storing. In the kitchen, gone are the days of just preserving the roots in vinegar; beets are also great roasted, pureed for soup, or added to cakes.

	SPRING	SUMMER	FALL	WINTER
SOW				
HARVEST				

TIME TO HARVEST: 12–16 WEEKS

SUITABLE FOR: BEDS AND CONTAINERS

30 plants

9FT (3M) ROWS
Sow 1½in (4cm) apart, thinning to 4in (10cm)

CONTAINERS
12 plants in each

1 Getting started

Beets can be bought as plug plants in the spring for a head start, but the plants are easily raised from seed. Most beet "seed" is actually a cluster of three or four true seeds, which germinate as a clump and should be thinned out. The exceptions to this are "monogerm" varieties that produce one seedling.

'Red Ace' produces large, dark red roots that are easy to grow and are good for storing.

'Chioggia Pink' has red-skinned roots with pink and white flesh. It has a sweet flavor.

'Boltardy' is widely grown and produces firm, round roots. It is resistant to bolting.

'Forono' is a reliable variety to grow for tender baby roots. It is suitable for containers.

Beet seeds are large and easy to handle, allowing you to sow one per module. Keep the soil moist after sowing.

Thin the seedlings as they grow to leave the strongest per module. Monogerm seed, sown singly, won't require thinning.

Plant out the seedlings as soon as possible so the plants develop fully in the soil. Try to avoid disturbing the roots.

2 Sowing under cover

To give them a head start, beets can be sown under cover. Fill modular trays with seed compost, firm gently, water it well, then allow it to drain. Make a ¾in (2cm) deep hole in each module using a dibber or pencil, and drop one seed into each. Firm the compost, water lightly, and place the tray in a propagator. As soon as roots start growing through the base of the cells, harden off the seedlings, and plant them out 4in (10cm) apart.

> **TIP** Soak seeds in warm water for 30 mins before sowing to help germination.

3 Sowing outside

Beets can be sown directly in the soil, provided it is warm enough. Turn over the site to remove any weeds, then rake it to a fine tilth. Along a garden line, create drills 1in (2.5cm) deep using the edge of a hoe or rake. Water the base thoroughly, then sow the seeds roughly 1½in (4cm) apart. Cover with soil, firm gently, and water in lightly.

Sow the seed at regular intervals, *spacing it by hand. The soil should be at least 46°F (8°C) before sowing, otherwise germination will be slow.*

Thin the seedlings *to 4in (10cm) apart by pulling them up or pinching them off completely. The "thinnings" can be used as salad leaves.*

Carefully weeding by hand *close to the plants is safer than using a hoe, which can easily damage the top of the swelling roots.*

Water plants at the base, *and avoid splashing the leaves, which can encourage disease. Plants on lighter soils should be watered more regularly.*

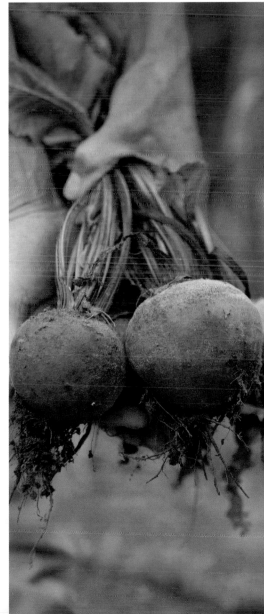

4 Weeding

Beets are fairly pest and disease-free, but remember to regularly hand-weed around the plants to prevent weeds from establishing. If left, weeds will compete against your crop for moisture and nutrients and will slow their growth; they also attract pests.

5 Routine care

Seedlings should be watered regularly, and although mature plants are drought-resistant, the roots are more tender if the soil is kept moist. Don't overwater though, since this will encourage the production of excess leaves at the expense of roots.

6 Harvesting

Roots can be harvested as soon as they reach a usable size or can be left to grow larger to be used as required. To harvest, carefully lift them from the ground, wash off any soil, and twist off the leaves. Surplus, undamaged roots can be stored in wooden boxes lined with newspaper. Place 1in (2.5cm) of sharp sand in the base, then a layer of roots. Add more layers to fill the box, then store in a cool, dry shed or garage.

Young roots are best enjoyed fresh, *so only harvest them on the day you intend to eat them.*

STEP-BY-STEP Carrots

This ever-popular root crop is just as happy growing in a container as it is in the soil, more so if yours is a little rocky. Carrots are a useful crop that can be enjoyed for almost 12 months of the year—with baby "pullings" in early spring and substantial maincrop roots that store well into winter. Their high sugar levels and crunchy texture make carrots a children's favorite. They are also rich in vitamin A, which promotes good eyesight.

	SPRING	SUMMER	FALL	WINTER
SOW				
HARVEST				

TIME TO HARVEST: 12–20 WEEKS

SUITABLE FOR: BEDS AND CONTAINERS

24–150 plants

9FT (3M) ROWS
Depending on variety, grow at 1¾–5in (2–12cm) apart

CONTAINERS
50 plants in each

1 Getting started

Carrots come in a wide variety of shapes, sizes, and even colors. They are grown from seeds, and if harvested young, they can be ready in a matter of weeks. Round varieties are the best choice for growing in containers or in shallow or rocky soils; larger maincrop varieties need deep, moist beds.

'Carson' *is a maincrop variety that produces large tasty roots that are good for storing.*

'Parmex' *produces bite-size, sweet-tasting, round carrots. It is ideal for container growing.*

'Purple Haze' *crops early, yielding unusual purple-skinned roots with contrasting flesh.*

'Bangor' *is a maincrop carrot with large chunky roots. It has good flavor and stores very well.*

2 Sowing seeds

To sow direct, turn over the soil to remove weeds, firm it, then rake it level. Make drills with a hoe, water the base, and sow the seed, then cover with soil and water. Carrots can also be sown into short drills in deep containers.

Make seed drills *¾in (2cm) deep, 4–8in (10–20cm) apart, depending on the variety. Check the packet first.*

Sow seeds thinly, *about ¼in (5mm) apart. Tip them from the packet or from the palm of your hand.*

3 Growing on

Carrot seed can be notoriously slow to germinate, so be patient. It is also important to keep the soil or compost well watered until your seedlings have emerged. If sowing early crops outside in spring, these can be covered with garden fabric to provide insulation. Where space allows, seed sown in containers can be kept under cover until germinated, then moved outside to grow. If not, cover with fabric instead.

Remove garden fabric *on milder days to let in the sunlight. Cover seedlings if hard frost is predicted.*

4 Thinning out

As they grow, thin the seedlings to the recommended distances for your particular variety. In general, maincrop varieties require much wider spacings than early carrots. Very young seedlings can be pulled, but those with developing taproots should be pinched off to prevent leaving holes in the soil ideal for carrot fly eggs (see below).

Check the seed packet *before thinning the seedlings since some varieties require more space, and therefore more thinning, than others.*

Weed regularly, *because removing fully grown weeds can disturb the crop. As carrots mature, their foliage will help to suppress weeds..*

Use stakes to support carrot fly netting, *and also bury the base 2in (5cm) into the soil, all the way around, to prevent flies from sneaking under.*

5 Routine care

Water plants during dry spells, but don't overdo it. This promotes leafy growth at the expense of roots. Regularly hand-weed near plants. Weeding releases the scent of the leaves, which attracts carrot fly, so it is best done at dusk when the pests are inactive.

6 Protecting plants

Carrot fly larvae (see p.238) can be a troublesome pest, eating the roots, especially on crops sown in late spring. To prevent the low-flying adults from laying eggs at the base of plants, erect a barrier of fine insect mesh about 24in (60cm) high around the beds.

7 Harvesting

Carrots are ready to pull once they reach the desired size. Early sowings are ready when they are roughly finger-thickness and are pulled from the soil by hand. Harvest maincrop varieties when they measure about 1½in (4cm) across, easing them out with a fork.

 TIP *Eat early carrots fresh; maincrop roots can be stored like beets (see p.143).*

If using a fork to lift carrots, *be careful not to disturb neighboring plants still growing.*

STEP-BY-STEP Turnips

This vegetable is undergoing a revival, with top chefs and gardeners alike rediscovering what these sweet, tender roots have to offer. Baby crops can be harvested in as little as six weeks, or plants can be left in the ground to mature fully. Turnips can also be grown for their leaves, or turnip "tops." These can be treated like a cut-and-come-again crop and will provide several flushes of tasty leafy greens through the leaner months.

	SPRING	SUMMER	FALL	WINTER
SOW				
HARVEST				

TIME TO HARVEST: 6–10 WEEKS

SUITABLE FOR: BEDS AND CONTAINERS

9FT (3M) ROWS
Plant 4in (10cm) apart
30 plants

CONTAINERS
10 plants in each

1 Getting started

Turnips prefer a site with moist, rich, well-drained soil that contains plenty of nitrogen, so dig in plenty of organic matter like well-rotted compost or manure in the season before growing. Sow turnips that will be harvested as baby roots alongside slow-growing crops such as parsnips or sweet corn.

'Purple Top Milan' *should be pulled early at 2in (5cm) wide. The roots have a sweet flavor.*

'Snowball' *has pure white roots that are sweet and tender. Lift the roots at six weeks.*

'Primera' *roots have purple tops and should be pulled small. They have sweet, tender flesh.*

'Atlantic' *produces purple and white roots that can be harvested young or left to mature.*

Hardy varieties *can be sown under cover at the beginning and end of the growing season, giving you roots during almost every month of the year.*

Harden the seedlings off, *and plant them out once their roots fill the modules. Space the plants 4in (10cm) apart, with 12in (30cm) between rows.*

2 Sowing under cover

Fill module trays with seed compost, firm gently, and water well. Let the soil drain then make a ¾in (2cm) deep hole in each cell. Sow four seeds per hole, cover over, and water in. Alternatively, fill large containers with compost, and make drills ¾in (2cm) deep. Sow seed thinly along the base, or sow a few seeds every 4in (10cm). Thin the seedlings to one per cell, or one every 4in (10cm); harden off, and plant out when they are large enough to handle.

TIP *To prevent a glut, sow seed little and often for a small but steady supply.*

3 Sowing outside

Alternatively, you can sow turnip seed directly outside between mid-spring and late summer. Create a seedbed by digging over a patch of soil to remove any weeds and incorporating a base dressing of high nitrogen granular fertilizer. Firm gently, rake level to create a fine tilth, then create drills ¾in (2cm) deep and 9–12in (23–30cm) apart.

Water the drills well, *and then sow seeds thinly along the base. Cover them back over with a thin layer of soil, and then water them in lightly.*

Carefully thin the seedlings *to leave a strong specimen every 4in (10cm). Use the thinned turnip seedlings as a leafy green or in salads.*

Fine insect-proof mesh *should be used to protect crops from flying pests such as flea beetles during all stages of their growth.*

Pull out competing weeds *by hand to avoid damaging the young turnip roots. Check the rows regularly so weeds can be pulled up when young.*

4 Routine care

Flea beetles can be a problem, especially in hot, dry weather, so cover drills with insect-proof mesh. Keep plants well watered and fed as they grow. Container plants and those on light soils can be fed periodically with a high-nitrogen liquid fertilizer to boost yields.

5 Weeding

It is important to keep the seedlings weed-free since weeds compete with the seedlings for light and nutrients and may harbor disease. Weed around the plants by hand to prevent damaging the roots, and use a hoe to remove weeds between the rows.

6 Harvesting

Pull individual "baby" roots of fast-growing summer crops once they reach the size of a golf ball—leaving them to grow any larger can result in a woody texture. Hardy winter types can be left to grow larger so that they can then be lifted in the fall as and when they are needed. It is possible to store turnips in boxes of sand, but they are only likely to keep for a couple of weeks because they have fairly thin skins.

Early roots are ideal for harvesting *when they reach about 1½–2in (4–5cm) in diameter.*

STEP-BY-STEP Parsnips

A delicious staple of the winter kitchen, parsnips are a worthy addition to any vegetable plot. An impressive number can be grown on just a small patch of ground, and they are very easy to cultivate—simply ensure that you give them enough water and space. Although they take a long time to grow, they are extremely hardy and can be left in the soil well into the colder months; exposure to frost is, in fact, said to make the roots taste sweeter.

	SPRING	SUMMER	FALL	WINTER
SOW				
HARVEST				

TIME TO HARVEST: 32–36 WEEKS

SUITABLE FOR: BEDS

11–15 plants

9FT (3M) ROWS
Plant 8–12in (20–30cm) apart

1 Getting started

Parsnips grow best in light soils that are free from rocks and not compacted—this reduces the risk of the roots becoming crooked or forked. Pick a site that was manured the previous fall—do not apply manure just before sowing. It can cause root tips to become scorched, which results in forked roots.

'White Gem' *has relatively short roots with white skin and excellent flavor.*

'Gladiator' *is an exhibition variety, known for its sweet, smooth-skinned roots.*

'Avon Resistor' *produces short roots that are uniform in size and have a good flavor.*

'Tender and True' *roots are large, smooth-skinned, and show some resistance to canker.*

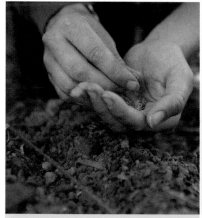

Sow the seed in mid- to late spring, *as soon as the risk of frost has passed. Seed sown earlier than this may struggle to germinate.*

Thin seedlings—*the youngest can be pulled out, but those forming taproots should be pinched off to avoid leaving holes in the soil, ideal for carrot flies.*

2 Sowing seeds

Because they develop a long taproot, parsnips are best sown direct. Prepare the soil, then sow four or five seeds every 8–12in (20–30cm), ¾in (2cm) deep. Space rows 12in (30cm) apart. Seedlings can germinate slowly —often taking up to 10–14 days—so be patient. Save space, and mark your rows by sowing fast-growing salad leaves or radishes between your parsnip seedlings. These can be harvested well before the parsnips mature.

TIP > *Buy new seed each spring because parsnip seed viability is very short.*

3 Protecting plants

As part of the carrot family, parsnips are prone to carrot fly attack. Prevent this by pinching off the surplus seedlings at soil level rather than pulling them, which can leave holes for the female fly to lay her eggs in. Also, erect a barrier of fine insect-proof mesh at least 24in (60cm) in height around your plants (see p.238).

Bury the insect-proof mesh *2in (5cm) deep in the soil, completely surrounding the plants, so that the carrot flies can't get underneath it.*

Regular watering *will encourage the roots to grow evenly—if they are allowed to become dry, later watering may cause the roots to split.*

Lift parsnips gently *to avoid damaging them. In very dry conditions, roots will emerge more readily if the soil is moistened beforehand.*

4 Routine care

Keep plants well watered as they develop to ensure good-sized, even roots. Hand weed around the plants to avoid disturbing their roots. When the plants are established, they will be better able to out-compete weeds. Parsnips do not require any additional feeding.

5 Harvesting

Early parsnip varieties will be ready to lift in early fall; later types can be harvested during winter. Roots can grow very deep, especially on open, light soils, so insert a garden fork next to each root, and use it to gently ease the root out of the soil.

Storing the roots

Late-maturing parsnips can be left in the ground until required. In very cold areas, cover the plants with a mulch of straw so that when you come to dig the roots up, the ground is not frozen solid. Mark plants with a stake so that they are easier to find. Roots left in the soil come spring can be stored in sand as for beets (see p.137).

STEP-BY-STEP Rutabagas

These plump, round roots are delicious roasted or mashed like potatoes and provide welcome fresh crops in fall and winter when the vegetable patch is pretty bare. These are slow-maturing plants, traditionally best suited to larger gardens, where they can be left to grow. However, rutabagas can also be sown densely to produce "baby" roots that can either be eaten within a few weeks, leaves and all, or left longer for small, sweet roots, 2in (5cm) across.

	SPRING	SUMMER	FALL	WINTER
SOW				
HARVEST				

TIME TO HARVEST: 20–24 WEEKS

SUITABLE FOR: BEDS

12–15 plants

9FT (3M) ROWS
Plant 8–10in (20–25cm) apart

1 Getting started

Rutabagas require a relatively long growing season and will take five or six months to mature fully. Dig in plenty of well-rotted organic matter such as compost or manure in the fall before growing, and ensure that you rotate rutabagas, including them in the same rotation group as other brassica crops.

'Brora' *roots are fast-growing and have good disease-resistance. The yellow flesh is very tasty.*

'Best of All' *is a reliable variety, giving medium-sized, purple roots with yellow flesh.*

'Virtue' *is an excellent choice. It produces reddish roots that have delicious yellow flesh.*

'Marian' *produces deep purple roots that have an excellent flavor and good disease-resistance.*

Sow seed thinly along your rows *before covering it over and watering in. Multiple rows should be spaced 12in (30cm) apart.*

Once seedlings begin to appear, *gradually thin them out, leaving the strongest to grow. Eventual spacing should be around 8–10in (20–25cm) apart.*

2 Sowing seeds

Because they develop a relatively long taproot, rutabagas are best sown directly into the ground rather than in modules or seed trays. In mid- to late spring, prepare the site for sowing by digging it over thoroughly to remove any weeds and large rocks, then firm it gently, and rake it level. Make a drill ¾in (2cm) deep, and water it well. Sow your seeds along it, cover them over with a little more soil to level the soil surface, and then firm down gently.

TIP *For baby rutabagas, sow seed densely then thin to 3–4in (8–10cm) apart.*

3 Growing on

Rutabagas are exceptionally hardy crops, although very early sowings may need protection if there is a risk of frost. Cover them with a single or double layer of horticultural fabric, or a cloche or cold frame, to offer insulation and speed up growth. Ensure that the plants remain well watered under their protective covering.

Rutabagas are fully hardy, *but cover early sowings with garden fabric to protect them from frost as a precaution, especially in colder regions.*

Cover plants *with wire or plastic netting to deter large pests such as pigeons. Use finer mesh to protect against flea beetles and cabbage root fly.*

Hand-weed or hoe *between the plants regularly to prevent competing weeds from checking growth; be careful not to damage the roots.*

4 Protecting plants

Rutabagas are prone to the same pests and diseases as other members of the brassica family. Flea beetles can be very damaging to plants during hot weather; where at risk, cover over rows with fine, insect-proof mesh to prevent access to the plants.

5 Routine care

It is important that rutabagas don't slow in growth due to a lack of moisture, so keep plants well irrigated, especially during dry spells. Apply a 2½–3in (6–7cm) deep mulch of organic matter to lock in soil moisture —this is especially useful on light soils.

6 Harvesting

In early to mid-fall, roots will become large enough to harvest. Use a garden fork alongside to gently pry each root out of the soil. If you don't have storage space, rutabagas can be left in the soil all winter, under a layer of straw. However, it is almost impossible to lift roots when the soil is frozen, so if you want to lift rutabagas in advance in fall, they can be stored in boxes of sand or kept in a shed or garage until required.

After lifting your rutabagas, *clean them thoroughly, and cut the stems off before storing.*

STEP-BY-STEP Potatoes

Whether you prefer yours roasted, baked, fried, mashed, or new and slathered in butter, potatoes are a delicious, must-grow crop in any garden. This extremely popular vegetable is very easy to grow and can be grown in large containers if you don't have ample amounts of bed space. Potatoes store well, and your crop can be enjoyed for months. There is a huge selection of tasty varieties, classed, in order of maturity, as early, main, and storage types.

	SPRING	SUMMER	FALL	WINTER
SOW				
HARVEST				

TIME TO HARVEST: 12–22 WEEKS

SUITABLE FOR: BEDS AND CONTAINERS

4–6 plants

9FT (3M) ROWS
Plant 18–30in (45–70cm) apart

CONTAINERS
2 plants in each

1 Start under cover

Potatoes bought for planting are called "seed potatoes" and are available to buy in mid- to late winter. Early types may benefit from being pre-germinated before planting, to give them a head start. This simply means allowing the "eyes" to sprout before the tubers are planted out. Place your seed potatoes "rose-end"—the end with the most eyes—upward in an egg carton, and position this in a cool, well-lit place such as a windowsill.

Choose seed potatoes *that are certified disease-free and of good quality to maximize your chances of healthy, productive plants.*

If stored in a cool, dry, frost-free place, *the tubers will begin to develop "chits" within a few weeks. They are then ready to plant out.*

Place the tubers *into the soil, ensuring that they are planted with the rose-end facing up.*

Water the chitted tubers *in well before covering them to help them establish quickly.*

Cover the tubers with soil, *leaving the surface raised up into a slight mound.*

2 Planting out

Seed potatoes can be planted in the ground or in containers. The main season to plant outside is early spring for early varieties, and mid-spring for main types. Dig over and weed the soil, and work in some general purpose fertilizer. Dig a drill about 6in (15cm) deep, and place your potatoes along the bottom, spaced 18–30in (45–70cm) apart. Cover over with 8in (20cm) of soil to create a slight mound.

TIP	*The closer the potatoes are planted together, the smaller the tubers will be.*

3 Container-growing

Alternatively, potatoes can be planted in containers, such as specially designed potato "barrels," large tubs, or plastic sacks. Use a 50:50 mix of multipurpose compost and good garden soil, placing a 6in (15cm) layer of this in the base. Lay the potato tubers on top, and then cover with a further 4in (10cm) of soil. Water them in well.

As long as you make drainage holes *before planting, a plastic barrel makes an ideal, and space-saving, growing container for potatoes.*

Plastic sacks make good growing containers *because they can be emptied and folded away once all the potatoes have been harvested.*

Potatoes are hardy, *but emerging shoots can be damaged by harsh frost. Cover plants with garden fabric when cold weather is predicted.*

Earth up potatoes *three or four times during summer. Containers should be earthed up until the compost reaches just below the rim.*

4 Routine care

Water plants well, and feed using an all-purpose granular fertilizer. Young plants need weeding but soon develop a smothering canopy of foliage. After flowering, green, tomatolike fruits, may appear—these are poisonous and should not be eaten. Check plants regularly for potato blight (see p.246).

5 Earthing up

Plants will need "earthing up" as they grow: draw the soil up around the stem to leave the top 4in (10cm) of the plant visible. This encourages the plant to produce greater yields and prevents the growing tubers from becoming exposed to sunlight, which makes them green and inedible.

6 Harvesting

Begin harvesting early potatoes in early summer—generally they will be ready to lift once their flowers develop; leave main types until late summer or early fall. Lift soil-grown plants gently with a fork, taking care not to damage the tubers. Container-grown plants can either be tipped out all at once or excavated to remove the tubers as you need them—gently refirm the compost afterward, and water well.

Harvest potatoes on a dry day *if possible, and leave them to dry in the sun for a few hours.*

Potatoes

1 'Accent' This yellow-skinned first early potato bears reliably high yields. It has moderately good disease resistance, and the tubers suffer less slug damage than other varieties.

2 'Charlotte' A second early, this yellow-skinned salad potato is reliable and has a good flavor. Higher yielding than others of this type, individual tuber-size is also impressive.

3 'Red Duke of York' This versatile first early variety can be lifted and eaten young as a new potato or allowed to mature for baking. It has red skin and creamy-white flesh.

4 'Belle de Fontenay' This early maincrop variety is renowned for being a great salad potato. The yield of knobby tubers is good, and the flesh is yellow and waxy.

5 'Pink Fir Apple' An heirloom maincrop variety, it produces knobby, red-skinned tubers that have a waxy texture and a good flavor. It is widely grown as a salad potato.

6 'Concorde' Renowned for its high yields, this first early variety is quick to bulk up, producing waxy tubers with yellow flesh. The tubers show some resistance to slugs.

7 'Foremost' This early variety produces high yields of tasty, firm, white-fleshed tubers with good scab resistance. They store well under cover if kept dry and well-ventilated.

8 'Yukon Gold' A second early, it has great flavor and can be used in a variety of different ways in the kitchen: boiled as a new potato, or baked, roasted, or mashed.

9 'Ratte' A good alternative to 'Pink Fir Apple', the tubers have smoother skins, making them easier to prepare in the kitchen, and mature earlier. It has a tasty salad-potato flavor.

Other varieties
'Mimi'
'Anya'
'Maris Bard'
'Maris Piper'
'Lady Christl'
'Edzell Blue'

1

2

3

6

Alliums

The unique characteristic of this group is unmistakable—no other crop has such a distinctive flavor or aroma, released from every part of the plant. These are versatile crops in the garden and highly valuable in the kitchen too. Grow enough, and you can easily be self-sufficient in onions all year thanks to their excellent storage qualities; likewise shallots, if you prefer something a little stronger. Leeks aren't just the mainstay of the winter plot, they can last until spring, and there are also fall varieties to grow. The sweetness of garlic completes the group—lift it in the summer for fresh cloves, or plait and store them through the winter.

STEP-BY-STEP Onions

No vegetable garden is complete without onions, and there are many to choose from, including red-, white-, and brown-skinned varieties. Onions need a long time to mature fully, and sizable bulbs can be achieved by sowing seeds under cover early in the year. However, an easier method is to raise plants from "sets" that are planted in spring or fall. Overwintered crops of hardy, often Japanese, varieties offer a useful early harvest.

	SPRING	SUMMER	FALL	WINTER
SOW				
HARVEST				

TIME TO HARVEST: 22–24 WEEKS

SUITABLE FOR: BEDS

0   3ft   6ft   9ft

30–60 plants

9FT (3M) ROWS
Plant or thin to 2–4in (5–10cm) apart

1 Sowing under cover

For larger bulbs, sow seeds under cover from mid-winter to early spring. Fill seed trays with seed compost, firm gently, and water well. Make a hole in each cell ½in (1cm) deep, and sow two seeds in each. The seeds don't require additional heat but should be kept moist. Germination will take a week or two. Thin the seedlings to leave the stronger in each module.

TIP	*For smaller, earlier bulbs, sow three or four seeds per cell and don't thin them.*

Sowing seeds in modules, *removes the need to prick the seedlings out as they develop.*

Thin seedlings *once large enough to handle. They should pull easily from the compost.*

Harden off *and plant out in spring—the same time when "sets" are planted out.*

Spring sowings can bolt *in cold weather. Don't sow too early in the year, when a cold snap may occur, and choose a bolt-resistant variety.*

Thin out the seedlings *gradually as they develop until they reach their final spacing. Leave only the strongest, and use the thinnings in your salads.*

2 Sowing outside

This method of raising onions is now less common since the introduction of "sets," which offer the crop a useful head start. Sow seeds in spring for summer crops, or in late summer for Japanese overwintering varieties. Dig over the soil to remove weeds, firm it down, and rake the surface level. Prepare a drill ¾in (2cm) deep. Water the base well, and sow thinly along it. Cover, water in, and once the seedlings have emerged, thin them out to leave one every 2–4in (5–10cm).

3 Planting sets

Sets are very small onion bulbs that are planted in either fall or spring. Each one bulks up in size to produce a larger bulb. Fall-planted sets of winter-hardy varieties mature to produce larger bulbs than those planted in the spring. Push the sets into prepared soil, 2–4in (5–10cm) apart, positioning the tip of the set at soil level.

The space between your sets *will determine the eventual size of your onion bulbs—plant them further apart if you want larger results.*

Firm the soil gently around the sets, *leaving the tips showing above the soil surface. Water them in lightly to settle the sets in.*

It is important *to keep crops well weeded, especially while they are young. Weed around them by hand to avoid damaging the bulbs.*

Onion bulbs are ready to harvest *once the stems and leaves have naturally died back. Lift on a dry day to discourage rotting.*

4 Routine care

Onions are very sensitive to plant competition, so ensure you weed regularly between your bulbs. Keep the soil evenly moist, especially if you want good-sized bulbs. Fall sowings and plantings benefit from an application of high-nitrogen fertilizer in late winter.

5 Harvesting

Harvest onions when they reach full size, once the stems have collapsed and bent over. On a dry day, gently lift them partly out of the soil using a fork. Leave them on the ground for a week or so to dry out; dry them indoors on racks if it is wet.

Drying the bulbs

Lay the onions out on a wire rack to dry. Ensure that this is kept off the ground so that air can circulate around the bulbs. Leave them in a light, dry place such as a greenhouse or on a windowsill. Once the outer skins rustle, you can either braid your bulbs and hang them up, or store them in net bags until needed.

Onions

1 'Sturon' This popular, brown-skinned onion produces mid-sized bulbs with flavorful, juicy flesh. The bulbs are resistant to bolting and keep well after harvesting.

2 'Ailsa Craig' A reliable variety, this onion develops large, globe-shaped bulbs with a mild flavor. Use them fresh—the bulbs don't store well. Plants can be raised from seed or "sets."

3 'Senshyu' This hardy Japanese variety can be planted in the fall to harvest in early summer. It is a reliable onion and gives a good harvest of tasty, flat-bottomed bulbs.

4 'Centurion' Plant this variety in spring for an early crop of rounded, brown-skinned bulbs in summer that store well for short periods. The flesh is crisp with a good flavor.

5 'Hi Keeper' This is a Japanese variety to plant in fall and overwinter outside, ready to harvest in early summer. It can also be sown in spring to harvest mid- to late summer.

6 'Red Baron' This variety gives a reliable crop of small to medium-sized, red-skinned bulbs in summer. It has a stronger flavor than many other red onions and stores well.

7 'Setton' Producing large, brown-skinned bulbs in late summer, these onions have a good flavor and store well. It is a reliable new variety that crops heavily. It is mainly sold as "sets."

8 'Shakespeare' Plant this variety in the fall for harvesting the following summer. It produces brown-skinned, mid-sized bulbs that are excellent for storing. It has good flavor.

9 'Golden Bear' This variety produces large brown-skinned bulbs that mature in midsummer. It gives a good crop that stores well and is resistant to onion white rot disease (see p.242).

Other varieties
'Bedfordshire Champion'
'Hercules'
'Hytech'
'Marco'
'Stuttgarter Giant'

STEP-BY-STEP Shallots

These small bulbs couldn't be easier to grow—simply plant sets during the fall or spring, and each will divide up, producing a cluster of new bulbs. If their skins are properly dried, storage life is extremely long, giving you useful bulbs with an intense flavor for many months of the year. Shallots are delicious used whole in casseroles, when they melt in your mouth, or roasted with meat or vegetables, when they take on a caramelized, sweet flavor.

	SPRING	SUMMER	FALL	WINTER
SOW				
HARVEST				

TIME TO HARVEST: 20–36 WEEKS

SUITABLE FOR: BEDS

15 plants

9FT (3M) ROWS
Plant out 8in (20cm) apart

1 Getting started

Shallots are most commonly grown from "sets"—small bulbs that, when planted, bulk up by splitting into numerous smaller bulbs. Alternatively, shallots can be grown from seed, either sown under cover in winter, or sown direct in mid- to late spring. Ensure that you give them rich, well-drained soil.

'Longor' *bulbs have pinkish flesh and good flavor. They are uniform in size and shape.*

'Red Sun' *is a high-yielding variety with red skins and red-flushed, crisp flesh.*

'Golden Gourmet' *is a mild-tasting variety, and the large, yellow bulbs can be eaten raw.*

'Mikor' *bulbs have brownish skin and pink flesh. The large bulbs are good for cooking.*

2 Sowing under cover

Fill a tray with seed compost, water well, and leave it to drain. Sow the seeds in small clusters, and cover them with ½in (1cm) of compost. Water lightly, and place the tray in a propagator; germination will take a week or two.

Plants sown from seed *under cover in winter should be ready to transplant in mid-spring.*

Once the seedlings emerge, *they will need thinning to leave the strongest seedling per cell.*

3 Planting sets

Plant your sets, either in late fall or spring, directly outside in an open, sunny site that has been turned over to remove weeds. Push them into the soil, leaving the tip of each bulb protruding just above the surface. Plant them at their eventual spacing—leaving 8in (20cm) between sets in each direction.

TIP *Cover sets with netting to protect against birds.*

Buy certified, virus-free sets *to boost your chances of growing successful, healthy crops.*

4 Sow and plant out

Seed can be sown direct once the soil has warmed up at the end of spring. Dig in plenty of well-rotted manure or compost. Create a drill about 1in (2.5cm) deep, and sow seed thinly along it. Cover with soil, and water in. Harden off your indoor-grown seedlings once their roots fill their modules, and plant out 8x8in (20x20cm) apart.

Sprinkle the seed thinly along each drill—sow plenty, as seedlings will be thinned out once they are established.

Thin the seedlings, pulling the weakest ones out gently by hand, leaving approximately ¼in (2cm) between them.

If your seedlings need transplanting to their final position, dig them up gently and replant them 8in (20cm) apart.

Weed the seedlings by hand or with an onion hoe. Keeping them well ventilated will prevent diseases such as downy mildew (see p.242).

Leave the bulbs to dry on the soil surface for a few days after lifting, and then carefully split into individual bulbs before you store them.

5 Routine care

Keep plants well watered and well weeded. Overwintered shallots should have a granular high nitrogen fertilizer sprinkled among the plants during spring—chicken pellets are ideal—to boost yields. There is no need to feed spring planted shallots.

6 Harvesting

Leaves will turn yellow and wither in mid- to late summer—a sign that the bulbs are nearly mature. Stop watering at this point to encourage the bulbs to dry and set strong skins for long storage. Lift gently with a fork, taking care not to damage the individual bulbs.

Drying the bulbs

To store well, shallots should be dried fully on a raised rack in a greenhouse or a covered area for at least two weeks. After this, cut the stem off each bulb to leave a ½in (1cm) stump, rub off the loose outer skin, and store them in a net bag or cardboard box in a cool, dry, frost-free place until required.

STEP-BY-STEP Green onions

Green onions bring a unique flavor to salads, so make sure your plot has space for a row or two. These small plants are amazingly productive and surprisingly hardy, allowing you to extend the season with both early and late sowings. Green onions can either form a small bulb or grow more like a miniature leek, producing cylindrical, non-bulbing stems. There are also red-stemmed, pickling, and Japanese varieties to choose from.

	SPRING	SUMMER	FALL	WINTER
SOW				
HARVEST				

TIME TO HARVEST: 10 WEEKS

SUITABLE FOR: BEDS AND CONTAINERS

0   3ft   6ft   9ft

150 plants

9FT (3M) ROWS
Plant out ¾in (2cm) apart

0   16in

CONTAINERS
40 plants in each

1 Getting started

Green onions are grown from seed, either sown directly in the soil or into large containers during spring and summer. Early and late crops can also be raised under cover, or sown into greenhouse borders, containers, or growing bags. Small crops can also be grown on warm windowsills during the winter.

'Guardsman' *has long, well-blanched stems and dark green leaves. It is a vigorous variety.*

'North Holland Blood Red' *produces striking red stems that deepen in color with age.*

'White Lisbon' *is the most commonly grown green onion and is good for container growing.*

'Summer Isle' *crops relatively late. Its mild flavor makes it ideal for eating raw.*

Seed can be sown *under cover from early spring to fall; sow in repeat batches to provide a steady supply.*

If necessary, *encourage and protect germinating seeds by placing pots in a propagator. Keep them well ventilated.*

Seedlings in pots *will also need thinning when they reach about 3in (8cm) tall—thin to leave four or five per small pot.*

2 Sowing under cover

As certain varieties are very hardy, early- and late-season sowings can be made under cover to extend the harvesting period. Fill large containers, 12in (30cm) wide, with seed compost, firm gently, water well, and allow to drain. Mark out drills ½in (1cm) deep and 4in (10cm) apart using a trowel or short length of bamboo pole. Sow seeds ½in (1cm) apart along the base, cover over with more compost, and lightly water in. As the seedlings emerge, thin out to leave one strong plant every ¾in (2cm). Protect the young crop against slug damage with a light sprinkling of pellets.

3 Sowing outside

If sowing green onions outside, prepare the soil thoroughly by digging it over to remove weeds and any crop debris, firm it gently, and rake it level. Mark out drills ½in (1cm) deep and 4in (10cm) apart. Water the base of the drill well, and then sow seeds ½in (1cm) apart along its length. Cover them over with soil, and water in lightly.

A late summer or early fall sowing *of a winter hardy variety will produce crops in spring. Cover plants with fabric during harsh winter weather.*

Once seedlings are 3in (8cm) tall, *thin them out to leave one every ¾in (2cm). These thinnings can be used in salads in the same way as chives.*

Watering is crucial *both indoors and out, while green onion plants are young—drought can severely stunt the development of seedlings.*

Keep plants well weeded—*weeds will compete with the young plants for water and nutrients and may encourage disease.*

4 Under cover crops

Crops can be grown under cover in containers to give an early or late harvest. Water them well, and feed with a diluted general purpose liquid fertilizer as they mature. Keep the plants well-ventilated to deter fungal diseases, such botrytis (see p.244).

5 Routine care

Keep crops well-watered since dry conditions can cause plants to become bulbous. Green onions are very sensitive to weed competition, so hoe between the rows, and hand-weed regularly. In cold areas, protect winter crops using garden fabric or a cloche.

6 Harvesting

Harvest individual plants when their stems are pencil-thick, gently lifting them with a hand fork and refirming the soil so that other plants in the row can continue to grow. Green onions don't store well, so only lift them as and when they are needed.

| TIP | *Green onions prefer an open, sunny site—they do not do well in shade.* |

Green onions reach a harvestable size *after about eight weeks. Resow for a constant supply.*

STEP-BY-STEP Leeks

These mildly flavored onion relatives are an invaluable leafy alternative to brassicas during winter. Rather than producing bulbs, the long white stems or "shanks" of leeks are blanched by earthing up soil around them as they grow. Plant breeders are constantly improving leek disease resistance and length of harvest, so choose from these types where possible; some varieties can even be closely planted to give deliciously tender "baby" leeks.

	SPRING	SUMMER	FALL	WINTER
SOW				
HARVEST				

TIME TO HARVEST: 30–32 WEEKS

SUITABLE FOR: BEDS AND CONTAINERS

11–15 plants

9FT (3M) ROWS
Plant out 8–12in (20–30cm) apart

CONTAINERS
5 plants in each

1 Getting started

Leeks are one member of the onion family that don't seem to mind root disturbance, so you can sow in clusters with the view to lifting the young plants "bare-root," and then planting into the crop's final position. This allows you to plant the final growing space with another crop until transplanting is required.

'Musselburgh' *is a well-established variety that reliably gives short, flavorful stems.*

'King Richard' *is a good choice for "baby" leeks, producing long, sweet, early stems.*

'Toledo' *leeks are late to crop and renowned for their uniform shape and size and good flavor.*

'Swiss Giant Zermatt' *has a mild flavor and can be pulled as "baby" leeks or left to mature.*

Seed can be sown under cover *in midwinter as long as seeds are given enough heat—ensure they are kept at a minimum of 50°F (10°C).*

Biodegradable individual pots *allow you to transplant seedlings straight into their planting holes without risking damage to the roots.*

2 Sowing seeds

To sow under cover, fill a tall, 6in (15cm) diameter pot with seed compost, firm gently, and water well. Allow to drain, and then sow your seeds thinly on top. Cover with another ½in (1cm) layer of compost, water in lightly, and place in a propagator. Alternatively, sow seed in biodegradable individual trays rather than pots. Seed can also be sown direct once the soil is suitably warm and workable in spring. Prepare a seedbed, and then create a short drill ¾in (2cm) deep. Water the base well, and then sow your seeds thinly. Cover with a little more soil to level, firm gently, and water in lightly.

3 Transplanting

Once seedlings are 8–12in (20–30cm) tall and pencil-thick, they can be transplanted or planted out. Prepare the site, then create holes using a large dibber ¾–1¼in (2–3cm) wide, 6in (15cm) deep, and between 8–12in (20–30cm) apart. Lift your leeks gently, trim the roots to about 1in (2.5cm) long, and then drop one plant into each hole.

After about eight weeks, *carefully lift the seedlings from their seedbed, being careful not to break the delicate leaves.*

Use a clean pair of scissors *to trim the roots to 1in (2.5cm) before you transplant them; their roots will continue to develop.*

Drop the seedlings *into their deep holes, ready for watering. For "baby" leeks with thin stems, space plants 4in (10cm) apart.*

Water transplanted leeks *thoroughly, but don't refill the planting holes with soil. This forces the plants to produce long white, tender stems.*

Mound up soil *around the developing plants to block out the light, blanching the stems. This will also help to keep the plants stable.*

4 Watering

When the seedlings are stood in their holes, pour water around them, allowing it to drag some of the surrounding soil back around the plants. Planting them like this blanches the base of the stems. Keep plants well watered during the summer months.

5 Routine care

Crops can be vulnerable to leek moth and onion fly (see p.238), so deter these pests by covering plants with insect-proof mesh. Leek yield can suffer if weeds are allowed to develop, so keep plants well weeded. Earth up soil around the stems to blanch them.

6 Harvesting

Lift leeks using a fork. They will stand in the ground for a while, but if you need the space for other crops, "heel" the leeks in: dig another hole, and stand them in it, covering the roots with soil. In wintry weather, place leeks in a bucket of soil in a shed or garage.

> **TIP** *Prevent leek rust from disrupting your crops by choosing a resistant variety.*

Leeks do not store well, *so try to use them as soon as possible once they are out of the ground.*

STEP-BY-STEP Garlic

This is one of the most versatile vegetables in the kitchen and is incredibly easy to grow, even in containers. Plant out individual cloves in a sunny location between mid-fall and early spring when beds are often empty, and you can look forward to harvesting mature bulbs from early- to midsummer. Once lifted, these can either be used while fresh, when they have a deliciously sweet flavor, or dried to use throughout the lean winter months.

	SPRING	SUMMER	FALL	WINTER
SOW				
HARVEST				

TIME TO HARVEST: 20–36 WEEKS

SUITABLE FOR: BEDS AND CONTAINERS

0   3ft   6ft   9ft

18–22 plants

9FT (3M) ROWS
Plant 6–7in (15-18cm) apart

0   16in

CONTAINERS
4 plants in each

1 Getting started

There are two types of garlic: "hardneck," which develop flower spikes, and "softneck," which don't, and subsequently have a longer storage life. Whichever type you choose, plant the cloves in light, well-drained soil. If yours is heavy, dig in bulky, well-rotted organic matter, such as composted bark.

'Solent Wight' *is a softneck-type that produces large, white, very flavorful bulbs.*

'Early Wight' *is a hardneck-type with early-maturing, easy-peel, chunky cloves.*

'Elephant' *is not a true garlic, but the large cloves are flavorful and ideal for roasting.*

'Mediterranean' *bulbs grow very large and taste especially good when eaten fresh.*

Final bulb size *is directly related to initial clove size, so plant the largest, and dispose of any that are very small.*

Push the cloves *into the compost, leaving the tip showing above the surface. Firm around them, and water in well.*

Cloves will sprout *after seven to ten days. Once the roots fill the pot, plant them outside, spaced 6–7in (15–18cm) apart.*

2 Planting inside

If planting under cover, do so in early spring. Break the garlic bulb, or "head," into individual cloves, fill pots with compost, and plant one clove per pot. Water in well, and allow to drain. Place the pots somewhere warm and bright; 50ºF (10ºC) is sufficient—excess warmth will cause sappy growth that will be more prone to disease. If you have a cold frame or sheltered spot outside, plants can be grown here once their shoots reach 4in (10cm) tall.

TIP	*Plant the bulbs in fall to grow over the winter for a larger harvest.*

3 Planting outside

Garlic cloves can be planted directly in the ground, any time between fall or spring. Choose a sunny, sheltered spot, and dig it over to remove any weeds. Work in a high-nitrogen granular fertilizer, gently firm the soil, and rake it level. Plant the cloves with their tips facing up, deeper than those planted under cover in pots.

Space bulbs *6–7in (15–18cm) apart each way; gently push cloves into the ground so that ¾in (2cm) of soil is above their tips. Water in well.*

Weed competition *can affect yields, so keep plants well weeded with regular hoeing or hand-weeding between the plants.*

Garlic bulbs *can be harvested during summer— those planted in the previous fall will be ready to lift sooner than those planted in spring.*

4 Routine care

Keep young plants well watered while they develop a strong root system. Once established, garlic is quite drought-tolerant, and too much water can actually impair its storage qualities, so only irrigate if there are prolonged dry periods. Keep crops well weeded.

5 Harvesting

Lift as soon as the top third of the foliage has turned yellow and begun to die—leaving plants in the soil for too long can cause them to resprout, which shortens their storage life. Gently ease them out of the soil with a fork, being careful not to damage the bulbs.

Drying the bulbs

In order to store well, garlic bulbs must be thoroughly dry. Lay them out on racks in a sunny, dry spot for at least two weeks, until the skins become crisp. Then hang them up in a cool, dry, well-ventilated place, either individually or by plaiting the stems together. Garlic can be stored this way for up to ten months.

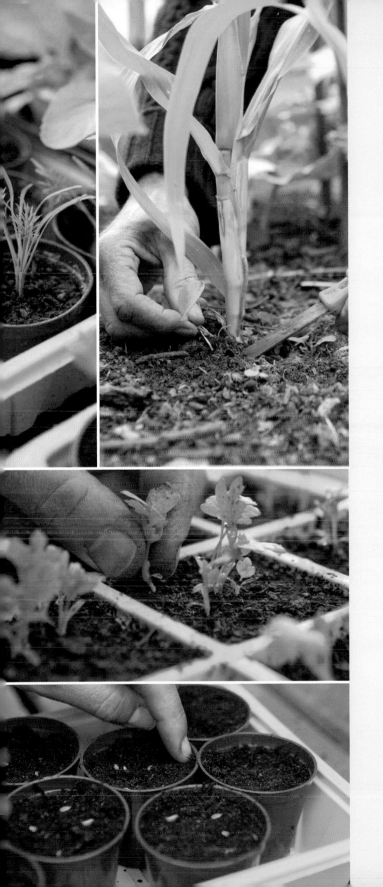

Other crops

Certain annual crops don't neatly fit into a group but have individual qualities and characteristics of their own. Some of the most unusual flavors can be found here—the aniseed tang of fennel, the fresh sugary taste of sweet corn, and the unmistakable taste and aroma of celery and celery root. Kohlrabi is always a conversation starter in the garden, looking and tasting like a turnip, held a few inches above the soil. Make room for these crops in your beds, and look forward to some extraordinary treats in the kitchen.

STEP-BY-STEP Sweet corn

Boiled and slathered in melted butter or grilled on a barbecue, sweet corn is a delicious treat in late summer and early fall. Pick and eat the sugary, tender cobs as soon as possible, since they are at their sweetest immediately after harvest. The flowers are pollinated by the wind, not insects, so grow them closely in blocks or groups. This is a productive crop, good for smaller plots, giving up to 32 tasty cobs from a block of plants, one yard (meter) square.

	SPRING		SUMMER		FALL		WINTER	
SOW								
HARVEST								

TIME TO HARVEST: 14–16 WEEKS

SUITABLE FOR: BEDS AND CONTAINERS

9FT (3M) ROWS
Plant in blocks, 12in (30cm) apart

11 plants

CONTAINERS
4 plants in each

Cardboard "growing tubes" *are ideal for sowing sweet corn. They are deep enough for the roots and can be planted out, tube-and-all.*

The seedlings will emerge *within a few weeks. They prefer rich, well-drained soil, so ensure that you dig in plenty of organic matter before planting out.*

1 Sowing under cover

Fill module trays or pots with seed compost, water well, and allow to drain. Sow one seed per cell or pot, ¾in (2cm) deep, water in lightly, and place in a heated propagator. Once the plants reach 4in (10cm) high, begin to harden them off. At the same time, prepare the ground by warming it with a cloche or cold frame. It is important to plant the seedlings out in a grid formation, 12x12in (30x30cm) apart.

TIP	*Keep different varieties separate or their flavor may be impaired.*

2 Sowing outside

If you don't have space to raise seed under cover, they can also be sown directly into their final location. The soil needs to be at least 50°F (10°C) before sowing, and you can encourage it to warm sooner by covering the area with cloches or cold frames. Water the soil well, and sow the seed in pairs into individual holes, ¾in (2cm) deep, spaced 12in (30cm) apart in a grid pattern. Keep the cloches in place until the seeds germinate in about two weeks.

Use cloches or cold frames *to warm the soil. Put them in place about two weeks before sowing.*

Sow two seeds *per hole for a greater chance of success, then thin to leave the stronger seedling.*

Always plant in blocks *so the wind can blow the pollen from flower to flower.*

3 Routine care

Sweet corn should be kept well-watered throughout summer, especially when the plants are in flower and the cobs are developing. It is possible to underplant sweet corn with low-growing crops like squash, but this will demand extra watering. Protect seedlings from slugs and snails, and weed young plants regularly until they establish.

Weeding is important in the initial stages, but as plants become established, they are increasingly able to compete against weeds.

Water at the base of plants so it soaks down to the roots. Plants are especially responsive to watering once the cobs start to fill in midsummer.

Earth up soil at the base of plants as they grow. This will help support the stems and prevent the roots being loosened by wind rock.

Using a fingernail, pierce a kernel to check the color of the sap. If it is milky, the cobs are ready to harvest, if not, give them a few days longer.

4 Providing support

These are tall plants reaching up to 6ft (2m) and may need support, especially in more exposed gardens. Earth up soil around the base of the stems, and insert stakes around the edge of the blocks, joining them with string to form a flexible frame.

5 Checking the cobs

In order to enjoy the cobs at their sweetest, it is important to see if they are ripe before harvesting. A good indication is when the tassels emerging from the cobs begin to turn brown. Gently peel back the outer leaves of the cobs to check the maturity of the kernels.

6 Harvesting

The cobs should be picked as soon as they are mature—they turn starchy and lose sweetness if left on the plant too long. Twist off the cobs when they are ready, and eat them as soon as possible since their sugar levels start falling almost immediately. Picked cobs keep best if the outer leaves are not removed and can be refrigerated for a few days until needed. Surplus cobs can be frozen if necessary.

Firmly twist the ripe cobs from the plants — you can expect each plant to produce two cobs.

Sweet corn

1 'Indian Summer' This heritage variety produces kernels that can be either yellow, white, or brown, which gives the cobs a multi-colored appearance. It grows best in warmer areas.

2 'Minipop' This variety is grown for its baby cobs, picked at finger-size. It is planted more closely than conventional varieties; the plants may bear more than one stem, giving a larger crop.

3 'Lark' Cropping from late summer onward, this variety bears tender, thin-skinned kernels that can be eaten cooked or raw. It is reliable and a good choice for cooler areas.

4 'Sundance' This variety produces large cobs, 8in (20cm) long, packed with sweet-tasting kernels. It is a reliable, early-maturing variety with shorter stems, suitable for cooler regions.

5 'Butterscotch' With shorter stems than many varieties, 'Butterscotch' is 5ft (1.5m) tall and suitable for more exposed sites. It matures early, bearing sweet cobs that freeze well.

6 'Lapwing' This variety gives a large crop of well-filled cobs in late summer and early fall. The bright yellow kernels are sweet-tasting and tender and are carried on large cobs.

7 'Mirai 003' Producing smallish cobs, 6in (15cm) long, filled with especially sweet and tender kernels that can be eaten cooked or raw, this variety crops well even on poorer soil.

8 'Swift' This is an early variety that produces large cobs filled with sweet-tasting, thin-skinned kernels. It is a reliable variety with sturdy stems and crops well in cooler regions.

9 'Northern Extra Sweet' This variety crops especially early, so it is ideal for areas with shorter summers. The plump kernels are sweet and tender and are packed on cobs 8in (20cm) long.

Other varieties
'Bodacious'
'Early Xtra Sweet'
'Extra Tender Sweet'
'Mirai Bicolor'
'Prelude'

STEP-BY-STEP Kohlrabi

This unusual-looking vegetable is a type of brassica and is closely related to the more familiar crops, cabbages and Brussels sprouts. Instead of its leaves however, it is grown for its mild-tasting "bulbs"—which are actually swollen stems—and it is growing increasingly popular with gardeners. It is very easy to grow, is quick-maturing, and can be grown alongside slower crops to make best use of limited space. It will also crop in containers.

	SPRING	SUMMER	FALL	WINTER
SOW				
HARVEST				

TIME TO HARVEST: 6–12 WEEKS

SUITABLE FOR: BEDS AND CONTAINERS

9FT (3M) ROWS
Plant 10in (25cm) apart
12 plants

CONTAINERS
3 plants in each

1 Getting started

Kohlrabi is raised from seed, which can be started off under cover in spring to give early crops a head start. Later crops can be sown directly where they will mature and will be ready to harvest in a few weeks. As a brassica kohlrabi is prone to club root disease, which can reduce yields (see p.242).

'Purple Danube' *bulbs are round with bright purple skins and crisp, white, tender flesh.*

'Quick Star' *produces pale green bulbs that are slow to bolt and are relatively small.*

'Superschmelz' *bulbs are very large and sweet-tasting and can reach up to 8in (20cm) across.*

'Kolibri' *produces purple-skinned bulbs with sweet, juicy flesh. Good for a late harvest.*

Sow seeds under cover *until around mid-spring, after which they can then be sown directly outside. Sow into modules or small pots.*

Kohlrabi can be prone to bolting *if exposed to sudden drops in temperature, so it's important to harden off plants gradually before transplanting.*

2 Sowing under cover

Early sowings can be made under cover, ready to transplant outside later. Fill trays with seed compost, firm, water well, and allow to drain. Then make a ½in (1cm) deep hole in each cell using a dibber or pencil, and place two seeds in each. Keep in a well-lit spot until emerged, then thin each cell to leave the stronger seedling. While hardening the seedlings off, warm the soil where they are to be planted with a plastic or fabric cloche.

TIP *Sow the seed successionally so that you don't end up with a lot all at once.*

3 Sowing outside

During the summer months, mark out drills ¾in (2cm) deep using the back of a hoe or rake, water the base well, and then sow a pinch of seed every 10in (25cm). Cover the seed over with soil, and lightly water in. Germination takes a week or two; once the seedlings emerge, protect them from slugs with a light sprinkling of pellets.

Being fairly robust, *kohlrabi can be sown direct from late winter. Purple-skinned varieties are said to be more cold-tolerant than green-skinned types.*

Once the seedlings emerge, *thin them out to leave the strongest per cluster, or "station," at a final spacing of 10in (25cm) between plants.*

Kohlrabi are brassicas *and suffer with the same pests, including cabbage white butterfly caterpillars (see p.238). Net as a precaution.*

Handweed next to your plants *to prevent damaging the stems. Do this on warm day so that weed seedlings quickly shrivel.*

4 Routine care

Although kohlrabi is a fairly drought-tolerant crop, keeping the soil constantly moist will produce the most tender roots: growth checks result in woodier harvests. You may need to cover the plants with fine mesh to deter pigeons and cabbage white butterflies.

5 Weeding

Keeping plants weed-free is beneficial for many reasons: it will discourage competition for moisture, as well as keeping your plot neat and discouraging the spread of disease, so pull out weeds next to the plants by hand, and hoe between the rows.

6 Harvesting

Although some crops will be ready to harvest in about six weeks, the swollen stems will generally take around 12 weeks to fully develop. Kohlrabi can be harvested when they are between golf-ball and tennis-ball size—this is when they are most tender. Cut the bulb off whole, just above the root. You can store kohlrabi at the end of the season. Simply trim off the leaves, and store in sand as for beets (see p.143).

Once the bulbs are large enough, *cut them off—their quality can deteriorate if they are left.*

STEP-BY-STEP Florence fennel

The fleshy stems of Florence fennel form a "bulb" with a mild aniseed taste, making this a unique flavor in the vegetable patch. In the kitchen, it can be used in a variety of dishes and is excellent for braising, stir-fries, and soups. The key to successfully growing Florence fennel is to keep it growing quickly: ideally, don't sow it until early summer and then water and feed it well. This ornamental vegetable flourishes in small spaces.

	SPRING	SUMMER	FALL	WINTER
SOW				
HARVEST				

TIME TO HARVEST: 12–20 WEEKS

SUITABLE FOR: BEDS AND CONTAINERS

11 plants

9FT (3M) ROWS
Plant 8in (20cm) apart

CONTAINERS
3 plants in each

1 Getting started

Don't be tempted to sow too early in the year, or the plants may bolt: late spring should be the earliest. Florence fennel can be grown in containers of multipurpose compost, but these must be large enough to provide constant moisture, so opt for a minimum diameter of 16in (40cm) for three plants.

'Zefa Fino' *produces large rounded bulbs that are slightly flattened. They have good flavor.*

'Perfection' *bears large bulbs with an excellent flavor and good bolt-resistance.*

'Finale' *bulbs are large and flattened in shape, with good bolt-resistance and excellent flavor.*

'Sirio' *produces large, rounded, slightly flattened white bulbs with an aromatic scent.*

Florence fennel seed should be sown *under cover from late spring onward. Ensure that you keep the soil moist at all times.*

To discourage a glut, *sow Florence fennel seed little and often. Sow seed into a small number of pots every two weeks to encourage a steady supply.*

2 Sowing under cover

Sow this early crop under cover, into modules or small pots of moist seed compost. Seed can be unreliable, so sow three seeds per module or pot, ½in (1cm) deep, and then thin to leave the strongest as the seedlings emerge. As soon as your module- or pot-raised plants begin filling their container with roots, start to harden them off gradually. Place them outdoors during the day, and bring them back in at night for seven to ten days.

TIP	*Choose a bolt-resistant variety; the plants are prone to premature flowering.*

3 Sowing outside

Seed can be sown directly later in the summer. Prepare the soil by digging it over to remove any weeds, firm it gently, and rake it level. Create drills 1in (2.5cm) deep, 12in (30cm) apart, and water thoroughly. Sow seed in clusters of three or four, cover with soil, firm gently, and water in lightly. Thin to leave the strongest seedling per cluster.

Sow clusters of seeds *every 12in (30cm). Cover the soil with newspaper to keep it from drying out: check daily and remove once seedlings appear*

Transplant indoor-sown seedlings *12x12in (30x30cm) apart in midsummer. Enrich the soil well before planting, and water plants in well.*

Plants need constant moisture *to develop good-sized "bulbs." In warm, moist conditions the plants can develop extremely rapidly.*

Earth up around the bulbs *to block out sunlight and create whitened, tender crops. The mulch will also help to retain moisture.*

4 Routine care

Keep the plants well watered at all stages of growth. A diluted general-purpose liquid feed can be applied to containers or if your soil is light. Keep plants well weeded because they grow upright and can't easily smother out weed growth.

5 Blanching stems

If you want the plants to develop to full size, water them regularly, and then, when the bulbs are about 3in (8cm) in diameter, earth them up, gently pulling soil up around the bases. This blanches the stems slightly and will give them a sweeter flavor.

6 Harvesting

You can harvest Florence fennel at all stages of growth—from "baby" bulbs that have a diameter of roughly 2in (5cm) and can be ready in as little as six weeks, to full-sized mature plants with bulbs approximately 6in (15cm) across, which will have been growing for between three and four months. The leaves can be cut in moderation at any time, or simply pull up the plants whole as they are needed.

Lift plants whole, *or cut them off at the base with a knife the cut stump will then resprout.*

STEP-BY-STEP Celery

While old fashioned "trenching" celery is challenging to grow, the introduction of self-blanching varieties has made this crop more manageable for gardeners. The blanched, tender stems are a key addition to summer salads, while the plants are also surprisingly hardy and will stand well into the fall. Celery needs to be planted closely to exclude the light and blanch the stems, which makes this a highly productive crop for small spaces.

	SPRING	SUMMER	FALL	WINTER
SOW				
HARVEST				

TIME TO HARVEST: 18 WEEKS

SUITABLE FOR: BEDS

0   3ft   6ft   9ft

15 plants

9FT (3M) ROWS
Plant in a block, spacing them 8in (20cm) apart

1 Getting started

Celery requires a long growing season, so seed is best started off under cover in early to mid-spring. If you don't have a suitable growing environment, you can purchase plug plants later in the spring. Celery needs rich, well-drained soil but isn't suitable for containers since it would need watering too frequently.

'Tango' *is an excellent self-blanching variety. Its tasty, long white stems resist bolting.*

'Celebrity' *stems are self-blanching with a good flavor and succulent texture.*

'Green Utah' *is a self-blanching type that produces tall, green, slightly variable stems.*

'Victoria' *produces fleshy, mid-green stems that are vigorous, tall, and self-blanching.*

To encourage germination, *seed should be kept moist and placed in a heated propagator for a couple of weeks, until they germinate.*

Celery seedlings *sown in early to mid-spring should be ready to transplant between late spring and early summer, once they are strong enough.*

2 Sowing under cover

Fill seed trays with seed compost, water well, and allow to drain. Sow the seeds thinly over the surface, but don't cover them with compost because they require light to germinate. Germination can be slow, so place the trays in a heated propagator set at 59°F (15°C). As soon as seedlings emerge and are large enough to handle, prick them out into individual module trays—don't let them get too big before this, or they are more likely to bolt. Water the plants in well, and continue to grow in a warm location under cover. A growth check caused by cold weather can also induce bolting.

3 Planting out

When plants are about 6in (15cm) tall, harden them off for the move outside. Celery requires moist soil, so prepare the site before planting by digging in plenty of well-rotted organic matter such as manure or garden compost to improve moisture retention. Just prior to planting, work in a granular general-purpose fertilizer.

Place plants outdoors *during the day, and bring them back under cover at night for two weeks. As you begin to do so, prepare the soil for planting.*

Plant out in blocks, *8in (20cm) apart in each direction. This dense planting will encourage the celery to blanch. Water the plants in well.*

Keep the plants well weeded. *Remove any weeds that grow in and around the blocks of plants by hand to avoid damaging the stems.*

Applying an organic mulch, *2–2½in (5–6cm) deep around your plants can help to lock in soil moisture. It will also help keep down weeds.*

4 Routine care

Keep plants well watered during the growing season—plants bulk up during some of the hottest and driest months of the year, and a lack of water can result in stringy, overly pungent stems. Keep slugs from attacking your plants with a thin scattering of pellets.

5 Blanching stems

If densely planted, the stems partially shade each other from the sunlight, causing them to become blanched. Plants on the outside of the bed are less shaded and will develop green stems; blanch these plants by wrapping their stems with cardboard.

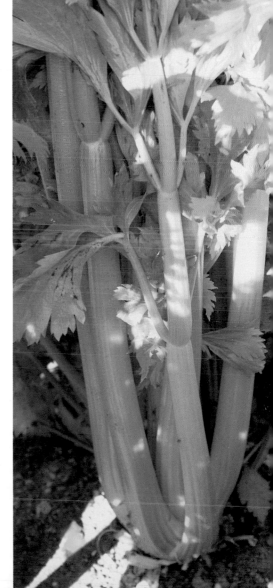

6 Harvesting

You can begin harvesting celery in late summer, as soon as it is large enough. Water the plant well, and then dig it up whole—stems can be broken off as needed. Cover plants with fabric or a sheet as the nights become cooler, but harvest before frosty weather.

| TIP | *Wash celery well before use. Soil can accumulate between the stems.* |

Harvest plants whole *with roots intact. They last better this way, cut stems soon brown.*

STEP-BY-STEP Celery root

This unusual root vegetable has enjoyed something of a renaissance in recent years and has now graduated to almost gourmet status. What it lacks in looks, celery root more than makes up for in flavor—a nutty, celerylike taste that is pleasantly mild. Roots can be grated raw, boiled, and mashed; sliced and braised in milk and butter; or added to soups and casseroles. The long storage life of this crop makes it a great winter staple.

	SPRING	SUMMER	FALL	WINTER
SOW				
HARVEST				

TIME TO HARVEST: 30 WEEKS

SUITABLE FOR: BEDS AND CONTAINERS

11 plants

9FT (3M) ROWS
Plant 12in (30cm) apart

CONTAINERS
3 plants in each

1 Getting started

Like other stem vegetables celery root prefers an open site and rich, well-drained soil, so dig in well-rotted organic matter in the season before planting. Celery root is prone to bolting, so choose resistant varieties, plant out strong seedlings after cold weather has passed in late spring, and keep plants well watered.

'Monarch' *bears strong yields of high quality white roots with good flavor that store well.*

'Diamant' *shows good resistance to bolting. Its medium-sized roots have excellent flavor.*

'Prinz' *is an exceptional variety, known for its flavor, bolt-resistance, and storage qualities.*

'Mars' *bears large, high-growing roots that have dense, flavorful flesh and keep well.*

Plants need a long season *to mature fully, so sow seed under cover in early to mid-spring for fall–winter crops.*

After sowing, *place the seed trays in a propagator, and ensure that they have a minimum temperature of 50°F (10°C).*

Celery root *can be slow to appear, but once the seedlings are large enough, thin to leave the stronger one per module.*

2 Sowing seeds

For large roots it is best to sow celery root seed under cover to extend the growing season. Fill trays with seed compost, firm gently, water well, and allow to drain. Make a hole in each cell ½in (1cm) deep, and sow two seeds into it. Cover with compost, and water lightly, then place in a propagator. Keep the compost moist to ensure germination. Grow on under cover and, once the seedlings' roots fill their modules, begin to harden them off.

TIP *Plant out in late spring so plants can establish before the warmth of summer.*

3 Planting out

Celery root can be planted out into large containers of multi-purpose compost, but the easier option is to grow the plants in the ground. Dig the soil to remove any weeds, and add some well-rotted organic matter, such as garden compost, well before planting. Firm gently, and plant seedlings 12x12in (30x30cm) apart. Water them in well.

Harden off the seedlings *by placing them outside during the day and under cover at night for a week to ten days.*

The swollen stems *will need plenty of space to develop, so ensure that seedlings are planted at least 12in (30cm) apart.*

Keep the plants *well watered. Celery root is native to boggy areas, so these conditions need to be replicated in the garden.*

Plants can be mulched *with a 2¼–3in (6–7cm) layer of compost, but do not let this come into contact with the exposed crown.*

Plants will form *small offshoots that compete with the main crown and impede its growth. Carefully remove these as you spot them.*

4 Feeding

To obtain good-sized roots, it is important to keep celery root evenly watered at all stages of growth. Its food requirements are fairly low, so there is no need to apply heavy doses of fertilizer. A half-strength general-purpose liquid feed every two weeks is sufficient.

5 Routine care

As plants develop, remove the outer leaves gradually so that the crown is exposed. Celery root is relatively free from pests or diseases, but celery leaf miner may be a problem—it causes dry, blotchy patches on leaves. Pick off affected leaves, and dispose of them.

6 Harvesting

Celery root roots can be lifted from fall onward. It is best to lift the roots as and when you need them, because they will keep better in the ground than if lifted and stored. Gently insert a fork under individual plants when harvesting, and tease the root carefully out of the soil. During the winter months, cover the crowns with a mulch of straw to protect them from the worst of the weather.

Be careful *not to damage the root when prying it out—insert the fork 4–6in (10–15cm) away.*

Perennial crops

For a long-term investment in the garden, dedicate some space to perennial vegetables. This group reliably emerges each spring, bears a crop, then dies back in the fall, year after year. Given an open, well-prepared site, asparagus crowns can crop for up to two decades, and the resulting spears are the ultimate in vegetable decadence. Globe artichoke hearts also deserve gourmet status and have architectural foliage that will match any garden ornamental. Add deliciously creamy Jerusalem artichokes and vibrant pink rhubarb to the group, and you have a luxurious collection of crops.

STEP-BY-STEP Asparagus

Asparagus is a luxury crop among vegetables, being available for just ten weeks of the year in a brief and uniquely delicious harvest from spring to early summer. It is easy to grow in most gardens, but it takes time to establish. Be patient however, and you'll be rewarded for the next 20 years with an annual supply of succulent shoots, or "spears," fresher than any you can buy. Asparagus is a great long-term investment, but not ideal for small plots.

	SPRING	SUMMER	FALL	WINTER
PLANT				
HARVEST				

PLANTING TO HARVEST: 2–3 YEARS

SUITABLE FOR: BEDS

0   3ft   6ft   9ft

7–8 plants

9FT (3M) ROWS
Plant out 16in (40cm) apart

1 Getting started

Asparagus can be raised from seed in spring if you want a lot of plants and are happy to wait for them to grow large enough to crop. The quicker option is to buy young plants, either bare-root to plant out in fall or spring, or pot-grown specimens that you can plant at any time if you keep them well watered.

'Gijnlim' *is an early-cropping variety that gives a reliable harvest of thick green spears.*

'Connover's Colossal' *is a traditional variety, grown for its high yield and good flavor.*

'Jersey Knight' *gives a good crop of thick, flavorful stems. It is a modern variety.*

'Purple Pacific' *bears attractive purple-flushed spears that are sweeter than many green types.*

Asparagus plants *grow in the same location for up to 20 years, so prepare the soil well before planting, and remove all perennial weeds.*

Mounding the soil *at the base of the planting holes helps ensure good drainage. This isn't needed if your soil is light and sandy; the holes can be flat.*

2 Planting out

Bare-root asparagus plants are known as "crowns" and should be planted as soon they are available in spring. Before planting, prepare a hole or trench 12in (30cm) wide, 4in (10cm) deep, and mound up the base so it slightly lower than the soil surface. Spread the "crowns" out on top of the mound so that the central growing point is at soil level, with the roots below. Fill the hole with soil, firm it in gently, and water the plants in well.

TIP *Avoid berry-bearing female plants, which give a smaller crop than males.*

3 Growing on

Mulch new plants with well-rotted organic matter such as garden compost after planting, and apply some granular general purpose fertilizer. Keep plants well-watered and weeded during their first year. The plants take time to establish and should not be harvested during their first year, then only lightly in their second.

Ferny asparagus growth *makes an attractive backdrop in the garden. If space is limited, plant it at the back of your ornamental borders.*

Mulching plants *with organic matter helps retain moisture and suppresses weeds. The mulch also releases nutrients to your plants.*

Check plants every few days *to cut the young spears at their best. These grow very quickly and soon become tough and inedible.*

4 Routine care

Established plants are drought-tolerant and only need watering in very dry spells. Mulch plants in fall with organic matter, and apply granular general purpose fertilizer in spring and again after harvesting. The tall foliage may need support on windy sites.

5 Harvesting

Once fully established—after 3 years—plants can be harvested each spring for about ten weeks. Cut all spears, thick and thin. This encourages more to develop. Slice them off just below soil level using a sharp knife, once they are roughly 8in (20cm) tall.

Overwintering plants

After harvesting the shoots for ten weeks, stop cutting, and allow the plants to develop their "fern"—their tall, feathery top growth. Allow them to grow all summer, giving the plants time to bulk up and recover. The "fern" will turn yellow and die back in the fall, at which point it should be cut off at the base.

STEP-BY-STEP Globe artichokes

As attractive as they are tasty, these eye-catching perennial plants produce a mass of architectural foliage before bearing tasty, thistlelike flowerheads. This makes them just as beautiful in the flower garden as the vegetable patch. Quality not quantity is the name of the game, since each plant only bears a few heads. However, the artichoke "scales" are absolutely delicious braised and then individually dipped into hollandaise sauce.

	SPRING	SUMMER	FALL	WINTER
PLANT				
HARVEST				

PLANTING TO HARVEST: 64–68 WEEKS

SUITABLE FOR: BEDS

0	3ft	6ft	9ft

2 plants

9FT (3M) ROWS
Plant 5ft (1.5m) apart

1 Getting started

Globe artichoke plants can be grown from seeds or "offsets" of existing plants (see step 3), but the simplest method is to buy pot-raised seedlings from garden centers or nurseries. You may find that this limits your selection since the varieties available may be few, so don't rule out the other two methods.

'Gros Vert de Laon' *is best propagated from offsets to give flavorful, attractive round heads.*

'Green Globe Improved' *is a reliable, vigorous plant that bears firm, tasty heads.*

'Purple Globe' *produces small heads that are tasty although variable in quality.*

'Concerto' *bears attractive, spineless purple heads that have an excellent flavor.*

For larger quantities of plants, *sow into seed trays. Ensure that the seeds are sown at a depth of ¾in (2cm) and ¾in (2cm) apart.*

Once the seedlings *have their first true leaves, they can be pricked out and repotted. Plant each seedling in its own pot so that it has sufficient space.*

2 Sowing seeds

Raising globe artichokes from seed in early to mid-spring will provide plants that will crop in their second year—remove any heads that develop this first growing season. Fill a 3½in (9cm) diameter pot with seed compost, water it well, and allow it to drain. Make holes ¾in (2cm) apart and ¾in (2cm) deep using a pencil or dibber, and then drop a seed into each. Cover over with more compost, water lightly, and place in a heated propagator.

TIP *Dig in plenty of well-rotted manure, and apply fertilizer before planting.*

3 Planting out

Harden off seed-raised plants in late spring. Offsets can be propagated at this time, too: gently lift an established plant, cut off a section that is complete with roots and leaves using a sharp knife, and transplant it immediately to its new location. Plant both offsets and seed-raised plants with a spacing of about 5ft (1.5m).

Harden off globe artichoke plants *by placing them outside for seven to ten days, but bringing them back under cover overnight.*

Blackfly may be a problem *and will swarm flower buds and stems. Wash them off by hand, or apply an appropriate insecticide.*

Harvest globe artichokes whole *while they are still young and tight. You may get a secondary crop after the main head has been cut.*

4 Routine care

Keep plants well watered until established so that they develop a strong root system. Ultimately, plants become extremely drought-tolerant and won't require additional irrigation, but these first two months are an exception. Remove any weeds that appear.

5 Harvesting

The largest bud will be at the tip of the spike; smaller ones often develop later on any sideshoots. Harvest each artichoke once it is a good size, but before the scales begin to open and the purple flowers appear. Cut with a knife or shears—the stalks are tough.

Overwintering plants

Once all the buds have been harvested, cut the stems back to ground level. The plants are hardy, but severe winters can kill them, especially if the soil is wet. Apply a thick mulch of bark or straw to protect them: cut back the leaves, and lay the mulch on top. The mulch can be dug into the soil in spring.

STEP-BY-STEP Jerusalem artichokes

Towering above other vegetables in the garden, this perennial relative of the summer sunflower bears attractive, bright yellow flowers. They are grown for their delicious knobbly tubers, which are harvested in the fall and are usually expensive to buy. Jerusalem artichokes are very easy to grow and can form a sizable clump in a season—they are best confined, or they may become invasive. Unsuitable for containers, they are best grown on larger plots.

	SPRING	SUMMER	FALL	WINTER
SOW				
HARVEST				

TIME TO HARVEST: 30–36 WEEKS

SUITABLE FOR: BEDS

0   3ft   6ft   9ft

11 plants

9FT (3M) ROWS
Plant 12in (30cm) apart in a grid pattern

1 Planting tubers

Jerusalem artichokes are planted as bare tubers, which can either be bought from seed suppliers—or from the supermarket if you don't want a named variety. Before planting in early spring, prepare the site by digging it over to remove weeds. Plant each tuber 6in (15cm) deep, and space them 12in (30cm) apart each way. Large tubers can be cut into two or three pieces, each with a distinct growing bud. Cover with soil, and water the tubers in.

Plant the tubers into individual holes *with the growing point, which is usually swollen and slightly pointed, facing upward.*

Tubers can be started off in pots *if your soil is too wet to work in early spring. Keep them outside, and plant out as soon as conditions allow.*

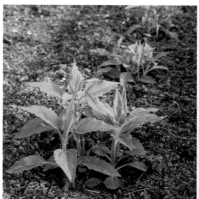

The new shoots grow quickly in spring, *but protect them from slug damage with a sprinkling of pellets. Mature growth is less vulnerable.*

Developing plants form dense clumps *and may compete with each other for moisture. Water regularly until they reach full height—10ft (3m).*

2 Routine care

Shoots will appear after a few weeks. Once these are 8–12in (20–30cm) high, earth up soil around the plant to help support the stems. Keep plants well watered, especially during dry periods, otherwise tubers will become extremely knobby and small. On lighter soils, apply a thick mulch to help retain moisture. Weed young plants until growing strongly—they will then out-compete most neighboring plants.

TIP *If your garden is exposed, use this crop as a productive summer windbreak.*

3 Providing support

Jerusalem artichoke stems are sturdy but may need supporting as they reach full height. Insert tall stakes around the edge of the clump or bed, about 6ft (1.8m) high, and tie string around them to form a flexible frame. This will also help keep plants tidy. Cut back any stems that are damaged by the wind using clippers.

Larger clumps may withstand the wind, *but it's worth providing support as a precaution. Damaged plants will still crop, but less freely.*

The flowers are attractive *and if your plants are in a prominent position, compromise your harvest a little by leaving a few to open.*

Once they have been cut back, *the stems will act as a marker, showing you where to dig for tubers during the winter months.*

4 Removing flowers

In late summer, cut back the tall stems to 5ft (1.5m) high to prevent them from rocking in the wind and loosening the tubers. At the same time, maximize the yield by removing all the flowers, which otherwise divert energy away from the developing tubers.

5 Cutting back

As the leaves begin to turn yellow in the fall, the plants start to take nutrients down the stems to store in the tubers, indicating that they are nearly ready to harvest. Once the leaves begin to yellow or fall, cut the stems to below 12in (30cm) in height.

6 Harvesting

Jerusalem artichoke tubers should be lifted as required. Since they have relatively thin skins and will not store very well, they are best left in the ground and then dug up as needed. Any tubers left in the ground will regrow the following year, so if you plan on growing another crop in that location, thoroughly dig over the site to make sure you remove them all at the end of the winter.

Use the tubers fresh *during winter—they are cold-hardy and their flavor improves after frost.*

STEP-BY-STEP Rhubarb

Although often thought of as a fruit because it is used in desserts, this crop is actually a vegetable and is incredibly easy to grow. The enormous leaves have their own architectural merit in the ornamental garden, but the pink-flushed stems are really what rhubarb is about. Best harvested young and tender, these can be made into jams, pies, chutneys, and, of course, cobblers. Mixed with sugar and perhaps a little ginger root, the taste is just sublime.

	SPRING		SUMMER		FALL	WINTER
PLANT						
HARVEST						

PLANTING TO HARVEST: 16–25 MONTHS

SUITABLE FOR: BEDS

```
0              3ft          6ft          9ft
```
3 plants

9FT (3M) ROWS
Plant at least 3ft (1m) apart

1 Getting started

Rhubarb is best bought as a young plant—it can be raised from seed, but plants grow very large, and few people want more than one. Plants are available bare-root to plant between fall and spring. Pot-grown plants can be planted at any time, providing they are kept well-watered afterward.

'Champagne' *produces long, red-tinged stems that have a sweet, sharp flavor, ideal for cooking.*

'Timperley Early' *is an early variety that is good for forcing. It has thick, juicy red stems.*

'Victoria' *gives a later, sweet-tasting harvest and is a good choice to grow in cooler regions.*

'Cawood Delight' *gives a smaller crop of richly-flavored and colored stems.*

Plant pot-grown plants *at the same depth as they were in their pots; bare-root plants should be planted with the crown level with the soil.*

Bare-root plants *are particularly susceptible to drying out during dry spells, even in fall and spring. Keep moist, and mulch as a precaution.*

2 Planting

Before planting, prepare the site thoroughly by digging in plenty of well-rotted organic matter, such as garden compost or manure, especially if your soil is light. Rhubarb is a long-lived crop, so also be careful to remove any perennial weeds (see p.236). Dig a hole large enough for the roots, then plant, firm in gently, and water well. Plants should be kept well-watered and weeded during their first year until fully established.

TIP	*Rhubarb will tolerate light shade, so make use of these areas.*

3 Routine care

Mulch plants in spring with well-rotted organic matter, but avoid piling it around the crown since this can encourage decay. Older, congested plants can be divided in fall to promote healthy new growth. Lift the plant with as much root as possible, split it into sections with a spade, and replant only one or two vigorous outer shoots.

Mulching around plants with straw *helps to retain moisture and keeps the stems clean by preventing soil from splashing up onto them.*

Forced stems are blanched *in the darkness within the forcer. Only force the earliest stems, and allow later ones to develop normally.*

Harvest the stems while young *but always wear gloves—the leaves are poisonous. Discard the leaves, and only use the stems for cooking.*

4 Forcing stems

Rhubarb can be "forced" to give an earlier harvest by placing a "forcing pot" or an upturned bucket over the plant before it emerges. The new stems then grow up into the dark forcer, making them sweet and tender. Remove the forcer after two weeks of harvesting.

5 Harvesting

New plants can be harvested after their first year. Harvest by sliding your index finger or thumb down the curved center of a stem until you reach the base, then gently twist to remove. Harvest until midsummer, when stems become tough and stringy.

Growing on

The plants need time to recover after cropping, so leave them to grow from midsummer onward. Cut out any stems that develop flowers, and remove any yellowing leaves as they occur. In fall, cut the plant to the base, and mulch well with organic matter. Although poisonous to eat, the spent growth is safe to compost.

Culinary herbs

Growing fresh herbs can be very
productive, even in smaller plots,
giving a steady supply of leaves and
stems that will add flavor to your
homegrown fruits and vegetables.
Grow as wide a selection as you
have space for, whether in beds,
baskets, or containers, and
experiment with different flavor
combinations. Mint is a classic
partner for new potatoes and peas,
but try it with broad beans or
strawberries, and you'll be hooked.
Annual and perennial herbs put on
a show with their abundant summer
foliage, but also grow evergreen
plants, such as bay and rosemary,
that will ensure a continuous supply
right through the winter.

STEP-BY-STEP Annual herbs

Growing annual herbs from seed is easy and rewarding and will provide you with exciting new flavors to use in the kitchen. You can obtain a good crop from even a tiny space since they don't require a dedicated bed and can be planted next to your other crops or in mixed beds or containers. Crops such as basil, dill, cilantro, and parsley—which is grown as an annual—are ideal for pots, where the free-draining environment suits them perfectly.

	SPRING	SUMMER	FALL	WINTER
SOW				
HARVEST				

TIME TO HARVEST: 10–14 WEEKS

SUITABLE FOR: BEDS, CONTAINERS, AND GROWING BAGS—UNDER COVER OR OUTSIDE

15–30 plants

9FT (3M) ROWS
Plant 4–8in (10–20cm) apart

CONTAINERS
5–7 plants in each

1 Getting started

Annual herbs generally prefer rich, well-drained soil, so if you are growing them directly in the ground, dig in some well-rotted organic matter and horticultural grit before planting. Give containers and window boxes a warm, sunny spot—place them close to the kitchen for easy access during cooking.

Basil is excellent with tomatoès or in pesto. It is commonly green, but red types are available.

Parsley has both flat- and curly-leaf forms. It is useful in cooking and as a garnish.

Dill produces feathery leaves with a delicious mild aniseed flavor. It makes a useful garnish.

Cilantro leaves and seeds have a distinctive flavor and are used in a variety of cuisines.

Sow seed under cover from early spring, but check individual seed packets since the timing varies for different varieties.

Once the seedlings emerge, prick them out to 2in (5cm) apart, so that they have more space to grow.

Once seedlings are 6in (15cm) tall, harden them off. Transplant directly, or plant in containers, a window box, or hanging basket.

2 Sowing under cover

Fill pots or trays with compost, water well, and allow to drain. Sow your herb seeds thinly on top, cover with a ¼in (0.5cm) layer of compost, water lightly, and place in a propagator. Once seedlings are large enough to handle, thin them, or prick out. If you have sown in pots, ease the compost out, and gently split it into clumps, each containing three or four seedlings. Plant each clump in a larger pot of compost, water in well, and grow on under cover.

TIP	Pinch off the growing tips regularly to delay leafy herbs from flowering.

3 Sowing outside

Alternatively, your herbs can be sown directly into garden soil. Choose a well-drained, sunny spot, and dig this over lightly to remove any weeds. Firm gently, and rake level, then create drills ½in (1cm) deep, water these well, and then sow seeds thinly along the base. Cover with more soil, firm gently, then lightly water in.

Herb seed can be sown *directly in the ground from spring onward, but check the seed packets because the timing varies between different herbs.*

Once the young herb seedlings appear, *carefully thin them out to 4–8in (10–20cm) apart, depending on the variety you have sown.*

Keeping your herbs well watered *will encourage rapid, tender growth, which is ideal for eating raw or cooked, and will delay flowering.*

Keep plants well weeded *to reduce competition for nutrients, light, and water. Pull out weeds by hand when young.*

4 Watering

Keep the herbs well watered—pay particular attention to those planted in containers. These will dry out more quickly than those planted in the ground. Annual herbs generally don't need any extra feeding, but if leaves begin to look yellow, give them an dose of diluted liquid fertilizer.

5 Routine care

Keep the plants well weeded. Basil will initially create a single stem but will then naturally branch out to become bushy—speed up this process by pinching off the growing tip. Parsley, cilantro, and dill naturally form a rosette of leaves. Protect plants against slugs with a light scattering of pellets.

6 Harvesting

Leaves can be harvested as soon as they are large enough, although it's important not to over-crop the plants or this will impede their growth—take just a few leaves from each plant at any one time. Herbs such as basil and cilantro are particularly fast-growing, so you may want to make two or three sowings throughout the spring and summer to ensure a fresh succession of tender leaves.

Treat plants as cut-and-come-again crops, *snipping the leaves for use as they are required.*

STEP-BY-STEP Perennial herbs

Perennial herbs range from low creeping plants to large shrubs and can either be planted around the garden or given their own dedicated bed. Most also grow well in containers, allowing you to keep them within easy reach of the kitchen for handy picking. Rosemary, sage, and thyme are all valuable ingredients, and as they can be used either fresh or dried, you can enjoy them all year long. Grow plenty to ensure a constant supply.

	SPRING	SUMMER	FALL	WINTER
PLANT				
HARVEST				

TIME TO HARVEST: 12–16 WEEKS

SUITABLE FOR: BEDS AND CONTAINERS

0   3ft   6ft   9ft

11 plants

9FT (3M) ROWS
Plant out 12in (30cm) apart

0   16in

CONTAINERS
3–8 plants in each

1 Raising new plants

Perennial herbs are widely sold, but if you want several plants, they are easy to propagate yourself. For plenty of new plants, sow seeds into pots or trays, following the instructions given on the packet (once established, fennel and chives will seed themselves freely). Many creeping herbs can be propagated easily since the spreading stems often have roots; these can be cut off, potted, and grown as new plants. Established clumps of herbs, such as mint, can also be lifted and split in the spring or fall.

Sowing plants from seed *is ideal if you want lots of the same herb—maybe for an herb lawn.*

Rooted stems *provide a quick and easy way to propagate your own herbs. Just pot them up.*

New herb plants *may be large enough to divide when you buy them. Split them into clumps.*

Herb planters *are ideal for growing a mixture of plants. Plant the side pockets first.*

Choose a mixture of plants *that creep or grow upright to make best use of the space.*

Fill with compost *to within 2in (5cm) of the rim of the pot to make watering easier.*

2 Planting a container

Most perennial herbs grow well in containers, and smaller plants can be planted together in the same pot. Many originate from the Mediterranean region and require good drainage, so plant them using a 50:50 mix of sharp grit and soil-based compost. Give them a sunny location, and keep plants well watered. Feed only occasionally to avoid encouraging soft, flavorless growth.

> **TIP** *Some perennial herbs can be short-lived, especially in cool, wet regions.*

3 Planting in beds

Most herbs prefer well-drained soil, so dig in some horticultural grit if yours is heavy, and choose a sunny site. These herbs rarely require additional feeding, so don't improve the soil with compost or fertilizer, which encourages weak growth. Mint is a spreading herb and can be invasive, so it is best planted into a large container sunk into the soil.

Dig planting holes *deep enough so that new plants are at the same depth as in their pots.*

Tease the roots out *away from the root ball to encourage them to grow into the surrounding soil.*

Water plants well *until they establish fully. Pinch off the tips to encourage bushy new shoots.*

Water young plants well—*once established many herbs, such as sage, rosemary, and marjoram, are relatively drought-tolerant.*

Harvest leaves and shoots *using scissors or a sharp knife. Harvest plants regularly to encourage a constant fresh crop of new growth.*

4 Routine care

Most herbs need little care once established. Stake taller plants as they grow, and weed low-growing herbs so they don't become smothered. Cut back mint and marjoram in summer to encourage tasty new growth, and remove any flowers that appear, which encourage plants to become tough.

5 Harvesting

Once well established, perennial herbs can be harvested as and when required. Pinching off the growing points of mint, thyme, sage, rosemary, and marjoram will not only provide you with the most tender foliage, it will also encourage plants to bush out. Individual chive leaves can be cut when needed.

Drying herbs

Perennial herbs are ideal for drying to use throughout winter. In summer, cut and bunch the stems, and hang them up somewhere warm, dry, and well-ventilated. Shorter stems, such as thyme or marjoram, can be laid out on wire racks. Dry the growth over 24–48 hours, and store it away from the light in sealed containers.

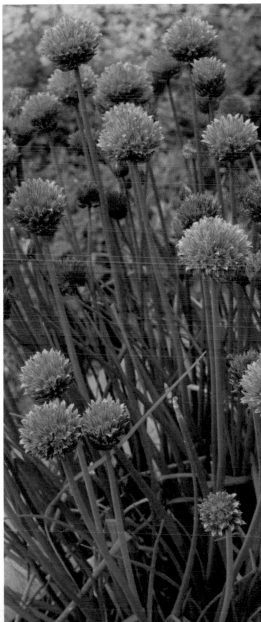

Perennial herbs

1 Parsley The leaves of this popular and useful herb are excellent used in a variety of dishes; curly types (shown) have a milder flavor than flat-leaf types. This is a biennial herb that flowers and dies after two years. Sow seed each spring to ensure a constant supply.

2 Fennel Not to be confused with Florence fennel (see pp.172–173), almost every part of this herb has a culinary use. It is also highly decorative and does not look out of place in ornamental borders if you don't have space for a herb bed.

3 Chives If you do not have a lot of space, this attractive herb makes an excellent container plant. A member of the onion family, chives have a mild onionlike flavor. The flowers and stems can be used in a range of dishes.

4 Rosemary Both highly ornamental and extremely versatile, this is a must-have shrubby herb for any garden. The aromatic leaves are excellent for use in stews, particularly with lamb. It needs a sunny site and well-drained soil to grow well but can be short-lived.

5 Thyme There are upright and creeping types of this staple herb, but the former are easier to harvest for culinary use. The flavorful leaves are excellent for use in a variety of dishes and should be harvested as required. It is a good choice for pots.

6 Sage There are several varieties of this shrubby herb, including purple-leaf and variegated types. It has many uses in the kitchen and is easy to grow when given a sunny spot and well-drained soil. It can be short-lived in cooler areas.

7 Marjoram Closely related to oregano, this versatile, creeping herb can be used in a variety of dishes; the leaves have a spicy flavor and are often used in Mediterranean cuisine. The flavors are strongest when planted in a sunny location.

8 Mint This vigorous, upright herb can be invasive when planted in borders and is best contained to a large pot sunk into the soil. There are several varieties to grow, including peppermint and spearmint. All are easy to grow in most soils.

9 Bay Commonly seen trained into standards or as topiary, a bay tree makes a great addition to the garden. The evergreen leaves are used in many dishes. It is easy to grow but can become large, so keep plants well pruned.

Vegetable crop planner

Use this table to check when to sow and harvest your vegetable crops. The precise timings will vary slightly for each region, so adjust them to suit your own site and conditions. Sow most seeds under cover until the risk of frost has passed.

CROPS		SPRING			SUMMER			FALL			WINTER		
		EARLY	MID	LATE	EARLY	MID	LATE	EARLY	MID	LATE	EARLY	MID	LATE
TOMATOES	SOW	■	■										
	HARVEST					■	■	■	■	■			
PEPPERS	SOW	■											■
	HARVEST				■	■	■	■	■	■			
CHILI PEPPERS	SOW	■											■
	HARVEST					■	■	■	■				
EGGPLANT	SOW	■	■										
	HARVEST						■	■	■				
PEAS	SOW	■	■	■									
	HARVEST				■	■				■			
RUNNER BEANS	SOW		■	■	■								
	HARVEST					■	■	■	■				
GREEN BEANS	SOW		■	■									
	HARVEST					■	■	■					
FAVA BEANS	SOW	■											
	HARVEST		■	■	■								
CUCUMBERS	SOW	■	■										
	HARVEST					■	■	■					
ZUCCHINI	SOW		■										
	HARVEST					■	■	■					
SUMMER SQUASHES	SOW		■										
	HARVEST					■	■	■					
WINTER SQUASHES	SOW	■	■										
	HARVEST							■	■	■			
PUMPKINS	SOW	■	■										
	HARVEST							■	■				
SUMMER/FALL CABBAGES	SOW	■	■										■
	HARVEST					■	■	■	■				
WINTER/SPRING CABBAGES	SOW	■	■										
	HARVEST									■	■	■	■
CAULIFLOWER	SOW	■	■					■	■				
	HARVEST				■	■	■						
CALABRESE BROCCOLI	SOW	■	■										
	HARVEST					■	■	■					
SPROUTING BROCCOLI	SOW	■	■										
	HARVEST	■											
BRUSSELS SPROUTS	SOW		■	■									
	HARVEST									■	■	■	■
KALE	SOW		■	■	■								
	HARVEST							■	■	■	■	■	■
LETTUCE	SOW	■	■	■	■	■	■	■					
	HARVEST		■	■	■	■	■	■	■	■			
CUT-AND-COME-AGAIN SALAD	SOW	■	■	■	■	■	■	■					
	HARVEST		■	■	■	■	■	■	■	■			■
MICROGREENS	SOW	■	■	■	■	■	■	■	■	■	■	■	■
	HARVEST	■	■	■	■	■	■	■	■	■	■	■	■
ASIAN GREENS	SOW				■	■	■						
	HARVEST					■	■	■	■				

CROPS		SPRING			SUMMER			FALL			WINTER		
		EARLY	MID	LATE	EARLY	MID	LATE	EARLY	MID	LATE	EARLY	MID	LATE
SPINACH	SOW / HARVEST												
SWISS CHARD	SOW / HARVEST												
CHICORY	SOW / HARVEST												
ENDIVE	SOW / HARVEST												
WATERCRESS	SOW / HARVEST												
RADISHES	SOW / HARVEST												
BEETS	SOW / HARVEST												
CARROTS	SOW / HARVEST												
TURNIPS	SOW / HARVEST												
PARSNIPS	SOW / HARVEST												
RUTABAGA	SOW / HARVEST												
POTATOES	SOW / HARVEST												
ONIONS	SOW / HARVEST												
SHALLOTS	SOW / HARVEST												
GREEN ONIONS	SOW / HARVEST												
LEEKS	SOW / HARVEST												
GARLIC	SOW / HARVEST												
SWEET CORN	SOW / HARVEST												
KOHLRABI	SOW / HARVEST												
FLORENCE FENNEL	SOW / HARVEST												
CELERY	SOW / HARVEST												
CELERY ROOT	SOW / HARVEST												
ASPARAGUS	SOW / HARVEST												
GLOBE ARTICHOKES	SOW / HARVEST												
JERUSALEM ARTICHOKES	SOW / HARVEST												
RHUBARB	SOW / HARVEST												
ANNUAL HERBS	SOW / HARVEST												
PERENNIAL HERBS	SOW / HARVEST												

GROW YOUR OWN Fruit

STEP-BY-STEP Strawberries

This fruiting perennial is extremely popular, and deservedly so, with varieties that produce sweet homegrown fruit from late spring until the first frost. Strawberries grow well in containers and growing bags, making them perfect for small spaces. They are also easy to propagate from plantlets or "runners," and can even be brought indoors to produce off-season crops. Strawberries are delicious cooked or can be enjoyed sprinkled with sugar.

	SPRING	SUMMER	FALL	WINTER
PLANT				
HARVEST				

FLOWERING TO HARVEST: 2–4 WEEKS

SUITABLE FOR: BEDS, CONTAINERS, HANGING BASKETS, AND GROWING BAGS

11 plants

9FT (3M) ROWS
Plant 12in (30cm) apart, 18in (45cm) between rows

GROWING BAGS
5 plants in each

1 Getting started

There are two main types of strawberries to consider. Junebearing varieties are the tastiest, and crop in a single flush in early to midsummer. "Everbearing" or "perpetual" strawberries produce their main harvest in summer, then give smaller subsequent flushes of fruit until the first frost.

'Pegasus' *is a summer-fruiting variety that freely produces large, sweet, glossy berries.*

'Symphony' *is a late-season, summer-fruiting variety, grown for its heavy crops.*

'Konona' *is a summer-fruiting variety that is easy to grow and yields huge, succulent berries.*

'Flamenco' *is a perpetual variety that crops heavily from midsummer to fall.*

To plant bare-root *strawberries, spread the roots out, and work soil in between them. Ensure the crown of the plant sits on the soil surface.*

Planting through plastic sheeting *will suppress weeds and help conserve moisture during summer. It will also keep the developing fruit clean of soil.*

2 Planting

Strawberries are available to buy bare-root or pot-grown. They can be planted in spring, although planting in fall gives them longer to establish before their first crop. Choose a sunny, sheltered spot, and if planting directly into the soil, fork it over to remove all weeds. Leave 12in (30cm) between plants, 18in (45cm) between rows. If planting into growing bags, space plants 8in (20cm) apart; in containers and baskets, 4in (10cm) apart.

TIP *When planting into containers and baskets, use soil-based compost.*

3 Mulching

As plants growing in beds begin to flower, lay a mulch of straw or hay around them so the developing fruits are held away from the soil. This keeps them clean and ensures good air movement, which deters rotting. Alternatively, use "collars" around individual plants, or plant through weed-control fabric.

Straw was traditionally *used to lift the fruits from the soil, thus straw-berry. It is cheap and easy to buy, and can be composted at the end of the season.*

Ready-made strawberry collars *are ideal if you only have a few plants and can be used from year to year. You can easily make your own.*

Support bird netting *above the plants with stakes so they cannot grow through it, otherwise the fruit would be vulnerable to attack.*

Pick the fruit *when it is fully colored but still firm to the touch. Leave the leafy crown in place until you eat the fruit to prevent decay.*

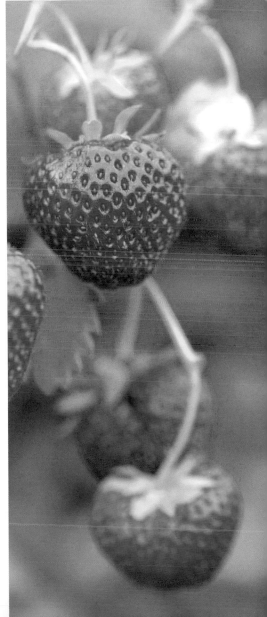

4 Protecting the fruit

Birds will attack the fruit as soon as they start turning red; erect net tunnel cloches over rows, or create small cages over single plants. Check netting regularly, and keep it taut so birds don't become entangled. Protect against slugs and snails by lightly spreading slug pellets around plants.

5 Harvesting

As soon as individual strawberries turn completely red, pick them. Do this by pinching them off at the stalk rather than holding the fruit itself to prevent bruising, which may subsequently rot. The berries will keep fresh for a few days in a cool place or can be frozen either cooked or raw.

6 Propagating plants

After fruiting, summer varieties send out stems or "runners," with small plantlets along their length, which can be used to propagate new plants. Plunge small pots of compost near the plantlets, and peg them into it. Keep them moist until fall, when they will be well-rooted. Cut the joining stem, and continue growing the new plant.

Anchor the plantlet *in place with a bent piece of thick wire, such as from an old clothes hanger.*

STEP-BY-STEP Raspberries

You could be forgiven for thinking that raspberries demand a lot of space—visit any grower and you'll see vast rows of canes. However, for the majority of people this actually yields too much fruit, and a smaller plot can easily meet your needs. Both summer- and fall-fruiting varieties are available, allowing you to enjoy sweet, tart berries from midsummer right through to the first frost. Raspberries are also very easy to grow.

	SPRING	SUMMER	FALL	WINTER
PLANT				
HARVEST				

FLOWERING TO HARVEST: 6–8 WEEKS

SUITABLE FOR: BEDS AND CONTAINERS

0   3ft   6ft   9ft

11 plants

9FT (3M) ROWS
Plant 12in (30cm) apart, with 3ft (1m) between rows

0   12in

CONTAINERS
3 plants in each

1 Getting started

Summer-fruiting raspberries crop from mid- to late summer; fall varieties fruit late summer to mid-fall, so plant both for the longest harvest. Summer raspberries should be planted against horizontal wires held 16in (40cm) and 32in (80cm) above the soil. Fall-fruiting varieties can be grown freestanding.

'Joan J' is a spine-free, fall-fruiting variety that stays compact and is suitable for containers.

'Cascade Delight' is a free-fruiting summer raspberry with large, rich-tasting berries.

'Tulameen' fruits in summer over several weeks and is a good choice for cooler areas.

'All Gold' crops in the fall, producing tasty yellow fruits that won't stain your fingers.

Plant new canes in evenly spaced rows, and provide suitable support for summer-fruiting varieties. Water and mulch after planting.

New shoots develop in spring after which the original woody cane can be cut to the ground. This will encourage further new canes to develop.

2 Planting

New raspberry canes are best planted in late fall and are generally sold bare-root or root-wrapped, which means they are lifted from the ground and bundled together loosely in compost. Raspberries prefer moist but free-draining soil and will tolerate a little shade. Dig plenty of well-rotted organic matter into the soil during the fall, allowing it to settle for two weeks before planting. Space the canes 12in (30cm) apart in rows at least 3ft (1m) apart.

TIP	Plant new canes to the same depth as the original soil mark on their stems.

3 Routine care

Keep plants well watered in the summer, and apply a tomato feed to promote a good harvest. Mulch near the base of the canes with composted organic matter to help retain moisture. As soon as the fruit starts to ripen, protect it from birds. Cover plants with a cage or netting, held taut using canes to prevent snaring birds.

Water the plants *once or twice a week during summer, even daily on light soils during dry spells. Avoid splashing the stems, which spreads disease.*

Birds soon attack summer raspberries *but are less interested in fall-fruiting varieties, which can even be grown without protection.*

Handle the berries *carefully when picking since they are easily damaged. Smashed fruit quickly spoils so is best eaten right away.*

After pruning in summer, *tie the new shoots onto the horizontal wires. These will fruit the following year, then be replaced by new growth.*

4 Harvesting

The berries are ready as soon as they turn fully red or yellow, depending on variety, and pull easily from the plant, leaving the central "plug" behind. Avoid picking on rainy days since wet fruit does not store well. Check your plants daily to ensure you harvest them at the perfect point of ripeness.

5 Summer pruning

Summer-fruiting raspberries are pruned right after the last fruits have been harvested, cutting the fruited canes to the base. Younger, unfruited stems produced that summer should be tied to the wires in their place. Keep only the strongest, and tie them in 4in (10cm) apart, to fruit next year.

6 Winter pruning

Fall raspberries are pruned in winter by cutting all the canes down to the ground. Alternatively, to encourage a staggered harvest the following year, cut a few canes down by only half their height in winter. The half-height canes will then produce an earlier crop in early to midsummer. These fruited canes can then be pruned out completely after harvesting.

Cut fall-fruiting canes *close to the ground. New shoots will appear in late spring.*

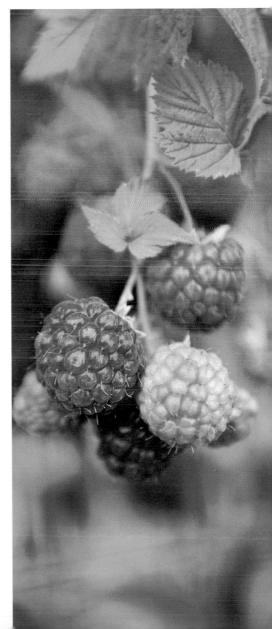

STEP-BY-STEP Blackberries and hybrids

Gone are the days of small berries, carried on large, vicious plants—modern blackberries have been bred to have fewer thorns, often none, and to give generous harvests of plump, tasty fruit. They are also easier to look after, being more disease resistant, and some new varieties fruit on new growth, making them easier to prune. Plant one of the blackberry hybrids as well, like a loganberry or a tayberry, and you will have a jam-maker's dream.

	SPRING	SUMMER	FALL	WINTER
PLANT				
HARVEST				

FLOWERING TO HARVEST: 6–8 WEEKS

SUITABLE FOR: BEDS AND BORDERS

0   3ft   6ft   9ft

1–2 plants

9FT (3M) ROWS
Plant 5–10ft (1.5–3m) apart, according to variety

1 Getting started

There are many blackberry varieties to choose from, with different qualities to suit your garden, including thornless plants. Hybrid berries are more distinct and result from cross-breeding blackberries with raspberries or with other related hybrids. For the largest selection, try mail order specialty fruit nurseries.

Blackberries *fruit from mid- to late summer, and there are many varieties, some being thornless.*

Loganberries *are best cooked with plenty of sugar and taste like tart raspberries.*

Boysenberries *are a hybrid of a loganberry and blackberry but taste much like the latter.*

Tayberries *are a cross between a raspberry and a blackberry and have delicious fruit.*

Make a hole *slightly wider than the root ball so you can firm the soil in after planting. Lower the plant in to check the depth.*

Remove the plant *from its container, and separate the roots to help them establish. Spread out those of bare-root plants.*

Pot-grown plants *are planted level with the soil surface; bare-root plants to the depth of the soil mark on their stems.*

2 Planting

Blackberries and hybrid berries are climbing shrubs and should be planted against a wall or trellis or a system of posts and wires, where their stems can be trained. To help plants establish quickly, they are best planted in the fall, while the soil is still warm and moist. Choose a sunny site, turn over the soil to remove weeds, and mix in some organic matter and granular, general-purpose fertilizer. Water well after planting.

TIP *Blackberries can be very thorny, so wear gloves when handling the plants.*

3 Routine care

Keep plants well watered during summer, and mulch them using well-rotted organic matter. If you use manure for this, no additional fertilizer is needed, Otherwise, apply a balanced granular fertilizer in spring. Net the fruits as they ripen, but ensure it's held taut to prevent birds from becoming snagged. Check the netting regularly for gaps.

A fruit cage is ideal *for protecting plants from birds, if you have space. If not, make a temporary structure using nets and canes until harvest.*

Unlike raspberries, *blackberries and the hybrid fruits pull off whole when picked and don't leave behind a white core. The juice can stain fingers.*

To help prune out fruited canes, *untie them from their supports first. This will make the cut stems easier to untangle and remove.*

4 Harvesting

Depending on variety or hybrid, the fruit ripens from mid- to late summer. For maximum sweetness, wait until the berries are fully colored, when it should be easy to pull them from the plant. Unless the fruit is to be eaten right away, pick the fruit while it is still firm and only during dry weather.

5 Pruning

Most blackberries and hybrids fruit on canes in their second year. These should be cut to the base in the fall after fruiting, while new unfruited canes that fruit in their first year of growth are tied in. New varieties that fruit on new summer growth can be cut completely to the ground in winter.

6 Training

Although these plants can be left to ramble, they are more manageable and take up less space when trained against horizontal wires. In winter or early spring, train unfruited stems produced the previous summer to form a fan on either side of the crown. This will encourage flower and fruit formation. Also tie in new season stems during summer to fruit next year.

Supporting wires *can be attached to walls and fences or stretched between two upright posts.*

STEP-BY-STEP Red and white currants

If you've ever seen a well-grown red or white currant bush, you'll know how bountiful they are—they can literally drip with fruit. Combine this with the fact that they are easy to grow, even in moderate shade, that the fruits freeze well and have a high pectin content (making them good for jams and jellies), and you can understand their value. They can also be planted against walls if space is limited, making them ideal for smaller gardens.

	SPRING	SUMMER	FALL	WINTER
PLANT				
HARVEST				

FLOWERING TO HARVEST: 10–12 WEEKS

SUITABLE FOR: BEDS AND CONTAINERS

0   3ft   6ft   9ft

4 plants

9FT (3M) ROWS
Plant bushes 32in (80cm) apart

0   12in

CONTAINERS
1 plant in each

1 Getting started

Red and white currants grow best in acid soil but will tolerate alkaline conditions. Plants are widely available grown in pots throughout the year or can be bought bare-root during fall. If deciding between the two types, red currants generally have a sharper, more acidic flavor; white currants are sweeter tasting.

'Jonkheer van Tets' *is an early variety that produces a large crop of rich, bright red fruit.*

'Red Lake' *produces long "strigs" of berries from midsummer. It is a large, vigorous shrub.*

'Blanka' *bears masses of sweet-tasting, pale yellow berries from mid- to late summer.*

'Versailles Blanche' *fruits in midsummer, giving a plentiful harvest of sweet-tasting berries.*

Plant red currants *so that all growth emerges from a short stem, or "leg," growing just above the soil surface.*

Fill in between the roots *of bare-root plants with soil; lightly tease out the roots of pot-grown bushes before planting them.*

Firm the soil after planting *to remove air pockets, ensuring the "leg" remains above the soil surface. Water in well.*

2 Planting

Currants establish best when planted in fall or spring, although container-raised plants can be planted at any time if kept moist. They can be planted in sun but also don't mind a shady spot and can be grown against north- or east-facing walls. Prepare the site by turning it over, space plants 32in (80cm) apart, then water well, and mulch after planting. In smaller plots, plant into 12in (30cm) wide pots filled with soil-based compost.

TIP *Plant pot-grown currants so the compost is level with the soil surface.*

3 Routine care

Plants will require regular watering in their first summer to encourage root establishment. After this time they become more drought-tolerant, but yields will be improved by regular watering in spring and summer. Mulch plants with rich, well-rotted organic matter, and apply a dressing of high-potash fertilizer every spring.

Organic mulch retains moisture, *reducing the need for watering during summer. It also degrades, providing nutrients for your plants.*

Birds love berries *and will repeatedly raid your plants. Net individual bushes, or consider buying a fruit cage if you have several plants.*

Harvest the fruit *as whole strigs rather than as individual berries; they are small and easily squashed. Eat the berries fresh, or freeze them.*

4 Protecting the fruit

Birds will quickly strip plants of berries, so erect a cage of netting over your bushes as soon as the fruits begin to ripen. (White currants turn from green to translucent white as they near maturity). Pull all netting taut to prevent birds from becoming trapped. Remove the net after harvesting.

5 Harvesting

The berries are carried on trailing stems or "strigs," which should be picked whole once all the berries along them have ripened. Pull the strig from the stem using your fingers, or carefully snip them with scissors. Check out your bushes every three or four days to harvest the berries at their best.

6 Pruning

Currants fruit at the base of stems that are at least a year old. In early to midsummer, prune the new stems back to 4–6in (10–15cm) to encourage more fruiting spurs, which will also help the fruit ripen and improve airflow. In winter, cut the pruned stems back to two buds above the cluster of buds at the base of the stem; also remove any dead or diseased growth.

Pruning encourages fruiting spurs *that develop in clusters at the base of cut stems*

STEP-BY-STEP Black currants

These robust bushes fruit in the summer, producing long stems or "strigs" of intensely flavored berries that are excellent when eaten fresh and even more so when cooked and made into preserves, pies, and summer drinks. Black currants are easy to grow and very reliable, even in colder areas, making them a good choice for beginning growers. They are also easy to prune, and modern varieties are prone to few pests or diseases.

	SPRING	SUMMER	FALL	WINTER
PLANT				
HARVEST				

FLOWERING TO HARVEST: 10–12 WEEKS

SUITABLE FOR: BEDS AND CONTAINERS

3 plants

9FT (3M) ROWS
Plant bushes 3ft (1m) apart

CONTAINERS
1 plant in each

1 Getting started

Black currants are widely sold throughout the year grown in containers, but they can also be bought and planted bare-root in fall. Bare-root plants are cheaper than pot-grown, which is helpful if you want several. Look out for modern, disease-resistant varieties, which have 'Ben' in their names.

'Ben Sarek' *is a free-fruiting variety with a compact style and is ideal for smaller plots.*

'Ben Connan' *fruits from midsummer and gives a good harvest of sweet, juicy berries.*

'Ebony' *is an early variety that crops from early summer. Its sweet fruit are especially large.*

'Ben Lomond' *crops freely from midsummer onward, producing large, sweet berries.*

Using a guide, *plant slightly deeper than the soil mark on the stem, or deeper than the level of the compost if pot-grown.*

Backfill the hole *with soil, making sure you don't leave large air pockets and that the plant is upright.*

Firm in gently, *and water in well. New black currant bushes should be pruned immediately after planting.*

2 Planting

The best time to plant is between fall and spring when the soil is warm and moist, although currants can also be planted in the summer if watered well. Choose a sunny, sheltered site, and weed it thoroughly. In smaller plots, plant into 12in (30cm) pots, filled with soil-based compost. Water plants in, mulch well, then cut back all the stems to soil level to promote sturdy new growth. If planting more than one bush, space them at least 3ft (1m) apart.

TIP *Plant black currants deeply so all the stems emerge directly from the soil.*

3 Routine care

Keep young plants well watered throughout their first summer; established plants are more drought tolerant but will crop better if watered during dry spells. Mulch plants in spring with well-rotted organic matter, such as garden compost, and apply a granular high-nitrogen fertilizer. Use canes to support fruit-laden stems.

Mulch plants *to help retain moisture in summer and to suppress weeds. As the mulch slowly breaks down, it releases nutrients to your plants.*

Support stems *using a simple frame of string and canes to prevent them from collapsing and snapping under the weight of summer fruit.*

Use netting *to keep birds from becoming trapped. Their feet can easily snag on loose nets.*

Ripe berries *pull easily from the bush, but handle them carefully. They are easily bruised.*

4 Protecting the fruit

Birds can strip plants of berries in a matter of days. As soon as fruit begins to ripen, protect your plants with netting, secured at the base, to keep birds from sneaking in underneath. Check the nets regularly for gaps.

5 Harvesting

Older black currant varieties ripen as individual berries and can be picked one by one when ready. Modern types are only picked when the whole stem, or "strig," is ripe. The strigs should pull easily from the bush.

6 Pruning

Black currants fruit mainly on one-year-old stems and can be pruned and picked at the same time. Cut stems that have fruited to the base, leaving the new growth to crop next summer. Plants pruned this way must be fed well in spring with a high-nitrogen fertilizer. An alternative method is to allow the stems to fruit for three years, then prune them to the base in winter. This leads to larger plants, less suited to smaller gardens.

Pruned growth

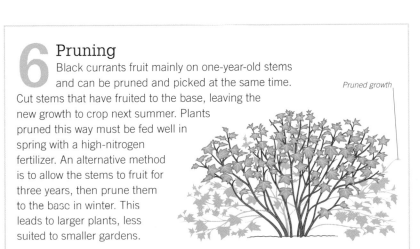

STEP-BY-STEP Gooseberries

This easy-to-grow fruit produces its main crop in early summer, but by using the tart fruitlets thinned in late spring in your kitchen, you can enjoy an even earlier harvest. There are culinary or dessert varieties to grow, while a few are dual-purpose and give you the best of both worlds. Gooseberries are reliable plants, and breeders are continually developing varieties with improved disease resistance, yield, and thankfully, fewer thorns.

	SPRING	SUMMER	FALL	WINTER
PLANT				
HARVEST				

FLOWERING TO HARVEST: 10 WEEKS

SUITABLE FOR: BEDS AND CONTAINERS

3 plants

9FT (3M) ROWS
Plant bushes 3ft (1m) apart

CONTAINERS
1 plant in each

1 Getting started

Young plants are widely sold pot-grown throughout the year, or bare-root during fall. There are many varieties to choose from, with fruit that varies in size, shape, taste, and color. However, some have sharp thorns, which you may want to avoid, especially in smaller gardens or if you have young children.

'Careless' *is suitable for eating fresh or cooking and gives an early crop of tasty green fruits.*

'Invicta' *fruits from early to midsummer, giving a heavy crop to cook or enjoy fresh.*

'Lancashire Lad' *needs good soil to crop well. It bears rich red fruit from mid- to late summer.*

'Hinnonmäki Röd' *is easy to grow and ideal for beginners. Its sweet-tasting fruit mature red.*

Dig a planting hole that is wide enough *so the roots of bare-root plants can be spread out fully and to fit the root ball of pot-grown bushes.*

Plant bare-root bushes *at the same depth as the soil mark on their stem; plant pot-grown plants so the compost is level with the soil surface.*

2 Planting

Pot-grown gooseberries can be planted throughout the year if watered well, although they establish best between fall and spring. Unlike many fruits they tolerate shade, so can be planted in north- or east-facing spots. Turn the soil over to remove all weeds, mix in some general purpose fertilizer, and water well after planting. Space plants 3ft (1m) apart. They can also be planted in 12in (30cm) wide containers, filled with soil-based compost.

TIP *Keep plants in pots well watered, especially when in flower or fruit.*

3 Routine care

Water new plants well in their first year, and water established plants during dry spells. In spring, mulch plants with rich organic matter, and add granular balanced fertilizer on sandy or alkaline soils. Protect the fruit from birds with fruit cages, or use netting held taut to keep birds out. Check regularly for gaps.

Wire hoops and bent canes *are ideal for supporting bird netting. The structure can be left in place all year or removed after fruiting.*

Picked gooseberries keep in the fridge *for about a week. For longer-term storage, they also freeze well and can be made into preserves.*

4 Harvesting

To encourage larger fruit, thin the developing gooseberries in late spring, and rather than waste them, use the sour-tasting "thinnings" for cooking. Take no more than half the berries and, if your bush has yet to establish a regular heavy cropping pattern, only take one quarter. Once the remaining berries are fully ripe, they can be harvested. Hold the berry by the stalk when picking, not the fruit, to avoid bruising and subsequent decay. Pick from your bushes regularly as they ripen to enjoy the fruit at its best.

5 Pruning

Gooseberries fruit at the base of stems that are at least one-year-old and are pruned twice a year. In midsummer, cut back all of the growth produced this year to 6–8in (15–20cm) long. In winter these pruned stems should be cut back further to leave only two or three buds each, which will then bear fruit the next year. At the same time, remove any dead, diseased, or damaged growth, as well as any thinner stems that look likely to droop on the ground once laden with fruit.

Pruned growth

STEP-BY-STEP Blueberries

Incredibly popular with gardeners, blueberries were one of the first crops to be crowned with "superfruit" status, thanks to their naturally high levels of health-giving antioxidants and vitamins. Give them an acid or "ericaceous" soil and plenty of water during the growing season, and blueberries yield abundantly. Even if you don't have an acid soil, they crop very successfully in pots, which also makes them an ideal choice for smaller gardens.

	SPRING	SUMMER	FALL	WINTER
PLANT				
HARVEST				

FLOWERING TO HARVEST: 8–10 WEEKS

SUITABLE FOR: BEDS AND CONTAINERS

0   3ft   6ft   9ft

4 plants

9FT (3M) ROWS
Plant bushes 75cm (30in) apart

0   12in

CONTAINERS
1 plant in each

1 Getting started

Blueberries are usually sold in pots and can be bought throughout the year. The plants are self-pollinating, so you only need one in order to produce a crop. However, they fruit more freely when cross-pollinated, so if you have space, grow two or more varieties that flower at the same time.

'Spartan' *produces a generous crop of large, richly-flavored berries in midsummer.*

'Bluetta' *is a compact variety, ideal for smaller gardens or for growing in containers.*

'Jersey' *is a tough variety for cooler areas. It must be grown near another variety to fruit.*

'Herbert' *fruits in late summer, giving a good crop of sweet, intensely flavored berries.*

Ease the plant *from its pot, and tease the roots away from the root ball to encourage them to grow into the surrounding soil.*

Plant the blueberry *so the surface of the compost is level with the surrounding soil. Firm it in gently, and water well.*

Mulch with organic matter, *such as composted pine bark, that will help provide and maintain acid soil conditions.*

2 Planting

Blueberries prefer boggy growing conditions and are best planted between fall and spring when the soil is moist. They also require acid soil with a pH below six (use a soil testing kit if you are unsure), otherwise they must be grown in containers filled with lime-free, ericaceous compost. Before planting, incorporate composted bark into the soil, and add sulfur chips to help maintain a low pH. Water plants in well, and keep moist.

TIP *To help retain moisture, line porous pots with pierced plastic sheeting.*

3 Routine care

Mulch plants in containers and borders in spring with well-rotted organic matter, such as leaf mold or composted bark. Water plants well throughout the year, especially when in flower and fruit, particularly those in pots. Feed plants every two weeks from early to midsummer with a liquid fertilizer suitable for acid-loving plants.

Use rainwater to water blueberries to help maintain the soil acidity. Tap water commonly contains lime, especially in hard-water areas

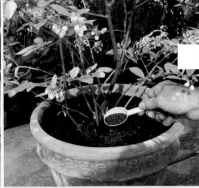

Acid-loving plants require specific fertilizers, which are widely available as liquid or granular feeds. Don't use conventional fertilizers.

Handle bird nets carefully when picking since the ripening fruit is easily knocked off

Blueberries ripen over a long period, and each shrub can be in fruit for several weeks.

4 Protecting the fruit

Blueberries flower in early spring, and it's worth protecting them against frost damage in cold areas with garden fabric. The ripening fruit should also be protected in summer from birds using taut netting or a fruit cage.

5 Harvesting

Check your plants every few days to ensure you pick the berries at their best. Ripe fruits pull easily from the plants but are also easy to squash, so take care. The berries are best enjoyed fresh, but any surplus can be frozen.

6 Pruning

Blueberries are usually grown as freestanding bushes, whether in containers or beds, and are pruned just before they come into leaf in spring. Remove lower branches and weak growth, along with any dead, diseased, or damaged shoots. The fruit is predominantly produced on one-, two- and three-year-old wood. Using sharp loppers or a pruning saw, remove less productive, older stems completely at the base.

Pruned growth

STEP-BY-STEP Apples

Apples are the classic garden fruit, and the availability of dwarfing rootstocks means even those with limited space can embrace apple growing. There are hundreds of different varieties to try. Many are widely available, each with individual flavors, disease-resistance, and cropping potential. Many can also be grown in containers, and for those with more time and experience, apples can be trained into neat, space-saving shapes, such as cordons.

	SPRING	SUMMER	FALL	WINTER
PLANT				
HARVEST				

FLOWERING TO HARVEST: 14–20 WEEKS

SUITABLE FOR: BEDS AND CONTAINERS

9FT (3M) ROWS
Plant trees 30in (75cm) apart, depending on rootstock
4 plants

CONTAINERS
1 plant in each

1 Getting started

Container-grown apples are available all year, whereas bare-root trees can be bought between fall and early spring. In order to produce fruit, apple flowers must be pollinated, and you will need at least two compatible trees unless there is already one growing nearby. Get advice before deciding what to buy.

'Cox's Orange Pippin' *is a well-known dessert variety that bears richly flavored fruit.*

'Greensleeves' *fruits freely in early fall, bearing sweet, tart dessert apples.*

'James Grieve' *is a dessert apple that fruits in early fall. It grows well in cool, dry areas.*

'Bramley's Seedling' *is a renowned culinary apple. It requires another variety for pollination.*

Lay a guide *across the hole, and plant at the same depth as the soil mark on the tree or the top of the compost if pot-grown.*

Backfill the hole *with soil, improved with organic matter, and firm it gently with your foot. Water the plant in well.*

Stake the tree, *before or after planting, and attach it using an adjustable tree tie. Nail the tie to the stake to hold it in place.*

2 Planting

Apple trees establish better if planted while dormant from fall to spring, although pot-grown trees can be planted at any time if kept moist. Choose a sunny, sheltered site, turn over the area to remove weeds, and add organic matter if the soil is sandy or heavy clay. Pot-grown and bare-root trees are planted using the same technique (see left). Apples on dwarfing rootstocks can also be planted into large containers of soil-based compost.

TIP	*Trees should be established after two years, when the stake can be removed.*

3 Routine care

Water trees well, especially in their first year, to help them establish. Trees in pots will always require regular watering; those in the ground will need less water once fully rooted. Mulch trees in spring with organic matter, and apply a high-potash granular fertilizer. Apply liquid high-potash feed to pot-grown trees in spring and early summer.

Regular watering is vital *for new apple trees. Watering mature trees during dry periods will also help to prevent the disease bitter pit (see p.244).*

Rich organic mulch *helps suppress weeds, retains moisture, and keeps the roots cool. It also releases nutrients as it degrades, feeding the tree.*

To help new trees establish, *remove any fruit that sets during its first year. Later crops can be allowed to develop once thinned.*

Harvest apples *regularly to enjoy them at their best. Early varieties are best eaten fresh, later varieties can be stored if you have a surplus.*

4 Thinning out

To encourage full-sized apples, thin the developing fruits in early summer, once they reach walnut-size. Thin dessert apples to one or two fruits per 6in (15cm); culinary types to one every 6in (15cm). Always thin out the central fruit, which can grow abnormally.

5 Harvesting

When fruit is ready to harvest, gently cup it in your hand, lift and twist. The fruit should come away without pulling; if it doesn't, try again in a day or so. Pick from the tree regularly as the fruit ripens, and handle the apples carefully to avoid bruising them.

6 Pruning

Established apples are pruned in winter. Prune out congested growth from the center to maintain an open shape, and remove dead, diseased, damaged, and weak growth. Cut back new stems by half to encourage fruit-bearing spurs at their base. Older fruit spurs should be thinned if they are congested.

Pruned growth

Fruiting spur

STEP-BY-STEP Pears

A perfectly ripe pear is a real indulgence, but picked fruit can go past its peak in a matter of days, so it's something you're unlikely to fully appreciate until you grow your own. Pears are as easy to grow as apples, and there are culinary and dessert varieties to choose, offering different flavors, textures, and storing qualities. The trees prefer a sheltered spot, and where space is limited, they can be planted and trained against walls and fences.

	SPRING	SUMMER	FALL	WINTER
PLANT				
HARVEST				

FLOWERING TO HARVEST: 16–20 WEEKS

SUITABLE FOR: BEDS AND CONTAINERS

9FT (3M) ROWS
Plant trees 30in (75cm) apart, depending on rootstock
4 plants

CONTAINERS
1 plant in each

1 Getting started

Pears are available in pots throughout the year, or bare-root in fall. You can also buy pre-trained trees to plant against walls. Most varieties must be pollinated before they will set fruit, so unless there are pear trees growing nearby, you will need to plant more than one. Get advice for compatible varieties.

'Concorde' *is easy to grow, has a good flavor, and stays compact. It is ideal for smaller plots.*

'Doyenné du Comice' *need a sunny spot but produces delicious fruit in mid-fall.*

'Beurré Superfin' *crops in early fall, bearing richly aromatic fruit. It is ideal for wall-training.*

'Packham's Triumph' *has richly flavored fruit in mid-fall. It grows best in a sheltered site.*

To plant a pear tree in a pot, *fill the bottom with soil-based compost, and incorporate some slow-release fertilizer.*

Tease out the roots *of pot-grown trees, and spread out those of bare-root plants. Fill around the roots with compost.*

Make sure the tree *is planted to the depth of the soil mark on the stem. Insert a stake for support, and water it in well.*

2 Planting

Pear trees flower in early spring and need plenty of sun to ripen the fruit, so choose a warm, sheltered site. Prepare the soil before planting by digging it up to remove weeds, and work in some granular general purpose fertilizer and organic matter. Once planted and staked, firm the soil gently, and water in well. Pears grown on dwarf rootstocks can also be planted in large containers, 24in (60cm) wide, filled with soil-based compost.

TIP	*Protect the blooms with garden fabric at night; remove it during the day.*

3 Routine care

Pears prefer to be kept moist, so water them well during their first year and during prolonged dry spells in the future. To help retain moisture and shade the roots, mulch around the trunk in spring with well-rotted organic matter, such as garden compost. Apply general purpose fertilizer in spring, followed by a high-potash feed in summer.

Water well *in summer, especially trees growing in containers. Don't allow trees to become dry while in flower or fruit, or the crop may be lost.*

High-potash feeds, *such as tomato fertilizer, encourage plants to flower and produce more fruit. Apply it as a liquid as the fruit develops.*

Pears naturally shed *some excess fruitlets in early summer, which is called "June drop." Wait until it has passed before thinning them further.*

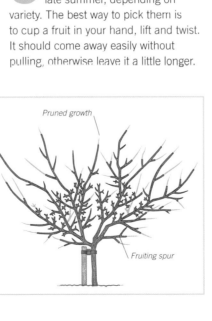

Early varieties *are picked underripe, while still hard, to ripen indoors. Pick later varieties only when they are completely ripe.*

4 Thinning out

Trees can set a heavy crop, which should be thinned to promote full-sized fruit. In midsummer, thin the fruitlets leaving one per cluster. As fruit swells, support heavily laden branches to keep them from snapping.

5 Harvesting

Fruits will begin ripening in late summer, depending on variety. The best way to pick them is to cup a fruit in your hand, lift and twist. It should come away easily without pulling, otherwise leave it a little longer.

6 Pruning

Established, freestanding pear trees are pruned in winter. Prune out congested stems in the middle of the tree to maintain an open shape. Also remove any dead, diseased, damaged, and crossing growth. Cut back stems produced in summer by half their length to encourage spurs to develop at their base —these will fruit next year.

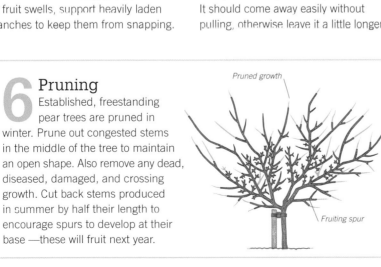

Pruned growth

Fruiting spur

STEP-BY-STEP Plums

Plums are deliciously sweet and juicy, and the trees fruit so freely that you're likely to have plenty, providing ample product for jams, canning, and freezing. Modern varieties grafted on dwarfing rootstocks are ideal for smaller gardens and can even be grown in containers. Plums, which include damsons, gages, and bullaces, are very easy to grow and need little pruning. If you choose a self-pollinating variety, you will only need one tree to produce a crop.

	SPRING	SUMMER	FALL	WINTER
PLANT				
HARVEST				

FLOWERING TO HARVEST: 14–16 WEEKS

SUITABLE FOR: BEDS AND CONTAINERS

2 plants

9FT (3M) ROWS
Plant trees 5ft (1.5m) apart, depending on rootstock

CONTAINERS
1 plant in each

1 Getting started

Bare-root trees can be bought and planted from fall to winter; those sold in pots can be planted at any time. Most varieties need to be cross-pollinated to set fruit so you will need to plant two or more. Self-pollinating varieties can be grown alone, though they will crop better when pollinated by a suitable type.

'Victoria' *is the classic plum and gives a heavy crop of tasty purple-red fruit in late summer.*

'Shropshire Damson' *is self-pollinating so you only need one tree. It crops in early fall.*

'Oullins Gage' *bears sweet, golden fruits in late summer that are good eaten fresh or cooked.*

'Langley Bullace' *crops freely in early fall, producing tart fruit for cooking.*

Place a guide *across the hole, and plant at the same depth as the soil mark on the tree, or the top of the compost if pot-grown.*

Backfill the hole, *working the soil in well between the roots of bare-root trees. Firm it gently as you go. Water the tree in well.*

Attach the stake *to the tree with an adjustable tie. Check all ties occasionally, and remove the stake after two years.*

2 Planting

Choose a sheltered, sunny site, turn it to remove weeds, and work in well-rotted organic matter, such as garden compost, and add some high-nitrogen granular fertilizer. When planting, stake the tree, firm it in gently, and water it well. Plums can also be planted in containers, although they must be kept well watered since they are sensitive to drought. Use a container at least 24in (60cm) wide, and fill it with soil-based compost.

TIP *Plums and gages can be eaten raw; use bullaces and damsons for cooking.*

3 Routine care

Water trees well in the first year and during dry spells in later years. Plums have relatively shallow roots and benefit from a thick mulch of organic matter in spring. They are especially hungry for nitrogen, which you can provide by mulching with well-rotted farm manure, which is rich in nitrogen, or apply a granular fertilizer.

New plum trees *need regular watering until well-rooted. Established trees can fend for themselves, except in dry spells or on sandy soils.*

Mulch trees, *but leave the base of the trunk clear to prevent decay. Use well-rotted material that will release nutrients to the tree.*

Leave the developing fruitlets *into early summer, in case any drop from the tree naturally. Then thin them out to promote larger fruits.*

Harvest the fruits *regularly when they are ripe to enjoy them at their best. If necessary, underripe plums can be stored for a few days.*

4 Thinning out

Plum crops can be variable since frost can kill the early flowers. In milder years when the crop is good, thin the fruit to 2–3in (5–8cm) apart to encourage full-sized plums. It will also help stop overladen branches snapping.

5 Harvesting

Leave plums and gages to ripen fully so they are as sweet as possible; bullaces and damsons can be picked while underripe. Watch out for wasps when picking, and cover trees with fabric if they become a problem.

6 Pruning

Plums are pruned as little as possible to protect the trees from the fungal disease, silver leaf (see p.244). As soon as fruit is harvested, use a clean saw or loppers to remove any dead, diseased, or damaged growth along with spindly or crossing stems. Then thin out the remaining branches, if necessary, to reduce congested growth.

Pruned growth

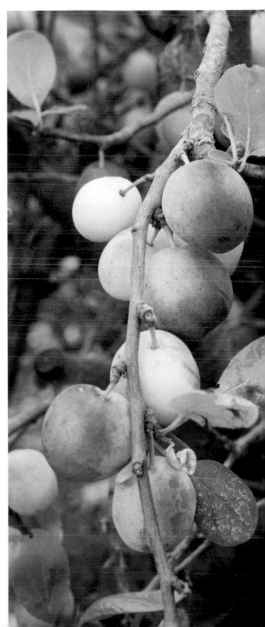

STEP-BY-STEP Cherries

Sweet cherries are a real treat when eaten fresh in summer, while sour-tasting tart varieties are excellent for pies and preserves. Whichever you prefer, recent progress with dwarfing rootstocks and self-pollinating varieties gives cherry lovers many options. Modern compact trees are easy to grow and are ideal for smaller gardens. Their small size also makes it easier to protect them against the fruit's traditional enemy—birds.

	SPRING	SUMMER	FALL	WINTER
PLANT				
HARVEST				

FLOWERING TO HARVEST: 10–14 WEEKS

SUITABLE FOR: BEDS AND BORDERS

| 0 | 3ft | 6ft | 9ft |

2 plants

9FT (3M) ROWS
Plant trees 5ft (1.5m) apart, depending on rootstock

1 Getting started

Pot-grown cherries are sold all year and can be planted at any time; bare-root trees are available to plant between fall and mid-spring. Self-pollinating varieties set fruit if grown alone, so you only need one tree. Conventional varieties don't, and you will need to plant two or more that flower at the same time for a crop.

'Lapins' *is a sweet, self-pollinating cherry that bears large, almost black fruit in midsummer.*

'Morello' *is an tart cherry that crops from late summer into early fall. It is self-pollinating.*

'Sweetheart' *is a sweet cherry with dark berries. It must be grown near a second variety to fruit.*

'May Duke' *is a sweet cherry with the sharper taste of an tart variety. It crops in midsummer.*

Place a guide *across the hole, and plant at the same depth as the soil mark on the tree or the top of the compost if pot-grown.*

Backfill the hole *with soil, which should be improved with organic matter, firm it in gently with your foot, and water in well.*

Insert a wooden stake, *and attach it to the tree using an adjustable tree tie; nail the tie to the stake to keep it in place.*

2 Planting

Sweet cherries require a sunny, sheltered site to grow well, tart types are less demanding and will even tolerate shade. To prepare the site before planting, turn over the soil to remove weeds, and add in sharp grit or composted bark to improve heavier soils. Insert a stake alongside your tree, then firm the soil gently, and water in well while planting. Although there are dwarf rootstocks available, cherries aren't ideal for growing in containers.

TIP *When choosing varieties, tart cherries are easier to grow in cooler regions.*

3 Routine care

Keep new trees well-watered during their first year, and water established trees in dry spells. Mulch in spring with well-rotted organic matter, ideally manure (if mulching with another material, provide additional feed by also applying general purpose fertilizer). To encourage a good harvest, feed the trees regularly in summer with a liquid high-potash feed, such as tomato fertilizer.

Cherries flower *in early spring when the blooms can be killed by frost. Cover with garden fabric, but remove on mild days to allow pollination.*

Protect trees with netting, *securing it at ground level to prevent birds from sneaking in. Wasps also like cherries; be careful when picking.*

Handle ripe fruits *gently to avoid bruising them. Cherries can be stored for up to a week if kept in an open plastic bag in the refrigerator.*

4 Protecting the fruit

Cherries are notoriously favored by birds, and it is important to net trees as soon as fruits show the first signs of color—a cage of netting over individual trees is ideal. Keep nets taut, and check them regularly for gaps.

5 Harvesting

Once the first fruits begin to ripen fully, cover the tree with a sheet of clear plastic to keep rain from getting to the cherries. Ripe fruits can absorb moisture through their skins, which encourages splitting and decay.

6 Pruning

To avoid the fungal disease silver leaf (see p.244), prune after fruiting, while the tree is still in leaf, but keep pruning to a minimum. To prune sweet cherries, only shorten overly long stems to keep the tree within bounds. To prune a tart cherry, cut one quarter of the fruited shoots back to the next branch, and remove any dead, weak, or damaged growth.

Pruned growth

STEP-BY-STEP Peaches and nectarines

If given a sunny, sheltered spot, peach and nectarine trees are wonderful conversation starters in the garden. One tree can yield a sizeable harvest of delicious fruit, which have a characteristically heady perfume when ripe. Many modern varieties are extremely compact, which makes them ideal for smaller gardens and also means they are easier to maintain. They also grow well in containers, allowing you to move them to the best spot possible.

	SPRING	SUMMER	FALL	WINTER
PLANT				
HARVEST				

FLOWERING TO HARVEST: 16–20 WEEKS

SUITABLE FOR: BEDS AND CONTAINERS

1–4 plants

9FT (3M) ROWS
Plant 2½–10ft (75cm–3m) apart, according to variety

CONTAINERS
1 plant in each

1 Getting started

Trees are available bare-root to buy and plant between fall and winter; pot-grown trees can be bought and planted at any time. Dwarf forms are sold pot-grown, and are the only types suitable for growing on in containers. All varieties are self-pollinating, meaning you only need to grow one tree to set a crop.

'Peregrine' *is a great peach variety for cooler areas and bears large fruit in midsummer.*

'Garden Lady' *is a dwarf peach, ideal for containers. It crops mid- to late summer.*

'Fantasia' *crops in late summer, producing large, delicious nectarines. It grows well in cool areas.*

'Lord Napier' *is a good nectarine for cooler sites. It bears large, tasty fruit in midsummer.*

2 Planting

If planting in the ground, choose a sunny, sheltered site, such as near a south-facing wall or fence. Dig up the soil to remove weeds, and incorporate some well-rotted organic matter. To plant in a container, use a pot 4in (10cm) wider than the original one, and plant into soil-based compost.

Use a cane *to check the planting depth. Plant bare-root trees level with the soil mark on the stem.*

Backfill the hole, *holding the tree upright, and support it with a stake and adjustable tie. Water in well.*

3 Routine care

Water trees during dry spells, mulch well, and apply high-potash fertilizer in spring. To prevent flowers from being killed by spring frosts, cover trees with garden fabric on cold nights, removing it on mild days so the blooms can be pollinated. To prevent peach leaf curl, shield trees from rain until late spring with clear plastic sheeting. Move container-grown trees under cover to protect them from frost damage and rainfall.

Ensure insects can reach *the flowers, or use a soft paintbrush to pollinate them yourself by hand.*

4 Thinning out

Trees often set a very heavy crop, which is best thinned to encourage fewer, but larger, fruits. Thin conventional varieties to about 6–8in (15–20cm) apart once the fruits are the size of walnuts; fruit on dwarf trees should be thinned to 4in (10cm) apart. As the fruit ripens, it often draws wasps, so hang sugary traps in the branches.

Homemade wasp traps *filled with a sugary liquid are easy to make. Hang them in the trees near to developing fruits to lure wasps away.*

Thinning the fruit *helps concentrate the tree's energy so that the remaining fruit grow larger and are more likely to develop fully.*

5 Harvesting

Begin harvesting fruits as they ripen from midsummer onward. Mature fruits will feel slightly soft to the touch and will release their characteristic scent. Ideally, leave the fruit on the tree to ripen as fully as possible, although you may find that wasp damage warrants earlier harvesting. To pick, cup the fruits in your hand, and twist gently.

TIP *If necessary, underripe fruits will ripen indoors on a sunny windowsill.*

Peaches and nectarines *are the same species and are grown and eaten the same way. The only difference is that peaches have fuzzy skins.*

6 Pruning

Peach and nectarine trees mainly fruit along the length of stems produced during the previous summer and should be pruned annually to promote new growth. Immediately after harvesting the fruit in summer, remove one third of the fruited stems from established trees to leave a framework of healthy, well-spaced, branches. To help prevent the disease silver leaf (see p.244), avoid pruning peach and nectarine trees at any other time of year, and use sterilized tools.

Pruned growth

STEP-BY-STEP Figs

Figs are a true taste of the Mediterranean, and although they need a sunny spot and take a long season to ripen fully, they give a good crop in most gardens. Left to their own devices, figs are large trees, but they can be kept to a more manageable size by restricting their roots, which also encourages them to fruit more freely. In colder areas figs can be grown in containers and protected during winter. They can also be wall-trained where space is tight.

	SPRING	SUMMER	FALL	WINTER
PLANT				
HARVEST				

FLOWERING TO HARVEST: 32–40 WEEKS

SUITABLE FOR: BEDS AND CONTAINERS

0   3ft   6ft   9ft

1–2 plants

9FT (3M) ROWS
Plant trees 5–10ft (1.5–3m) apart

0   24in

CONTAINERS
1 plant in each

1 Getting started

Figs are generally sold as container-grown plants and establish best when planted in mid-spring. There are several varieties to grow although few are widely sold, so you may need to contact a specialty supplier. Fig flowers don't need to be pollinated in order to set fruit, so you only need to grow one tree.

'Brunswick' *needs a mild site to crop well and bears large, sweet figs in late summer.*

'Panachee' *produces unusual-looking striped fruit. It is best trained against a warm wall.*

'Brown Turkey' *is widely available and grows well in cool areas. It crops in late summer.*

'Rouge de Bordeaux' *produces delicious figs but needs a sheltered, warm spot to grow well.*

Dig a hole, *and line the sides with stone slabs. To ensure good drainage, line the base with broken pots or stones to a depth of 8in (20cm).*

Plant the tree *at the same depth as it was in its pot, then backfill the hole with soil. Water the tree in well, and hammer in a suitable tree stake.*

2 Planting

If growing the tree directly in the soil, turn over the site to remove weeds, and incorporate sharp grit or composted bark (not manure) to ensure good drainage. To restrict the roots, create a planting pit, 24x24in (60x60cm), and plant the tree into it (see left). To plant into a container, choose one at least 24in (60cm) wide and deep, place stones or pieces of broken pot in the base for drainage, and fill it with soil-based compost.

TIP *Fig trees become more drought-tolerant once they establish fully.*

3 Routine care

New figs should be watered in their first year, but otherwise they thrive on neglect. Although the trees are fully hardy, the tiny fruitlets that overwinter from one year to the next (see below) can be damaged by frost. Cover free-standing and wall-trained trees with garden fabric if practical. The trees will benefit from annual pruning.

Fig trees grow well in pots *and can be brought under cover during winter in colder regions to protect the developing fruitlets.*

Remove any larger fruitlets in the fall. *Thinning them prevents the tree from wasting energy on fruits that won't reach maturity.*

Ripe figs soon spoil, *so eat them as quickly as possible to enjoy them at their best. Surplus fruit can be preserved or dried to eat later in the year.*

4 Thinning out

Our summers are too short for figs to ripen in one year. Instead, tiny fruitlets produced in late summer overwinter on the tree and mature the following summer. Any fruitlets larger than pea-size won't survive the winter however, and should be removed in late fall by snapping them off.

5 Harvesting

It is important to let figs mature as fully as possible before picking them since they won't ripen much more indoors. Ripe fruits hang downward from the branch, sticky sap appears at their bases, and they soften and emit a slight scent; they will pull easily from the tree. Birds may target the soft, ripe fruits.

6 Pruning

Young trees only need pruning to keep them in shape. Older trees are pruned twice in spring to promote fruiting and a healthy shape. In early spring, cut out some of the older stems to encourage new growth. Then, in late spring, pinch out the tips of this new growth to promote the formation of new fruits.

Pruned growth

Fruit crop planner

Use this table to check when to plant, prune, and harvest your fruit crops. Timings will vary for different regions, so adjust accordingly to suit your own site and conditions. When planting bare-root trees and shrubs, water them well afterward, even during winter.

CROPS		SPRING			SUMMER			FALL			WINTER		
		EARLY	MID	LATE	EARLY	MID	LATE	EARLY	MID	LATE	EARLY	MID	LATE
SUMMER STRAWBERRIES	PLANT (CONT)												
	PLANT (BR)												
	HARVEST												
	PRUNE												
EVERLASTING STRAWBERRIES	PLANT (CONT)												
	PLANT (BR)												
	HARVEST												
	PRUNE												
SUMMER RASPBERRIES	PLANT (CONT)												
	PLANT (BR)												
	HARVEST												
	PRUNE												
FALL RASPBERRIES	PLANT (CONT)												
	PLANT (BR)												
	HARVEST												
	PRUNE												
BLACKBERRIES AND HYBRIDS	PLANT (CONT)												
	PLANT (BR)												
	HARVEST												
	PRUNE												
RED AND WHITE CURRANTS	PLANT (CONT)												
	PLANT (BR)												
	HARVEST												
	PRUNE												
BLACK CURRANTS	PLANT (CONT)												
	PLANT (BR)												
	HARVEST												
	PRUNE												
GOOSEBERRIES	PLANT (CONT)												
	PLANT (BR)												
	HARVEST												
	PRUNE												

KEY	CONT: CONTAINER-GROWN PLANTS
	BR: BARE-ROOT PLANTS

CROPS		SPRING			SUMMER			FALL			WINTER		
		EARLY	MID	LATE	EARLY	MID	LATE	EARLY	MID	LATE	EARLY	MID	LATE
BLUEBERRIES	PLANT (CONT)	▪									▪		
	PLANT (BR)	▪									▪		
	HARVEST				▪	▪	▪						
	PRUNE											▪	▪
APPLES	PLANT (CONT)	▪	▪	▪	▪	▪	▪	▪	▪	▪	▪	▪	▪
	PLANT (BR)										▪	▪	▪
	HARVEST					▪	▪	▪	▪				
	PRUNE					▪	▪				▪	▪	▪
PEARS	PLANT (CONT)	▪	▪	▪	▪	▪	▪	▪	▪	▪	▪	▪	▪
	PLANT (BR)	▪									▪	▪	▪
	HARVEST					▪	▪	▪	▪				
	PRUNE					▪	▪				▪	▪	▪
PLUMS	PLANT (CONT)	▪	▪	▪	▪	▪	▪	▪	▪	▪	▪	▪	▪
	PLANT (BR)	▪								▪	▪	▪	▪
	HARVEST					▪	▪						
	PRUNE			▪	▪	▪							
CHERRIES	PLANT (CONT)	▪	▪	▪	▪	▪	▪	▪	▪	▪	▪	▪	▪
	PLANT (BR)	▪								▪	▪	▪	▪
	HARVEST				▪	▪							
	PRUNE			▪	▪	▪							
PEACHES	PLANT (CONT)	▪	▪	▪	▪	▪	▪	▪	▪	▪	▪	▪	▪
	PLANT (BR)	▪									▪	▪	▪
	HARVEST				▪	▪	▪						
	PRUNE			▪	▪								
NECTARINES	PLANT (CONT)	▪	▪	▪	▪	▪	▪	▪	▪	▪	▪	▪	▪
	PLANT (BR)	▪									▪	▪	▪
	HARVEST				▪	▪	▪						
	PRUNE			▪	▪	▪							
FIGS	PLANT (CONT)		▪										
	PLANT (BR)												
	HARVEST						▪	▪	▪				
	PRUNE	▪			▪								▪

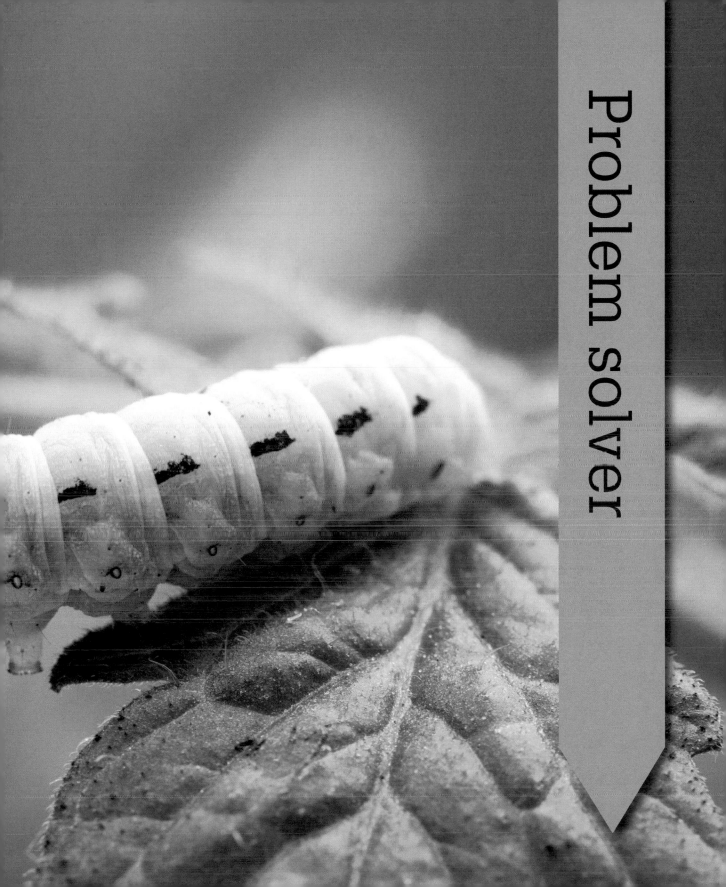

Problem solver

The organic approach

One of the best things about growing your own fruit and vegetables is that you can choose whether you want organic produce or not. Both organic and nonorganic approaches have their pros and cons, so weigh these up carefully. You may find yourself compromising and using a bit of both—hand-weeding here and applying weedkillers there, for example—when making decisions about your garden's management.

Different approaches

In simple terms, taking a nonorganic approach means using man-made fertilizers and pesticides to manage your garden. Organic gardening, on the other hand, involves using natural, non-artificial methods. The essence of organic gardening is to harness nature for your benefit, creating a balance between predators and prey, and using natural resources sensibly and sustainably, with as little impact on the environment as possible.

Feeding

There is a range of organic and nonorganic fertilizers available, but you can't beat organic matter such as well-rotted manure or compost for mulching and improving the soil.

Tackling pests and diseases

For nonorganic gardeners there is a variety of chemical sprays for targeting pests and diseases. Organic gardening requires more planning, and you may need to use a few methods to keep problems at bay. Sowing marigolds to draw aphids away from crops, known as companion planting, is one such pest control method, while biological control is another and is especially useful for undercover crops. Here, natural predators are used to prey on the pests. Another option is to plant sacrificial plants to shield valuable crops from damage. However, if these techniques fail to solve the problem, there are also organic sprays that can be used to target specific pests.

Plant diseases can often be difficult to control organically, so aim for prevention rather than cure.

Weed management

For the nonorganic gardener there is a range of highly effective weedkillers, but if you've chosen to go organic, or simply don't want to use chemicals near your crops, weeding manually is the best option. The saying that "one year's weed is seven years' seed" is a useful reminder to try to remove weeds before they can set seed.

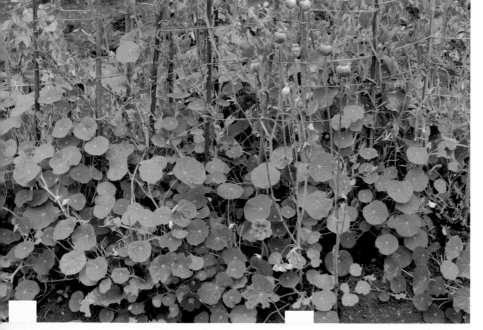

(left) **Nasturtiums** *are good companion plants, and are said to draw blackfly away from crops. Their edible leaves, flowers, and seeds have a peppery flavor.*

(right) **Applying a mulch** *of bark chips between plants will help to suppress weeds. Grow a mix of crops to discourage attack from pests.*

Preventing problems

Whether you decide to go organic or not, your primary aim should be to encourage resilient, healthy plants since these are best able to withstand competition from weeds. Make sure your site and soil are suitable for your crops: improve any compacted areas by digging in plenty of bulky organic matter, ensure that plants are well ventilated and not too crowded, and enrich nutrient-deficient plots with an appropriate fertilizer.

Common problems

Plants are affected by a number of factors, including nutrition, soil, and climate. If your plants look sickly, you may need to do some detective work to make an accurate diagnosis. For example, if your soil is sandy, or very acidic or alkaline, it may be prone to nutrient deficiencies (see p.246), while an overcropped site can be exhausted of a specific nutrient. Remember that blindly applying fertilizers in an attempt to solve the problem can be just as harmful to plants, not to mention environmentally unsound.

Soils may also contain pockets of compaction that impede root growth, or waterlogged areas that can cause roots to rot; "rain shadows" against walls or fences can cause dry spots. Digging in organic matter to improve the soil structure will help. Weather-related damage such as scorching of foliage by frost, sun, or wind can often look very dramatic, but this damage is often superficial and, because the root system is unharmed, plants will often resprout and recover (see p.244).

Preventing weeds

In an ideal gardening world we would keep weeds from appearing rather than simply controlling them once they've established. Realistically, this doesn't always happen, but there are ways to tackle both situations.

Weed-suppressing mulches are good at preventing unwanted growth —weeds will quickly exploit bare soil if you let them. Your options include man-made materials, such as weed control fabric or black plastic sheeting, flattened cardboard boxes, or recycled sheets of plastic—laying these on your plot in the fall will save you a vast amount of weeding come the spring. Alternatively, a 3in (8cm) thick layer of organic matter such as certified weed-free garden compost or well-rotted manure can also be effective and also has the benefit of

Mature zucchini plants *and other trailing crops suppress weeds naturally. Other plants that are good at this include potatoes, pumpkins, and vigorous leafy plants such as Swiss chard.*

__Preparation is key__, so dig over the soil well at the beginning of the season, and remove any weeds that may have developed.

releasing nutrients as it decomposes.

Crops are most vulnerable to weed competition when they are young, so try a smart technique known as the "stale seedbed" to trick weed seeds into germinating before this. Simply prepare your bed, water well, and keep moist. After one week a flush of weed seedlings will appear—remove these, then sow your chosen seed.

Dealing with weeds

There are a number of organic tactics to try when removing weeds. Manually digging them out with a hoe or hand fork is often the best method, but be aware that shallow-rooted crops such as cherries and raspberries can sucker profusely if their roots are damaged. Flame guns can be used to scorch annual weeds, and perennials can be smothered with mulch and then dug out completely. You can also choose from a number of highly effective non-organic weedkillers—follow the manufacturer's guidelines carefully.

Weeding tips

It is vital to do all you can to prevent and remove weeds from your plot, or they will compete with your crops for water, nutrition, and space, and may also harbor pests and diseases. Try to do so before weeds have a chance to flower and produce more seeds.

1 Hoeing and hand-weeding Using a hoe to weed between rows of plants will help you to cover large areas with relative speed. If possible, weed on a dry day, and leave the weeds on the soil surface to shrivel and die. If you are removing perennial weeds, do so with a garden or hand fork, and try to ensure that you remove the entire root so the weeds do not regenerate.

2 Feeding Strong, healthy plants are best able to compete with weeds, so prepare the soil in advance, and apply fertilizer to the soil if necessary. Dig in plenty of well-rotted manure or compost before planting as well.

3 Mulching with straw Even vigorous, leafy plants like potatoes will benefit from a mulch of material, such as straw, to prevent competing weeds from growing nearby.

4 Planting through plastic Many crops benefit from being planted through black plastic sheeting, which not only suppresses weeds but has the added benefits of keeping the soil warm and helping to keep it moist. This method is especially useful for crops that don't produce weed-suppressing foliage, like strawberries and onions.

Common weeds

1 Stinging nettle These tall-growing weeds can establish a deep network of roots, and their leaves deliver a painful sting. Dig them out completely to get rid of them.

2 Dock The broad, unattractive leaves of this perennial weed look bad in a vegetable patch. The plants have a long taproot, which should be entirely removed from the ground.

3 Creeping buttercup This common perennial weed is found in many gardens. It uses horizontal runners to creep across the ground—dig out its whole root system, or it will regenerate.

4 Shepherd's purse This annual weed produces characteristic purple heart-shaped seed pods—to prevent it from spreading, dig up and compost the plants before the seed pods form.

5 Groundsel This annual weed produces fluffy white seedheads from yellow, daisylike flowers. Dig the plants out before the seeds have a chance to disperse.

6 Goosegrass Also known as "cleavers," this sticky, clinging weed is covered with tiny hooks and can rapidly spread throughout a vegetable patch. It can be pulled up by hand.

7 Dandelion A common perennial weed, dandelions must be dug out before the seeds are released. Remove the taproot completely since any pieces left behind will regenerate.

8 Hairy bittercress Target this fast-growing annual while it is young and easiest to pull up. Do not allow the delicate seed pods to form. They split easily and will spread seed far and wide.

9 Creeping thistle This tough perennial is difficult to eradicate so you may need to consider using a chemical weedkiller.

10 Bindweed This perennial weed can be very tough to overcome. Ensure that you remove the entire root before destroying it. Consider applying a systemic weedkiller.

11 Annual meadow grass This common lawn grass is considered a weed in the vegetable patch—the best way to deal with it is to hoe it regularly to prevent it from flowering and setting seed.

12 Ragwort This rosette-forming annual weed has attractive yellow flowers but can produce a prolific amount of seeds; dig the plants out before these have a chance to form.

Avoiding pests and diseases

No garden is immune to attack from pests and diseases, but there are measures you can take to reduce the risk, and methods you can use, both organic and non-organic, to deal with problems as they arise. Maintaining good garden hygiene and encouraging strong crops by keeping plants well fed, well watered, and well ventilated is a good start. Keep in mind that it is easier to prevent pests and diseases rather than cure them.

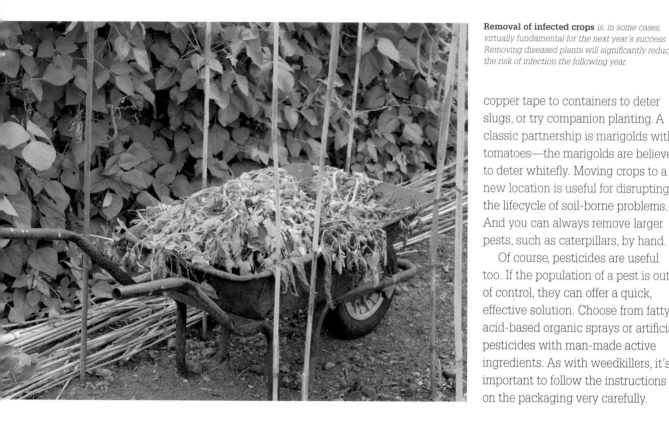

Removal of infected crops *is, in some cases, virtually fundamental for the next year's success. Removing diseased plants will significantly reduce the risk of infection the following year.*

copper tape to containers to deter slugs, or try companion planting. A classic partnership is marigolds with tomatoes—the marigolds are believed to deter whitefly. Moving crops to a new location is useful for disrupting the lifecycle of soil-borne problems. And you can always remove larger pests, such as caterpillars, by hand.

Of course, pesticides are useful too. If the population of a pest is out of control, they can offer a quick, effective solution. Choose from fatty acid-based organic sprays or artificial pesticides with man-made active ingredients. As with weedkillers, it's important to follow the instructions on the packaging very carefully.

Dealing with pests

Building up a population of beneficial creatures is a useful organic method for keeping pests at bay. Encourage them by providing habitats, such as ponds for frogs and suitable flowers for hoverflies. This can also attract other useful wildlife such as bees and butterflies. You may also want to use biological controls, such as parasitic

wasps to target whitefly, predatory mites to feed on red spider mite, and microscopic eelworms to infect slugs. Introducing the predator before the pests become too numerous is crucial, but the results can be very effective.

There are many other organic methods to try: create a barrier against pests by covering crops with insect-proof mesh or a tunnel cloche, attach

Dealing with diseases

The limited number of fungicides available to amateur gardeners means that avoiding or preventing plant diseases is a far better option than controlling them once they arrive. There is a range of organic and non-organic methods to try, but one of the most fundamental goals should be good garden hygiene:

keep pruning and digging tools sterilized. It also helps to keep plants well watered and well ventilated.

For non-organic gardeners, fungicides are also an option, but always follow the manufacturer's guidelines, and if plants are severely affected, consider consigning them to the garbage can as a lost cause.

Resistant varieties

Choosing resistant varieties and planting them in uncontaminated soil will also help to avoid infection. For some crops this can be very important: 'Kilaxy' cabbage shows good resistance to clubroot, which is critical since there is no fungicidal cure for this root disease, and its spores can survive in the soil for up to 20 years. There are resistant varieties within many crops, so keep on the lookout. Remember though, that resistance doesn't mean immunity, and plants may still succumb.

To prevent the risk of further contamination, *only compost disease-free plant material. As a further precaution, remove any diseased plants from your garden or burn them.*

Natural measures

Be proactive in your garden, and try to discourage pests from attacking. Daily walks among your crops will allow you to spot problems early, and once you spot the symptoms of a specific problem, you'll be well armed with the tools to make an informed plan of attack. For further, more specific pest and disease information, see pages 238–247.

1 Pollinating Planting nectar-rich, flowering annuals and perennials will attract hoverflies, whose larvae have a voracious appetite for aphids. As well as looking beautiful, these flowers will also attract pollinating bees and butterflies to the garden. Provide hibernation sites for them.

2 Beneficial wildlife Consider making your garden amphibian-friendly. A wildlife pond, log pile, or shady, damp corner will entice frogs and toads, which love to eat one of the garden's most common pests: slugs.

3 Insect-proof mesh Fine mesh is good for protecting crops such as brassicas since it will deter their common pest, cabbage white butterflies. Support the mesh on sticks, and bury it in the soil all the way around the plants to stop the pests from getting underneath.

4 Companion planting Rows of nasturtiums or marigolds planted around the plot not only look beautiful but may help to draw marauding pests, such as aphids, away from valuable crops.

Common pests

1 Wasps These common pests target the sweet flesh of ripe fruits, especially apples, pears, and plums. Hang jam and water traps from the branches of the trees to lure them away.

2 Cabbage caterpillars Nibbling the leaves and boring into the heart of the cabbages, these pests cause considerable damage. Pick them off, use netting, or apply an appropriate insecticide.

3 Onion fly These maggots attack the roots of onions and leeks and bore into the base of the vegetables, causing them to rot. Destroy infested plants. Rotate crops, and cover with fabric.

4 Leek moth There is no insecticide for these caterpillars, which mine the leaves and flesh of leeks and onions. Kill any that you find, and cover crops with horticultural fabric to deter them.

5 Colorado beetle This is a serious pest that can cause considerable damage. The yellow- and black-striped beetles eat the foliage of potatoes and tomatoes.

6 Pea moth Eggs are laid on plants in summer; the caterpillars hatch and burrow into the pods to eat the peas. Sow early or late types to avoid the adult moths, or protect plants with netting.

7 Carrot fly The maggots tunnel into carrots and parsnips. Use horticultural fabric to deter them, or grow resistant varieties.

8 Codling moth The caterpillars of this pest tunnel into apples and pears and feed on the cores. Use pheromone traps, and spray the fruits with an appropriate insecticide in summer.

9 Wireworms This pest is the larvae of the click beetle and will kill seedlings and feed on potatoes and onions. There is no available insecticide, so remove the larvae as you spot them.

10 Mealy cabbage aphids Massed on the underside of brassica leaves and sucking the sap out, this pest turns the foliage yellowish-white. Control it using an appropriate insecticide.

11 Whitefly The pest sucks sap from the underside of leaves and excretes honeydew, encouraging sooty mold to form. Use a biological control in greenhouses, or use insecticide.

12 Raspberry beetle Feeding on raspberries, blackberries, and other hybrids, this pest causes gray-brown patches to form on the fruits. Spray with insecticide; this pest is hard to control.

13 Pea and bean weevil This pest targets the leaves of peas and beans, eating neat "U" shapes out of the margins. As the majority of the leaf is unharmed, attacks are rarely fatal, but raise plants in pots if necessary, or spray with an insecticide.

14 Gooseberry sawfly Causing severe damage to gooseberries and red currants, this pest can completely strip plants of their leaves. Pick insects off, or use a biological or chemical control.

15 Plum fruit moth The pale pink caterpillars feed on the flesh of plums, damsons, and greengages. Hang pheromone traps in early summer to catch adult males—this can reduce damage.

16 Pear midge This pest lays its eggs in pear blooms; the maggots hatch and then feed inside the fruits, causing them to turn black and shrivel. Remove infested fruits as you spot them.

17 Capsid bugs Sucking the sap from apples and currants, this pest creates corky, brown patches on the skin of fruits. Chemical controls are available, but affected fruit is still edible.

18 Cabbage root fly The white larvae of this common brassica pest feed on roots and will severely damage young plants. There is no insecticide; the best defense is brassica collars.

19 Aphids Greenfly or blackfly are tiny, swarming, sap-sucking insects common on many plants and can distort new growth. Encourage natural predators, or apply a commercial insecticide.

20 Red spider mite Common in greenhouses, this pest causes the leaves of a range of plants to become mottled, turn yellow, and then drop. Use a biological control or a fatty acid spray.

21 Cutworms These brownish white caterpillars target the roots of seedlings and eat holes in root vegetables. There is no effective cure, so remove the pest by hand if you spot it.

22 Slugs and snails These very common pests will target leafy crops and seedlings, causing rapid damage. Deter them using gritty barriers or copper tape, set up beer traps, or use pellets.

23 Root aphids Carrots and lettuces are vulnerable to this pest, which sucks sap from roots, causing the plants to wilt. There is no cure, so rotate crops annually, and keep plants watered.

24 Asparagus beetles The adults and their larvae target the leaves and bark of asparagus plants and can rapidly defoliate them, causing the stems to die. Pick off any that you find, or apply an appropriate insecticide.

Common diseases

1 Scab This disease causes brown patches on the skins of apples and pears and can spread to leaves and branches. Rake up fallen leaves in the fall since it can overwinter.

2 American gooseberry mildew Powdery fungal patches on leaves, fruits, and stems are a symptom of this disease. Keep plants pruned and well watered to reduce the risk of attack.

3 Rusts These fungi cause disease on many plants. They cause bright orange pustules to form on leaves or stems; remove infected material, and rotate crops.

4 Bacterial leaf spot Yellow-ringed dead patches form on the leaves of crops such as brassicas and cucumbers. Remove and destroy affected leaves, and rotate crops in future years.

5 Clubroot This slime mold affects brassica crops. It causes roots to swell and foliage to wilt and can be fatal. Reduce the soil acidity with lime, and improve drainage.

6 Downy mildew This disease causes brown patches on the leaves of lettuces and brassicas with moldy growth beneath. Destroy infected leaves, and keep plants well ventilated.

7 Tomato blight Affecting mainly outdoor types, this disease causes stems, leaves, and fruits to discolor and rot: remove and destroy them. Spray with copper before symptoms are seen.

8 Cucumber mosaic virus Causing leaves to become mottled and distorted and stunting fruit growth, this disease affects a range of crops, so destroy infected plants if symptoms are spotted.

9 Onion neck rot Onions, shallots, and garlic bulbs will become soft and coated with a fuzzy gray mold. Rotate crops.

10 Onion white rot Able to survive in the soil for many years, it causes bulbs to rot and foliage to become yellow and wilt. Destroy infected plants carefully to avoid contamination.

11 Brown rot Affecting a range of tree fruits including pears and apples, the fungus rots the flesh and causes brown pustules to appear on the skin. Remove infected fruits promptly.

12 Fungal leaf spot This disease affects a range of crops such as celery and strawberries and causes gray, brown-ringed spots on leaves. Remove infected leaves, and destroy them.

13 Sclerotinia This disease causes crops such as celery to turn yellow and suddenly wilt, with moldy stems often containing black structures called sclerotia. It can persist in the soil for years so it is vital to remove and destroy infected plants promptly.

14 Strawberry viruses These cause a number of problems, such as yellowing leaves and stunted growth. Remove and destroy infected plants; rotate crops to deter future occurrences.

15 Canker This disease causes existing wounds in tree trunks to grow or distort, often causing resin to ooze from the bark. Prune the infected growth, and apply a copper fungicide.

16 Blossom end rot The result of a calcium deficiency, this disorder creates dark, moldy patches on crops such as tomatoes and peppers. Remove affected fruits, and water well.

17 Bitter pit Black spots or indentations will appear on the skins of apples, which can also develop bitter-tasting flesh. Keep any affected fruit trees mulched and well watered—the disorder is a result of drought-induced calcium deficiency.

18 Potato common scab Common in dry soils that lack organic matter, this disease causes unattractive corky, brown patches on the skin. Choose a resistant variety, and water plants well.

19 Scorch Caused by either hot sun or cold, dry winds; both can strip the plant of its moisture and cause it to become brown and crisp. Shelter plants, and water in the cool of the evening.

20 Raspberry cane blight This disease results in split, brittle canes and withered foliage. Cut any diseased wood out, and destroy it. Prune the plants to encourage good ventilation.

21 Powdery mildew Affecting a range of crops, from zucchini to currants, this host-specific disease causes a white coating on leaves and fruits; remove these, and water plants well.

22 Honey fungus This root disease can be fatal to trees; its honey-colored toadstools may appear in the fall. Any plant with white fungal growth should be dug up and destroyed.

23 Silver leaf Plum, cherry, apricot, and peach trees are at risk, developing a silvery appearance on the leaves; branches may die back too. Prune in summer to reduce the risk of infection.

24 Botrytis Gray mold is a common fungus that causes fluffy grayish mold on crops, which will rot and die back. Any infected material should be removed promptly and destroyed.

25 Chocolate spot This disease affects broad beans, resulting in dark brown or grayish spreading spots on the foliage, stem, and pods. Remove any infected plants, and destroy them.

26 Potato black leg Leaves become yellow, and stems rot and become black at the base; remove any infected plants, and destroy them. Rotate potato crops in future seasons.

27 Tomato ghost spot Although fruits do not become inedible, they develop faint yellow or green rings on the skin.

28 Damping off Deterred by growing crops in clean pots and watering them with tap water, damping off causes greenhouse seedlings to collapse and can affect their roots.

29 Parsnip canker This disease targets damaged roots, resulting in orange-brown growth at the top; spots can also appear on the leaves. Rotate crops, and choose resistant varieties.

30 Potato blight This disease causes patchy, rotten foliage and later spreads to the tubers—destroy infected foliage. Spray with copper before symptoms are seen. Choose a resistant variety.

Common nutrient deficiencies

1 Iron Yellowing leaves which later turn brown at the edges can indicate a lack of iron. Add chelated iron to the soil.

2 Calcium A lack of water or an acidic soil can inhibit a plant's uptake of calcium, resulting in disorders such as blossom end rot (pictured). Keep plants well watered, and lime the soil.

3 Magnesium Plants develop yellowing foliage that turns brown between the veins. Spray a solution of epsom salts on the leaves.

4 Boron This deficiency affects a variety of crops, causing roots to split and preventing sweet corn from developing properly. Apply borax to the soil, or use as a foliar spray for fruit trees.

5 Potassium A lack of this nutrient causes leaves to turn brown and plants to flower and set fruit poorly. This nutrient is easily leached from the soil, so apply tomato feed to plants.

6 Nitrogen The foliage of plants becomes yellow, and overall growth is weak. Dig in well-rotted manure, or apply fertilizer.

Useful resources

Seeds and plug plants

Gurney's Seed & Nursery Co.
P.O. Box 4178
Greendale, IN
47025-4178
(513)354-1491
www.gurneys.com

Park Seed Co.
One Parkton Avenue
Greenwood, SC
29647
(800)845-3369
www.parkseed.com

W. Atlee Burpee & Co.
300 Park Avenue
Warminster, PA
18974
(800)333-5808
www.burpee.com

Henry Field's Seed & Nursery Co.
P.O. Box 397
Aurora, IN
47001-0397
(513)354-1495
www.henryfields.com

J.W. Jung Seed Co.
335 South High Street
Randolpb,WI
53956
(800)297-3123
www.jungseed.com

Harris Seeds
355 Paul Road
P.O. Box 24966
Rochester, NY
14624-0966
(800)544-7938
www.harrisseeds.com

Territorial Seed Co.
P.O. Box 158
Cottage Grove, OR
97424
(541)942-9547
www.territorialseed.com

The Natural Gardening Co.
P.O. Box 750776
Petaluma, CA
94975-0776
(707)766-9303
www.naturalgardening.com

Johnny's Selected Seeds
955 Benton Avenue
Winslow, ME
04901
(877)333-6276
www.johnnyseeds.com

NESEED
3580 Main Street
Hartford, CT
06120
(800)825-5477
www.neseed.com

Eden Brothers
P.O. Box 1115
Dahlonega, GA
30533
(877)333-6276
www.edenbrothers.com

American Meadows Inc.
223 Avenue D
Suite 30
Williston, VT
05495
(877)309-7333
www.americanmeadows.com

premiumplantplugs.com
6300 North 160 Road
Beggs, OK
74421
(877)72-PLUGS
www.premiumplantplugs.com

Mountain Valley Growers
38325 Pepperweed Road
Squaw Valley, CA
93675
(559)338-2775
www.mountainvalleygrowers.com

Thompson & Morgan Seedsmen, Inc.
P.O. Box 397
Aurora, IN
47001-0397
(800)274-7333
www.tmseeds.com

Fruit trees and shrubs

Gurney's Seed & Nursery Co.
P.O. Box 4178
Greendale, IN
47025-4178
(513)354-1491
www.gurneys com

Willis Orchard Co.
P.O. Box 119
Berlin, GA
31722
(866)586-6283
www.willisorchards.com

Stark Brothers Nurseries & Orchards Co.
P.O. Box 1800
Louisiana, MO
63353
(800)325-4180
www.starkbros.com

Nature Hills Nursery, Inc.
9910 North 48th Street
Suite 200
Omaha, NE
68152
(888)864-7663
www.naturehills.com

Raintree Nursery
391 Butts Road
Morton, WA
98356
(800)391-8892
www.raintreenursery.com

Biological pest control

Buglogical Control Systems, Inc.
P.O. Box 32046
Tucson, AZ
85751-2046
(520)298-4400
www.buglogical.com

GreenMethods.com
93 Priest Rd.
Nottingham, NH
03290-6204
(603)942-8925
www.greenmethods.com

Gardens Alive!
5100 Schenley Place
Lawrenceburg, IN
47025
(513)354-1482
www.gardensalive.com

Planet Natural
1612 Gold Avenue
Bozeman, MT
59715
(406)587-5891
www.planetnatural.com

Arbico Organics
10831 North Mavinee Drive
Suite 185
Oro Valley, AZ
85737-9531
(800)827-2847
www.arbico-organics.com

Supplies and equipment

Gardener's Supply Co.
128 Intervale Road
Burlington, VT
05401
(888)833-1412
www.gardeners.com

Plow and Hearth
Route 230 West
Madison, VA
22727
(800)494-7544
www.plowhearth.com

Garden Tool Co.
10 Circle Drive
Fort Collins, CO
80524
(800)830-4019
www.gardentoolcompany.com

A.M. Leonard, Inc.
241 Fox Drive
Piqua, OH
45356-0816
(800)433-0633
www.amleo.com

Tractor Supply Co.
200 Powell Place
Brentwood, TN
37027
(877)718-6750
www.tractorsupply.com

Index

Main entries are indicated by **bold** page numbers. Main entries for crops include full details for sowing, growing, feeding, watering, cultivation, and harvesting. These details are not indexed separately.

Acknowledgments

The publisher would like to thank the following for their kind permission to reproduce their photographs:

(Key: a-above; b-below/bottom; c-centre; f-far; l-left; r-right; t-top)

Alamy Images: ableimages 118br, Andrea Jones Images 184bc, Bon Appetit 225c, Brigette Sullivan / Outer Focus Photos 178tl, 180fcr, Karen Cairns 203tr, 209cl, Nigel Cattlin 239crb, CJG 213c, Elena Elisseeva 221c, foodimagecollection 209ca, funkyfood London - Paul Williams 169br, Trish Gant 211tc, Anne Gilbert 118fbr, 163cla, Brian Hoffman 64cl, Marvin Dembinsky Photo Associates 223c, Peter Titmuss 181c, Rob Walls 118fcr; **Blackmoor Nurseries:** 222cr; **Corbis:** Klaus Hackenberg 210fcr, Jacqui Hurst 240br, Image Source 201ca, Ocean 120fcr, Emma Shervington 219c; **Dobies of Devon:** 44br, 58c, 58cr, 70cr, 75, 169c, 186cl, 186c, 202c; **Dorling Kindersley:** Alan Buckingham 13bc, 47crb, 47br, 49crb, 49br, 145crb, 200cr, 201br, 202cl, 202bc, 203tc, 203c, 203br, 204c, 205tc, 205fcr, 206cl, 206c, 206fcr, 207cla, 207ca, 207bc, 208cr, 208fcr, 210cl, 210c, 210cr, 211fcr, 212cl, 212c, 212cr, 212fcr, 214cl, 214c, 214cr, 214bl, 214fcr, 215tr, 215cla, 216c, 216cr, 216fcr, 216-217cl, 217cl, 218c, 218cr, 218bl, 218fcr, 219tr, 219cla, 219br, 220cl, 220c, 220cr, 221cla, 222cl, 222c, 222fcr, 224cl, 241cla, Caroline Reed 31tr, 213tr; Chauney Dunford 23br, 23fcra, 237ftr; Emma Callery 241tr; Jan Van Der Voort 237cra; Jo Whittingham 179ca, 185ca; Mel Shackleton 185cl; **DT Brown Seeds:** 76c, 76cr, 84c, 98cl, 108fcr, 158cl, 158c; **FLPA:** Nigel Cattlin 241tl, 243cra, 243clb, 243br, 246cra, 247br; **Fothergills:** 100fcr, 138c, 138cr, 140cl, 154c, 168tr; **GAP Photos:** Maxine Adcock 8cr, 155ca, Thomas Alamy 193c, Lee Avison 146c, BBC Magazines Ltd 129cla, 163c, Dave Bevan 126cr, 140bc, 247cra, Richard Bloom 27tr, Christina Bollen 187ca, Mark Bolton 231c, Elke Borkowski 26clb, 48bc, 170fcr, Jonathan Buckley 84cr, 142-143cr, 198-199, Chris Burrows 144cr, Simon Colmer 228-229, Sarah Cuttle 48bl, 131fcr, Lydia Evans 28bl, FhF Greenmedia 27br, 46cla, 130bc, 141fcrb, 145tc, Victoria Firmston 193bc, Suzie Gibbons 18clb, 24cr, Marcus Harpur 19cla, 155br, Michael Howes 99bc, Martin Hughes-Jones 176fcr, Lynn Keddie 63br, 131cla, Geoff Kidd 126fcr, 244crb, Michael King 27bc, 159bc, 186bl, 186bc, Fiona Lea 9br, Jenny Lilly 155bl, Howard Rice 168br, 185fcr, Gary Smith 11tl, 145cl, Friedrich Strauss 25tr, 27cr, 29tc, John Swithinbank 175bc, 193cla, Visions 128ca, Juliette Wade 19c, 88-89tc, 118bl, 177bc, Jo Whitworth 16-17ca, Mark Winwood 118c, 130fcr, 143c, 144bc; **Garden World Images:** Dave Bevan 239br, 242cra, 245, Sine Chesterman 225fcr, Francoise Davis 225tc, Giles DelaCroix 122c, Glenn Harper 224fcr, Martin Hughes-Jones 128fcr, Andrea Jones 224c, Trevor Sims 29bc, 64cr, 90-91cr, 122cl; **The Garden Collection:** Torie Chugg 64c, Liz Eddison 25tl, 27tc, Nicola Stocken Tomkins 25cra; **Getty Images:** Ben Bloom 223br, Richard Bloom 181cl, Brian Carter 244br, Sarah Cuttle 131ca, Michael Davis 170cr, FhF Greenmedia 118cr, Jan Tove Johansson 239tl, Photos Lamontagne 184c, Cora Niele 176cl, Howard Rice 187fcr, Gary K Smith 48, Mark Turner 118bc, Juliette Wade 182bc, Jo Whitworth 129fcrb; **iStockphoto.com:** 179clb; **Marshalls Seeds:** 62tr, 75bl, 80cl, 82cl, 97tr, 97bl, 97br, 104fcr; **Photolibrary:** 144fcr, 184bl, 184fcr; **Photoshot:** Photos Horticultural 80fcr; **RHS The Garden:** Tim Sandall 10bl; **Ron Ludekens:** 224cr; **Royal Horticultural Society:** 240tr, 245bl, 247tr, P. Becker 238br, 241crb, Andrew Halstead 241cra, Horticultural Science 243crb, 246tr, 247tl, 247cla, Joyce Maynard 239tr, 239cla, 240cra, 241bl, Pathology 242tr, 245clb; **Science Photo Library:** Dr Jeremy Burgess 245tl; **Suttons Seeds:** 48fbl, 76cl, 104cl, 104cr, 108c, 140c, 142fcr, 144cl, 160cl, 160cr, 168cra, 170cl; **Thompson & Morgan:** 45bc, 64fcr, 90cl, 98c, 99fbr, 100c, 100cr, 102cr, 122fcr, 142c, 154-155c, 155cr, 156c, 158cr, 160c, 169tr, 200fcr; **Tozer Seeds:** 56tr; **Victoriana Nursery Gardens/Stephen Shirley:** 46cb, 68c, 70fcr, 89tr, 89ca, 89bl, 89crb, 89fbr, 90c, 169crb, 172cl, 176cr, 186cr, 202cr, 220-221fcr

All other images © Dorling Kindersley
For further information see:
www.dkimages.com

Author's acknowledgements:
Chauney Dunford for politely and patiently answering all my queries and tolerating my 'green pen moments'; Alison Shackleton for sending an early cover design to motivate me during the late hours; and to my parents for their never-ending support.

Dorling Kindersley would like to thank:
Mark Winwood for his exceptional work growing and photographing most of the vegetables featured in this book; and his wife, Lizzie, for her help and patience.

Louise Furnival, Steve Hernandez, Alan Crick, Lucie Pendred and James Perkins for their kind help.

Becky Tennant for additional design assistance; Fiona Wild for proofreading; and Susan Bosanko for indexing.

Robin and Brenda Beresford-Evans, and the growers at Cannizaro Allotments, Wimbledon, London.

Dobies/Suttons, D.T Brown, Floranova, Marshalls/Unwins, Mr Fothergill's, Thompson & Morgan, and Victoriana Nursery Gardens for their kind permission to reproduce their images.